Napoleon's Police

Fouché

POL

Napoleon's Police

PETER DE *POLNAY*

W. H. ALLEN . LONDON . 1970

© PETER DE POLNAY, 1970
PRINTED AND BOUND IN GREAT BRITAIN
BY T. & A. CONSTABLE LTD
EDINBURGH
FOR THE PUBLISHERS
W. H. ALLEN & CO LTD
ESSEX STREET LONDON WC2
0 491 00124 X

Contents

Illustrations

A section of illustrations
appears between pages 112-113

Preface

While France was preparing to celebrate the second centenary of Napoleon's birth I sat in the Hôtel de Soubise, the seat of the Archives Nationales, engrossed in the police reports of the Consulate and the Empire. I was fascinated and horrified as before me emerged the other side of the medal of glory, for it was the police that kept Napoleon in power, and ruled the country while he was away at war, no mean achievement, especially as the West of France was frequently in revolt. The despicable methods the police used seemed frighteningly familiar, and no wonder: the modern conception of the police was born under the Consulate and the Empire, the Revolution the father, base human instincts the mother.

The police had to deal with practically everything. They and the gendarmerie brought in the conscripts without whom the years of conquest would have been barren years for the Corsican. The police controlled all spying and counter-espionage, had to frustrate English plots and intrigues, royalist plots and machinations, and be on the alert day and night while one plot after the other was hatched to assassinate Napoleon, a formidable organisation considering that the last head of the old regime's police, his task strictly

7

limited to Paris, did not even know a few days before the fall of the Bastille that there might be trouble ahead.

In the old regime the security of the realm was based on the *lettres de cachet:* a prerogative of the King on whose safety, and often on whose royal caprice, the police system rested. The King locked up Voltaire in the Bastille when his writings annoyed him; when he got over his annoyance Voltaire was released. There were no *agents provocateurs* under the Bourbons in the modern sense; police had nothing to do with Government policy. It was Joseph Fouché, the begetter of present-day police methods, who gave the police the new trend. France and the conquered territories swarmed with his *agents provocateurs.* In his conception the security of the State rested more on infiltration and counter-espionage than on straightforward spying as practised under the Bourbons.

It appears almost unbelievable how unsafe the great Napoleon's position was, and how much in peril his person was during the years the world feared him and kow-towed to him. (Nobody appreciated that better than he, but he had the meridional's fatalistic approach to it.) Already in 1793 the Vendée had risen against the Revolution; however that was an open rising: the people of the Vendée fought in the open, and were crushed in battle. The other movement, the Chouannerie, was far more dangerous, for it consisted mostly of conspiracies to eliminate the Usurper, and though in the last resort the Chouans were always thwarted, they never gave up, and helped by England and backed by the nobles and peasants of Normandy, Brittany, Anjou and Mayenne they fought and plotted till the Restoration. I have to admit that Chouans like Georges Cadoudal and La Haye-Saint-Hilaire rouse my admiration.

It is not my aim to paint an overall picture of the organisation and history of Napoleon's police as police methods are as repetitive as plotters' foolhardiness, but I feel that with the cases I give the reader will have a clear view of the other side of the medal. The bridge of Lodi and the sun of Austerlitz on the one side, detention even after acquittal, prison dungeons, deportation, the Emperor's promised pardon, the promise not kept, enforced residence, the firing squad and the guillotine on the other.

I have to express as much my thanks to the helpful staff of the Archives Nationales as to the equally helpful staff of the Bibliothèque Nationale de Paris, who truly aided me in my work, and I want to put on record my deep debt of gratitude to my wife Carmen for her help, inspiration and hard work while I did the research and wrote this book.

A

LIEUTENANTS-GENERAL OF POLICE

Reynie (Gabriel-Nicolas de La): March 29, 1667 to January 29, 1697.

Argenson (Marc-René de Voyer de Paulmy, marquis d'): January 29, 1697 to January 28, 1718.

Machault (Louis-Charles de, seigneur d'Arnouville): January 28, 1718 to January 26, 1720.

Argenson (Marc-Pierre de Voyer de Paulmy, comte d'): January 26, 1720 to February 18, 1721; April 26, 1722 to January 28, 1724.

Tachereau or Teschereau (Gabriel, seigneur de Baudry et de Linières): February 18, 1721 to April 26, 1722.

Ravot (Nicolas-Jean-Baptiste, seigneur d'Ombreval): January 28, 1724 to August 28, 1725.

Hérault (René, seigneur de Fontaine-l'Abbé et de Vaucresson): August 28, 1725 to December 21, 1739.

Marville (Claude-Henri Feydeau de, seigneur de Dampierre et de Gien): December 21, 1739 to May 27, 1747.

Berryer de Ravenoville (Nicolas-René): May 27, 1747 to October 29, 1757.

Bertin de Bellisle (Henri-Léonard-Jean-Baptiste, comte de Bourdeilles, seigneur de Brantôme, baron de Périgord): October 29, 1757 to November 21, 1759.

Sartine (Antoine-Raymond-Jean-Gualbert-Gabriel de, comte d'Alby): November 21, 1759 to August 24, 1774.

Lenoir (Jean-Pierre-Charles): August 24, 1774 to May 14, 1775; June 19, 1776 to August 11, 1785.

Albert (Joseph-François-Ildefonse-Rémond): May 14, 1775 to June 19, 1776.

Crosne (Louis Thiroux de): August 11, 1785 to July 16, 1789.

B

MINISTERS OF THE POLICE

Camus (Armand-Gaston): January 2, 1796 to January 4.

Merlin de Douai (Philippe-Antoine, comte de): January 4, 1796 to April 3, 1796.

Cochon (Charles, comte de Lapparent): April 3, 1796 to July 6, 1797.

Lenoir-Laroche (Jean-Jacques, comte de): July 6, 1797 to July 26, 1797.

Sotin de la Coindière (Pierre-Jean-Marie): July 26, 1797 to February 12, 1798.

Dondeau: February 12, 1798 to May 15, 1798.

Lecarlier: May 16, 1798 to October 29, 1798.

Duval (Jean-Pierre-Chevalier): October 29, 1798 to June 22, 1799.

Bourguignon-Dumolard: June 22, 1799 to July 20, 1799.

Fouché (Joseph, duc d'Otrante): July 20, 1799 to September 15, 1802; July 10, 1804 to June 2, 1810; March 21, 1815 to June 23, 1815; July 9, 1815 to September 25, 1815.

Savary (Anne-Jean-Marie-René, duc de Rovigo): June 3, 1810 to April 3, 1814.

Anglès (comte d'): April 3, 1814 to May 15, 1814.

Pelet de la Lozère (Jean, comte de): June 23, 1815 to July 8, 1815.

Decazes (Elie, duc de Glukesbourg): September 25, 1815 to December 29, 1818.

C

DIRECTORS OF THE POLICE DEPARTMENTS

Dubois: July 10, 1804 to October 1810.

Miot: July 10, 1804 to February 21, 1806.

Pelet de la Lozère: July 10, 1804 to April 8, 1814.

Réal (Pierre-François, comte de): July 10, 1804 to April 8, 1814.

POLICE PREFECTS

Dubois: March 8, 1800 to October 14, 1810.

Pasquier (Etienne, duc de): October 14, 1810 to April 8, 1814.

Bourrienne (Louis-Antoine Fauvelet de): March 12, 1815 to March 20, 1815.

Réal: March 21, 1815 to July 2, 1815.

Courtin: July 2, 1815 to July 9, 1815.

Decazes: July 10, 1815 to September 25, 1815.

DIRECTORS-GENERAL OF POLICE

Beugnot: May 18, 1814 to December 3, 1814.

Dandré: December 3, 1814 to March 20, 1815.

I

Lieutenants of Police

In 1667, on the recommendation of a commission of which Lamoignon, Colbert and Pussort were members, Louis XIV created the rank of lieutenant of police of Paris, at the same time abolishing the office of the civil and criminal lieutenants of the Châtelet whose functions often overlapped. The lieutenant of police also assumed some of the powers of the Provost of Paris. The Royal Edict, which was promulgated the previous December, determined the new magistrate's duties which consisted of keeping order, keeping the town clean, and sitting in judgment, when necessary, on beggars, vagrants and vagabonds, assisted by seven high officers of the Châtelet.

The lieutenant of police had to oversee the cleanliness of the streets and public places and the carrying of arms; he issued orders and led the operations in case of fire or flood; and was responsible for food reaching Paris regularly. The control of prices was his responsibility too. In short, he was a sort of avuncular guardian of the comfort and security of the law-abiding burghers and artisans of Paris who equally feared fire and pestilence, and the organised beggars of the *cours des miracles* (thieves' kitchens). He was responsible for the orderly conduct of markets, butchers, fishmongers, greengrocers, inns and brothels. Secret meetings were brought to his notice, and he dealt with cases of sedition, not to mention controlling shipping on the Seine. But he had absolutely nothing to do with Government policy or with the security of the realm. Yet it was the edict of 1667 that begot the police. In his responsibility for suppressing the printing and circulation of illicit books or pamphlets the lieutenant of police came nearest to the modern concept of police power.

In March 1674 the King created a second lieutenant of police, but as the two officers did not work smoothly together the two offices were fused in April 1675 and the remaining lieutenant became lieutenant-general of police. The *Guet*, that is the Watch, ceased to exist. Since the profession of spies, eavesdroppers and informers is as old as the hills the lieutenant did not encounter any teething troubles, especially as Gabriel-Nicolas de La Reynie,* the first lieutenant of police, was a man of great ability.

He was a Limousin born in 1625. Louis XIV's choice fell on him because Louis XIV knew how to choose his men. Even Saint-Simon, whose evil tongue wags down the ages, had only praise for him, saying that he ennobled his profession. The first lieutenant took up his duties on March 29, 1667. Like his royal master, de La Reynie was endowed with common sense. You cannot watch over the security of the citizens in dark streets, so he established the lighting of the streets at night, exept in summer and when there was a full moon. He brought some order into the large underworld of beggars and forced the Parisians to clean their streets, at the same time seeing that the tradesmen did not overcharge them for food.

When he was appointed, Paris was full of rumours of poisoning in high places, and it was de La Reynie who caught the Marquise de Brinvilliers, an angelic-looking noblewoman, who on the pretext of bringing them alms poisoned the sick in the Hôtel-Dieu, for the simple pleasure of seeing them die in torment. She was beheaded in the Place de Grève, her body burnt, and scattered to the wind. However, rumour had it that more important persons

* See A.

than the late marquise were guilty of poisoning and black magic.

The Government established a Chamber of Justice or *Chambre ardente de l'Arsenal* to try the poisoners. The Parliament of Paris (parliaments were law courts) protested without avail against its exceptional jurisdiction as it encroached on the Parliament's powers. The Government's reason was that as high personages might be involved the public should be kept ignorant of the arrests and trials. In January 1680 the King chose de La Reynie as president and prosecutor of the new tribunal. The lieutenant knew Paris inside out, the inhabitants had few secrets for him. His agents and inspectors kept him informed of the coming and going of foreigners. In July 1682 a Royal Edict proclaimed, that because the old rules were ineffective many impostors, calling themselves wise men, magicians and fortune tellers, had entered the kingdom, and on the pretext of casting horoscopes and fortune telling had done harm to ignorant and stupid people, by playing on their curiosity, making them impious and sacrilegious, and, as a result of their baneful influence turning the wretches into poisoners in order to fulfil their evil predictions. Because of their sinister actions all sooth-sayers, magicians and their like were ordered to leave the kingdom at once. The Edict pronounced the death penalty against every subject who took part in their evil deeds; and those who had any knowledge or information about poisonings would be prosecuted in the same manner as the guilty if they withheld information from the Chamber of Justice.

The Edict was not aimed so much at the poor as at the men and women in high places who indulged in black masses, poisoning, or mixing love potions in the food of their loved ones. De La Reynie arrested a nobleman whose name was never divulged, though his statement in which he told all remains. He gave the whole show away. He must have had an important position at Court because he dished up all the tittle-tattle and gossip at Court, and practically every detail of the doings of a woman called Voisin who was, so to speak, the arch-sorceress.

"Monseigneur," began his statement, "has in his hand the

lettre de cachet which delivers me from all fear and the consequences of the revelations I made to him. I will speak as a faithful subject of the King. I use this opportunity to renew my allegiance to his Majesty. Because of the order that has come from so high above, and because of my strong desire to recognise the services Monseigneur, the Lieutenant of Police, rendered me, I now appreciate how low I have fallen. . . . In my misery I cannot forget the cross I wear in my buttonhole [*either the Cross of Malta or the Cordon Bleu: Order of the Saint-Esprit, as the Order of Saint-Louis dated only from 1693*], and the family I belong to. I know that I am unworthy of both as my fatal passion and relationship with Voisin turned me into a wretch. When Monseigneur summoned me I was waiting for the awful hour to expiate my sad error, but the kind words of this great magistrate, in showing me how to rehabilitate myself and how to repay the favours granted, persuade me to repeat here all I told him. . . ."

The denunciation of Voisin followed. He left out nothing. Monsieur, the King's brother, and Madame, Henrietta of England, Monsieur's wife, had been in touch with Voisin. She told them their fortunes, gave them potions, for her to have children, for him to seduce young men, and even Marie-Thérèse, the pious Queen of France, had her fortune told by Voisin, who offered her a potion that would make the King love her alone. The Comtesse de Soissons, who now and then slept with the King, went in disguise at least thirty times to Voisin's lodgings, and had dealings also with Vigoureux, another sorceress and poisoner, an accomplice of Voisin. Mme de Soissons needed their occult help in regaining her waning influence on the King, and get hold of the late Cardinal de Mazarin's estate. "What a terrible profanity!" exclaims the nobleman in his statement as he relates Mme de Soissons promising Voisin hair, nail parings, two shirts, several stockings and one collar of his Majesty the King in order to make a "love doll." "Monseigneur knows to what horrible purposes those love dolls are put. I also think that in a phial she gave some of his Majesty's blood." De La Reynie had certainly made him talk.

Cardinal de Bouillon, he went on in his confession, wanted Voisin to put a spell on the King so as to receive the entire Province of Auvergne for his family. Marshal of France the Duc de Luxembourg asked Voisin to arrange a meeting between him and the Devil. Voisin was willing to arrange it, but the Marshal became frightened and called the meeting off. And so on, and so on, and when de La Reynie had finished with the nobleman he could report to the King that his mistress, Mme de Montespan, had also had dealings with Voisin and Satan. The sorceress was executed and Mme de Montespan fell from grace.

Though he was blazing a trail, de La Reynie already knew the tricks of the new profession of head of police. The nobleman's statement bears that out. De La Reynie was an inflexible official who executed all orders he received. When in 1685 the Edict of Nantes was revoked he filled the Bastille with Huguenots. He held the office of lieutenant-general of police for thirty years. When he left he was nominated to the Council of State. He died about June 1709 in his house in the rue du Boulay. Though he gave Paris street lighting he is better remembered as the scourge of the poisoners.

Marc-René de Voyer de Paulmy, Marquis d'Argenson, was the next police-lieutenant. He was born in Venice where, at the time of his birth, his father was the Ambassador of France. D'Argenson trained to become a lawyer since he belonged to the nobility of the gown, looked down on by the nobility of the sword, none the less a powerful proud caste. He took his oath as advocate before the Parliament of Paris in 1669. He advanced steadily, became lieutenant-general to the Tribunal of Angoulême when only twenty-five, and was so highly esteemed that when de La Reynie withdrew in 1697 Pontchartrain, the King's Minister, made him the new lieutenant-general of police. "Lighting, cleanliness and security," said de Harlay, the First President of the Parliament of Paris, when he made his courtesy visit, then closed the door to him

Crime was still rampant in Paris in spite of de La Reynie's efforts. D'Argenson decided to tackle it. The town was infested with beggars who thieved and killed whenever the opportunity arose. They lived in the *cours des miracles* and were well organised. In the old days the Watch gave them a wide berth, for it was dangerous penetrating into their lairs. D'Argenson approached the problem in a scientific fashion inasmuch as he used informers, recruiting them among the beggars themselves, an innovation which was praised at the time without anybody thinking of its sinister implications. The burghers were so pleased with the new system of policing the town that they overlooked the abuses it could give rise to. The lieutenant's army of informers, the *mouchards*, were so well drilled that nothing that happened in Paris escaped their vigilance, a far cry from the original idea of watching only criminals. The underworld nicknamed d'Argenson the Judge of Hell.

He was an exceedingly brave man who seldom missed a fire, and once when some men barricaded themselves in a house he went to speak to them, soothed them, and in the end they came out to surrender. He rose to great heights, becoming the President of the Financial Council after relinquishing his post as lieutenant of police, then Minister of State and Inspector-General of the Police of the Kingdom. He died in 1721, a member of the Academy of Sciences and of the French Academy, leaving behind the well organised body of police spies, his contribution to the development of the police. It was said of him that due to his spies he was acquainted with everything that went on in Parisian families. Louis-Charles de Machault succeeded him, then his second son Marc-Pierre who was less feared by the criminals than his father had been.

The next noteworthy lieutenant was René Hérault, Seigneur de Fontaine-l'Abbé et de Vaucresson, who was nominated in 1725. He concentrated his efforts on the persecution of the Jansenists and the authors of schismatic writings. A brother of his was a Jesuit father. He handled the police spies with admirable skill, always preferring their testimony to the protestations of the citizens.

A milliner had a sign put up outside her shop, representing a priest choosing bonnets while smiling at the sale-girls. That was reported to Hérault who was outraged as not only was the sign indecent, but, adding insult to injury, the milliner had the cheek to call the shop À *l'abbé coquet:* the coquettish abbé. He ordered an underling to fetch the abbé coquet meaning the sign. The underling went to an abbé called Coquet, arrested him and brought him to Hérault, and leaving the priest in the waiting-room announced that the Abbé Coquet was on the premises. "Put him into the attic," answered Hérault, still thinking of the sign. So the good abbé was taken to the attic and locked in. Next morning, tormented by hunger, the abbé started shouting for food. The underling returned to Hérault, saying, "Monseigneur, we do not know what to do with the abbé."

"Burn him," said Hérault. Eventually he discovered that the abbé was truly a priest, and a famished one at that. He apologised and gave him an enormous meal.

Hérault's main headache was a publication entitled *Nouvelles ecclésiastiques* which appeared from time to time. It was a continuous game of hide-and-seek with Hérault unable to catch the printer. It was rumoured that the publication was distributed by smugglers' dogs. It was also reported that one day while he and his henchmen were searching a house in the Faubourg Saint-Jacques the freshly printed sheets of the *Nouvelles ecclésiastiques* were carried out under his nose and thrown into his own carriage.

Claude-Henri Feydeau de Marville was a far more amiable lieutenant of police. He used to spend his evenings in the Comtesse de Noisy's mansion, thinking up practical jokes to amuse and annoy the old Prince de Conti, who also spent his evenings thinking up practical jokes. Mme de Noisy's son, aged sixteen, wanted to go to the ball at the Opera, and Mme de Noisy asked de Marville to keep an eye on him. Immediately the Prince de Conti went to see a dozen or so prostitutes to whom he gave tickets to the ball on the condition that they made the Lieutenant's life sheer hell. He described to them the disguise he would wear. They kept their promise, chasing de Marville all over the Opera House, and he could not get rid of them. He was certain that those girls were put up to it by the Prince de Conti. One day the Prince told him that he would be lunching the next day in a country house eight leagues outside Paris. The journey would take four hours, so he would leave at eight in the morning to arrive at noon. De Marville sent messengers to every village the Prince would drive through with the order to receive him with the respect due to his station; and in each village the Prince de Conti had to listen to addresses and answer them. He arrived in the country house at eight in the evening.

The Lieutenant's life was made rather difficult by Voltaire who at times could be more vindictive than any informer.

It is not the aim of this chapter to consider all the police lieutenants in turn since a number of them did not contribute to the evolution of the police. However, Nicolas-René Berryer de Ravenoville deserves mention as he developed the system of spying on the subject in a masterly manner. He was unafraid of the mighty if he could catch them out. De La Reynie would have shuddered at the very thought of opening a minister's private letters: Berryer had no such scruples. D'Argenson, the King's Minister, sent a letter to the Comtesse d'Estrade in the year 1748 in which he spoke with scant respect of Louis XV and Mme de Pompadour. The letter fell into Berryer's hands, he hurried with it to the King, and d'Argenson was dismissed.

Berryer had a special relationship with Mme de Pompadour in so far as he acquainted her with everything the police was doing, showing her all the secret reports he received, though never letting her know in what derision she was held by many poets and writers. He took it on himself to persecute her detractors, sending them to the Bastille by the shoal after obtaining *lettres de cachet* from the King. Mme de Pompadour regularly received reports on what was going on in the Parisian brothels. She would amuse Louis XV by reading them out to him. Berryer was so encouraged by the success of these reports that he concentrated most of the police's energy on watching the houses of ill-repute. That was an innovation.

His men haunted the brothels, checked on everyone that entered and put on record how long they stayed, all for the King's entertainment. The bawds had to send reports too, describing everything that took place in the houses they ran, and giving the name of each visitor. One Dufrêne, a notorious bawd of her time, would send in such reports as this, "On June 20, 1753 M. Cot..., mathematician to the King, living in Versailles, about forty years old, married. He came in at six o'clock and left at eight. He was with the little Raton from Mme Huguet." Or, "On the 21, M. de la R... governor of the King's menagerie, Knight of the Order of Saint-Louis, about forty years old, unmarried. He saw the little Adélaïde who lives at the sign of King Solomon in the rue Saint-Honoré." Another customer was the Baron de Ram..., also Knight of the Order of Saint-Louis, aged seventy. He saw a girl called Victoire, but, probably because of his ripe age, stayed only from six to seven.

M. de Crem..., Knight Commander of the Cordon-Rouge, Lieutenant-General of the Royal Armies, staying with his brother, the Treasurer of the States of Brittany, in the rue des Capucines, aged about fifty, spent an hour and a half with the same Adélaïde who lived in the rue Saint-Honoré at the sign of King Solomon. The Ambassador of Portugal, aged between thirty-six and forty, spent an hour with Agatha from the Desportes.

Mme de Pompadour and the King read the reports avidly, and when the men of quality, whom Berryer had watched, presented themselves at Versailles she must have believed that she knew their innermost secrets.

The power of the police was expanding as though it were part of progress. In 1755 the Government decided to enlarge the population of the colonies. Since the police had already in de La Reynie's time declared war on beggars and vagabonds, the police now thought that two birds could be killed with one stone. Berryer undertook to transport beggars and the children wandering in the streets and alleys of Paris to the colonies. The children were caught in large numbers, and when they had disappeared the rumour spread in the capital of eternal rumours that they had their throats cut by the police because the Dauphin, who was sick at the time, needed baths of blood to be restored to health. There was rioting before the police headquarters in the rue Saint-Honoré, and the windows of the church of Saint-Roch were smashed. A member of the police force was killed on the church steps.

Frightened, Berryer escaped through the back door; however his wife, who was of stronger fibre, appeared in a dressing-gown on the balcony, which act of courage so impressed the populace that calm returned to Paris. In 1758 Mme de Pompadour repaid Berryer for all he had done to entertain her by having him named Minister of the Navy. He was no more successful in the ministry than he had been in the police. But if one overlooks his lack of tact with vagrants and poor children one has to acknowledge that he made innovations while holding the office of lieutenant of police. "He made useful and deplorable progress," Dulaure said of him.

In the reign of Louis XV Paris was crowded with foreigners: Berryer considered it his duty to keep an eye on them; brothels multiplied: goings on in them were now strictly controlled without public morality benefiting from it; gaming dens needed police permits: none the less, there were twice as many as in the previous reign. The police spied on individuals: one could do little without it being reported, and, to quote Dulaure again, there were fewer daggers but more chains to carry. *Agents provocateurs* did not yet exist. Even Berryer would not have contemplated the use of them.

Antoine-Raymond-Jean-Gualbert-Gabriel de Sartine, Comte d'Alby, was probably the most efficient lieutenant of police since de La Reynie. Between 1759 and 1774 Paris was clean and well lighted. He did a lot for the town, including a free school of drawing for artisans and the building of the *Halle au blé*. He also improved the police system. A friend of his one day declared that he could come to Paris and spend several days there without the police knowing of it. Sartine made a bet with him, and when the friend arrived from Lyons, taking up residence in a district he had not frequented before, and which was far from his customary haunts, he received an invitation to dinner from Sartine a few hours after his arrival. The friend admitted that he had lost the bet.

Sartine followed in Berryer's wake inasmuch as he too sent reports to Versailles to amuse the King. A nobleman arrived every night in the Place Royale in a fiacre, got on the coachman's box, then climbed up to the balcony of an Irishwoman called Nicolson. "Then she hid him in her bed." Louis XV must have laughed. The net expanded with every new lieutenant of police. As Sartine was not satisfied with the adventures of prostitutes and other small fry, the love affairs of great ladies had to enter the police province too. Among his reports, for instance, the intrigue between the Comte de La Marche and the Princesse de Chimay was featured. Mme Du Barry did not escape his vigilance either. Sartine also excelled in having subversive literature destroyed. Among his trophies were the *Contrat Social*, *Lettres de la Montagne*, and a rather modern sounding book, *Les advantages du marriage des Prêtres*. He too finished at the Ministry of the Navy.

Jean-Pierre-Charles Lenoir became lieutenant of police in August 1774 when Turgot was Comptroller-General of Finance. The two men immediately fell out over the victualling of Paris. Turgot had his way with his new sytem of trying to save the economy of France. Lenoir resigned in 1775; as Turgot's plan did not work he was reinstated in 1776.

By then the police more or less controlled the lives of well-to-do families in Paris, that is to say they knew what exactly went on in their homes. Since nothing could be kept secret, and because Lenoir was of a friendly and affable disposition, many parents consulted him before their children got married. He would give them all details on the fortune and position of the intended. Parents also asked him to keep a watch on a son who led a debauched existence. Actresses were his favourites, and he willingly obliged them by having their husbands or lovers followed. He did all that on the cheap. Servants were under his thumb, for no servant could find employment if frowned on by the police. Newsvendors were authorised to sell newspapers and books only if they kept their eyes and ears open in the interests of the police. Among beggars many were left unmolested because they reported where their colleagues hid the loot after a theft or a robbery. Gaming dens were allowed to function if their proprietors kept the police informed of everything that went on in their establishments. One of Lenoir's new departures was to recruit spies among homosexuals. When one of them was caught *in flagrante* he was brought before him, and could choose between public disgrace and the trade of informer. If anybody had anything to hide, Lenoir spoke to him, and since Lenoir knew everybody's secrets more often than not the man would agree to work for him. Thus knights, counsellors of Parliament and magistrates spent their time spying on each other. Those dignified, substantial men cost the police nothing.

However, Lenoir did have an expensive spy, a woman who twice a week invited a large crowd of people to tea, then the next day called on the lieutenant of police and related everything that had been said at the party. She received 2,000 francs a year for this.

Like the other lieutenants of police in the second half of the eighteenth century Lenoir was kept busy by the books that were smuggled in from London and Geneva, not to mention Amsterdam. He appointed Camus de la Neville, a master of pleas, as a sort of censor to whom the booksellers had to bring every book they wanted to sell. If the books were condemned a bonfire was made of them in the Bastille. All works judged to be seditious were labelled philosophical, even if they enlightened no philosopher. After a time about fifteen copies of each condemned book were kept in the Bastille, though not for long as every month a number of them was torn up, and the paper sold. However, some escaped, and when the Bastille fell a large bundle of books was found under Lenoir's seal. Not one of them was of any significance whatever.

Lenoir kept an eye on the milliners, for the Government considered it in the interest of France for prices to be reasonable in order to encourage foreigners to buy French dresses, laces and ribbons.

The police lieutenant had become a powerful personage indeed. A noblewoman, having poisoned her sister-in-law, was arrested and brought before Lenoir who, without bothering to send her before a tribunal, locked her up for life in a convent. Yet the lieutenant's power was only local, and he and his police had nothing to do with the Government's policy. He did not know what went on in Versailles, and had he dared to send a spy to Court to find out, the spy would have been executed and himself put into the Bastille. The police were kept in complete ignorance in matters of State; the lieutenant was never consulted by the ministers. The King's safety was no concern of his; and how could it be in an age when anybody, as long as he wore a hat and carried a sword, could calmly walk into Versailles? When in 1757 Damiens stabbed Louis XV nobody was astonished by him having been able to enter the Castle, and no one was blamed for it. In a sense the police were still in their infancy.

Louis XV was so pleased with the useful work of the police lieutenant—Lenoir had improved the prisons, the hospitals and founded the Mont-de-Piété to save the poor from usurers—that he appointed police lieutenants in most of the large towns, but the municipal councils or the local lords bought them out, and thus their functions reverted to them. Lenoir left the police on August 11, 1785. The King raised him to the presidency of the Commission of Finances, and made him his private librarian.

He was succeeded by Louis Thiroux de Crosne, the last lieutenant-general of police, a man full of good intentions whose first achievement was the destruction of the Cemetery of the Innocents which was overcrowded with scarcely any room left for the fresh corpses, and a centre of pestilence. The Revolution was round the corner, yet Crosne was blissfully unaware of it, and remained deaf to the approaching thunder. For him books and plays were the only danger, especially plays, and he could not resist notifying the Government of every play he considered seditious, or inspired by the *philosophes*. He was convinced that he had his finger on the pulse of Paris; convinced too that he kept the Court informed of everything that went on in the town.

Louis XVI began to think that the truth was kept from him. In order to acquaint himself with public opinion he decided to read the political pamphlets which were distributed all over Paris under the noses of the police. In secret the King commissioned a book-seller called Blaizot to bring to Versailles every pamphlet that had appeared, and leave it in a prearranged place. That went on for two months, at the end of which the ministers noticed that the King was too well informed, the last thing they wanted. They used their own spies, soon discovering that it was Blaizot who brought the pamphlets to their sovereign master. M. de Breteuil, one of the ministers, had Blaizot sent to the Bastille charged with circulating forbidden books. Crosne, the police lieutenant, knew nothing of it. When Louis XVI found no more pamphlets waiting for him in the appointed place, he made inquiries, and discovered that on his own order Blaizot was detained in the Bastille. The King commanded his immediate release without, however, taking trouble to find out how and why the order was issued in his name, a good example of the state of affairs on the eve of the Revolution.

Till the last moment Crosne kept himself busy with plays, pamphlets and books. In his own way he scrupulously followed all orders emanating from Versailles. The Comte de Vergennes, the Foreign Minister, told him to lock up for life one Jean-Claude Fini who wanted to found an empire in the Caucasus, but as he had stolen eleven manuscripts that could interest the Government, Crosne thought it was preferable to put him into the lunatic asylum of Bicêtre. Marshal of France de Ségur complained to Crosne of the *Journal de Paris* because it had praised Guibert, Governor of the Invalides. In future, demanded the Marshal, the newspaper should write nothing about officers without his permission. Crosne at once summoned the editor, and gave him a good scolding. That was three years before the Fall of the Bastille.

Baron Breteuil sent him a letter on August 19, 1787. "It is the King's intention to close all clubs and salons. Please take immediate action to suppress them; if you need *lettres de cachet* I will send you as many as you need." Crosne obeyed, but achieved nothing. He leaves the impression that he was incapable of taking the clubs seriously, as if he had closed his window to the whirlwind of history. He knew the purpose a window served, whereas history was something that was outside his capability.

M. de Villedeuil, Minister of the Royal Household, wrote to him in June 1789, "An important person has denounced the public sale of a scandalous sheet, entitled *Le premier Coup de Vêpres*. It is essential to forbid its sale, and be good enough to stop its distribution." At once Crosne got busy; however, on July 14 the Bastille fell and his career came to an end. Soon his life, too.

On July 15 Bailly was publicly acclaimed mayor of Paris, Crosne resigned, Bailly took possession of the police headquarters, and the King accepted him, in fact signed his appointment. The police were put under him. Thus ended the lieutenancy of police after 122 years, Crosne the fourteenth and last lieutenant-general.

On his mother's advice Crosne left for England, but returned only to be arrested. He shared a cell with Angran-d'Aleroy, another magistrate, and was executed with him on April 28, 1794.

II

From the Revolution to Fouché

During the Revolution the police reverted to their municipal duties which in theory were similar to those before the Royal Edict of 1666. The laws of 1790-91 left to the voters the choice of the commissioners of police and their assistants. Public order and safety were in the hands of the National Guard.

The police of the Revolution and the Terror had travelled a long way from the Watch that Louis XIV had turned into the police of Paris. The Revolution gave immediate and logical birth to the *agents provocateurs* as though the legion of informers it had created at its very inception had not been enough for the purpose. Moreover, the revolutionary governments used the armies as their police. Their soldiers marched to the Vendée, Maine, Lyons and the South, carrying the guillotine with them.

Yet the police in Paris did not entirely founder in anarchy, though within two years after the Fall of the Bastille they had become completely political, that is to say their main activity consisted of tracking down the enemies of the revolutionary regimes. In 1792 the Legislative Assembly decided to take rigorous, preventative action against the émigrés whose number rose daily. The police were charged to deal with them. The passing of the

Passport Act took up much of the legislators' time. When it was passed the police were sent out to catch those whom the men in power wished to keep in France.

Eventually the Directory decided to reorganise the police. The Directors were inspired in their zeal to do so by their own unpopularity. Theirs was a feeble, insecure government, attacked by the news-sheets as much as by their enemies whether of the right or the left. The royalists remained a danger, the anarchists too, and the Directory had but one newspaper in which to defend the regime. There were too many meetings for their liking, and for a while they were like paralysed men watching the fire coming nearer, themselves unable to move. In the long run the State could be upheld only if a ministry of police were created and run by an energetic man who, as member of the Government, would, naturally, serve the Directors' interests. The man they turned to was Merlin (known as Merlin de Douai).*

Philippe-Antoine Merlin, later a Count of the Empire, was born on November 30, 1754, at Arleux, the son of a farmer, and was educated at the College of Anchim at Douai. He was a choirboy at the Abbey of Anchim, and due to a scholarship given by the monks he managed to finish his education. The monks gave him enough money to pursue his studies and become a lawyer at the Parliament of Douai. When the *Etats Généraux* were summoned in 1789 Douai sent him as one of the town's deputies. He joined the group round the Duc d'Orléans (Philippe Égalité), and made such a penetrating speech on feudal rights (January 5, 1790) that Mirabeau congratulated him, but by February 1791 Mirabeau turned against him because of his extreme views when a Bill on the émigrés was debated. "Silence your thirty voices," shouted Mirabeau. Robespierre, Pétion and Buzot were among those thirty voices. In September 1792 Merlin was elected to the *Convention Nationale*. Suspected of not being revolutionary enough he declared on October 7 that he had never committed the crime of serving Louis XVI, or wanting to. He was one of the many who voted for

* See B.

the King's death. By then he had turned against his erstwhile friend and protector, the Duc d'Orléans.

On April 6, 1793, the Convention returned a verdict according to which all members of the Bourbon family were to be arrested in order to be used as hostages by the Republic. Orléans, who had voted for the death of his cousin the King, would be no exception. On that day he was in his mansion, the Palais-Royal, in the company of M. de Monville who had always been a close friend of his, an epicure like himself. The two men were playing cards while Egalité's fate was being decided. When the hour of dinner arrived M. de Monville suggested that it was time to have the meal. They were served on the card table. Merlin acted as messenger between his late protector and the Convention. They were still dining as Merlin rushed in, announcing that the decree had been passed, consequently Orléans' fate was sealed. "Great God," exclaimed Orléans, touching his forehead, "how is that possible? After all the proofs I gave of my patriotism, all the sacrifices I made, how can I be the subject of such a decree? What ingratitude! What horror! What do you make of it, Monville?"

Merlin was watching them both. M. de Monville seasoned his sole, then squirted on it the juice of a lemon. "It is awful, Monseigneur," he said, "but what else can you expect? They took from your Highness all they could take, and as your Highness can do no more for them they treat your Highness in the same manner as I treat this lemon which has no juice left."

Having said that, Monville threw the two halves of the lemon into the fire-place, then reminded Orléans that soles should be eaten piping hot. Impressed, Merlin hurried back to the Convention; Orléans was executed on November 7, 1793.

Merlin was sent to Belgium, and while he was there a new Act created the revolutionary tribunals, the Convention having ordered the disarming of all suspected citizens. On March 28, 1793, two days after the decree establishing those tribunals, the Convention enjoined the municipality of Paris to deliver no more passports before the suspects were disarmed, which should be done at once, and the municipality was empowered by the same decree to arrest anybody considered suspect. In the following August, on the 12th to be precise, the Convention declared that all arrested suspects should be tried summarily, and all the municipalities of France immediately be informed. The decree originated from Danton. Merlin had gone to Brittany after his return from Belgium; but now was back in Paris where he was made a member of a legislative commission. He said that to "regularise the laws of March 28 and August 12 without taking away their arbitrary character was to undertake the lighting of chaos without bringing light". He was loudly attacked for his words, and eventually was forced to present a plan more pleasing to the members of the Convention. That was, as it were, the law on which the Terror was based. On September 17, 1793, the Act dealing with the suspects was finally passed, and cautious Merlin moved out of the limelight.

He remained silent during the Terror, reappeared only after Robespierre's execution, was elected President of the Convention, then made member of the Committee of Public Safety. In January 1795 he wanted the revolutionary tribunals reorganised and a return to the constitution of 1793. As the pendulum was swinging away from the extremists Merlin was not loath to move with it. In the department of the Nord he suppressed the Populist Societies. Due to him Liège and Belgium were attached to France, he became Minister of Justice, reformed criminal procedure, and his code remained in use till 1810. On September 4, 1797, he replaced Barthélemy as Director. The idea of the police ministry originated from him when his fellow Directors saw how insecure their position was.

He found a strange sort of police to reorganise. Though the municipal police had retained their five departments as in the time of the lieutenants-general most of the men were transferred in 1793 to the revolutionary committees, which numbered twelve. Virtue being officially the order of the day, the commissioners arbitrarily decided who was or was not virtuous. Mothers, married women and even young working girls, who refused the advances

of policemen, were herded as prostitutes to the prisons of the
Madelonettes and Petite-Force, where they remained till their
families claimed them, if the families found out where they were.
The police became so venal and disorganised that the Convention
had to interfere.

A decree of Fructidor 14 of the year II (August 31, 1794) set out
in detail how Paris was to be administered. Ministries having
ceased to exist, their functions were taken over by national commissions. The National Commission of Commerce was charged
with the feeding of Paris; the Commission of Public Relief
administered the hospitals; the Commission of Public Education
took over the elementary schools and all other educational establishments; the Commission of Public Works looked after the roads;
the Commission of Agriculture and the Arts looked after artisans,
workshops and all works unconnected with the armies; the Commission of Arms directed everything connected with war, ammunition and artillery; and the Commission of Civilian Administration
headed the police, the prisons and the tribunals. In short, in Paris
six different commissions took over the duties of the lieutenant of
police. (The number was seven, but the lieutenants had had nothing
to do with army matters.) It is important to record this because it
gives the lie to those who believed that Napoleon's police simply
took over and perfected the Royal police. Of that police nothing
was left by the time Merlin came on the scene.

With the new decree the police became dependent not only on
the municipality but on the general administration of the Republic,
which often brought about confusion; and as governments and
regimes changed, so the police had to change tactics. On top of that
the Convention put an administrative commission above the police
whose duty was to watch over public safety and general security.
The commission had twenty-four members, each paid 4,000
francs a year, and to them was attached a National Agent to direct
the police, and in cases of litigation the Police Tribunal took
charge of the municipal police. In matters concerning the émigrés
the civil committees controlled the police. These committees drew

up the lists of émigrés, issued certificates of citizenship and residence, and corresponded directly with the Convention and the National Commissioners over the heads of the police.

This utter confusion ended on August 15, 1795 when the number of the members of the Administrative Commission was reduced from twenty-four to three. In time, the Commission turned into the Central Office, which lasted till 1800 when the office of Prefect of Police was created.

During the Revolution many Acts were passed to restrict personal and civil liberty. The several Passport Acts were specially designed to achieve that. All French citizens had to register with the Paris police within twenty-four hours of their arrival, and it was for the police to decide whether they could stay or not. Theirs was completely an arbitrary power; if the citizen were ordered to leave the capital, he had no appeal. That Act was embellished on March 17, 1796, when a new Passport Act laid down that every citizen had to ask for a permit from his own place of domicile before embarking on a journey, then on arrival for a permit to stay, and anyone who did not or was unable to show a certificate of domicile was declared a vagrant and treated as any old tramp would be.

On Merlin's advice the Directory appointed a commission to report on the police. The commission's conclusions were put before the Councils of the Five Hundred and of the Ancients, where several acrimonious debates took place, each party paying lip-service to the necessity of maintaining order, but each wanting order maintained in its own interests, and according to its own interpretation of the duties of a police minister. Both the royalists and the true republicans feared fresh tyranny, whereas the constitutional party wanted the minister to have enough power to be able to keep the Directors in the saddle. After many debates a seventh ministry was added to the Government, the *Ministère de la Police Générale*. The gendarmerie was also established, and every town with more than five thousand inhabitants received a commissioner of police.

On January 2 the Directory designated Armand-Gaston Camus* as first police minister. He was minister precisely for two days, for on the second day it occurred to him that he could not be both minister and a representative of the people, so he resigned from the ministry. Merlin took his place.

He issued a proclamation to the people of Paris on the day he was appointed. "The Directory sent me to the General Police. I have calculated the weight of the burden I shall have to carry; confident in my courage, full of devotion to the public cause, relying on you and all good citizens, I accepted the task and took up the duty.

"Now, citizens, we must march forward.

"We have to regenerate an immense city.

"Regenerating it we will regenerate the first republic in the world. Paris has always been the model to all departments. Let us make Paris safe; let us establish cleanliness and morality; we will have a wise republic and purity will reign everywhere. . . . I will live only for the republic and the police."

He must quickly have tired of living for the police because he relinquished the ministry after four months, returning to the ministry of justice.

By establishing the ministry of police, Jacques Peuchet wrote in his *Mémoires tirés des archives de la police*, the Directory tried to turn a dishonest trade into a legal institution. A government pretending to believe in a free republic turned France into something worse than Venice had been under the Doges.

During his brief stay at the Ministry of Police Merlin hired a woman referred to as Amélie who came from good Provençal stock, and, therefore, would not arouse suspicion in royalist circles. He sent her to the Abbé Montesquiou, an important royalist. She threw herself at the Abbé's feet, and confessed that she, who belonged to the nobility, had sunk so low as to become the mistress of a director of the police. In her shame she was willing to do anything to redeem herself. The Abbé swallowed the story, told her

* See B.

to spy on the police to expiate her awful sin. She gladly consented. She took money from both sides, and only after Bonaparte's *coup d'état* on Brumaire 18 did the Abbé perceive that he had been her dupe.

A man called Dutour, who belonged to the police, appeared in the Police Ministry asking for higher pay, which was refused on the spot. So he decided to raise money elsewhere. He got in touch with the Chevalier d'Antibes, an ardent royalist, who was in Paris under the name of de Blondel, and whose fires of loyalty could easily be kindled. As one lived in extraordinary times one did not need to be a fool to believe the impossible. Dutour made d'Antibes believe that he was in the position to kidnap Barras, Reubelle, Larevellière, Lépeaux, Carnot and Letourneur, the six Directors. He said he had a number of faithful men at his disposal, all of them belonging to the police, and if they had enough money to make it worth their while they would walk into the Palais de Luxembourg, arrest the Directors, take them away, and then the royalists could settle their fate. The Chevalier parted with 40,000 francs, and waited in vain for the Directors to be brought before him. Meanwhile Dutour spent the money on good living. Through his royalist friends the Chevalier discovered that Dutour was a very subordinate member of the police. But what could he do? In fear of Dutour denouncing him to his superiors he left Paris in haste. On the other hand, Dutour was promoted because he could give his chief the names of the royalists he had met while taking the 40,000 francs from the gullible Chevalier.

Of Amélies and Dutours there were hundreds during the Directory, the Consulate and the Empire. Neither those in power nor those against it could do without them.

At the Ministry of Police Merlin was followed by Charles Cochon, later Comte de Lapparent. He wanted to suppress both the royalists and the anarchists. Babeuf's conspiracy gave him the opportunity to hit hard at the anarchists. However, the Directors always confused the anarchists with the royalists, believing that evil could come only from the right. Cochon knew through his agents that the conspirators of the left assembled nightly in the taverns near the Plaine de Grenelle, but he did not dare to take action, fearing that the Directors would prefer to listen to the conspirators' cries of innocence than to the police. So Cochon used his energy strictly against the royalists. He was an astute man, his spies infiltrated royalist circles, and when royalist agents had assembled in a house Cochon swooped down on them, seizing their papers and their persons. In spite of his success he was suspected of being in league with the enemies of the Directory. Moreover, Mme de Staël disliked him. It is said that it was she who persuaded the Directors to get rid of him.

Jean-Jacques Lenoir-Laroche took over the ministry on July 6, 1797, and was out on the 26th of the same month. It was not easy to be minister of police. In the short space of two years four different ministers, Sotin de la Coindière, Dondeau, Lecarlier and Duval, followed one another. On June 22, 1799, when Roger Ducos, Moulin and Gohier had become the Directors, Bourguignon-Dumolard was designated Minister of Police. His ministry was pretty inefficient, for which he could not be blamed. He was an honest man without any political axe to grind, wanting truly to serve his country. He was frustrated all the time by Sieyès and Barras, whose candidate for the ministry was Joseph Fouché. Due to Gohier's protection, Bourguignon-Dumolard held out till July 20, 1799. Then Fouché took over.

"Honest Bourguignon," said Fouché, "owed his elevation to Gohier; he was completely below his task."

While the police were marching, as it were, to the eminence personified by Fouché, the royalist counter-police became organised too. The chiefs were the Chevalier de Coigny, Hyde-de-Neuville, de Larue, the Abbé Godard, and Dupeyron, known as Marchand.

Coigny, who spent much time in England, was one of the first to get the counter-police going; Hyde-de-Neuville, who had been associated with the Vendée, came later. On his order on the night of January 20-21, 1799, the anniversary of Louis XVI's execution, a black flag was hoisted on the belfry of the Madeleine, in the cemetery of which the King was buried with his head between his legs as a sign of national disgrace. The fluttering flag had an enormous effect on the people, and brought many volunteers to the white flag of the Bourbons. Dupeyron, who had been employed on royalist missions during the Convention, was the director of movements of the counter-police, an important job since the members had often to move, and rapidly at that. Hyde-de-Neuville and a few others would rapidly have to escape to England if the police discovered their whereabouts. The agency's address became known to the police who seized all the agency's papers. So the counter-police had to start afresh.

Dupeyron laid down new rules. "One must keep and perfect the existing agency, but one must stop everything that had been left to the agents' arbitrary judgments." The most important thing was to create an organisation in which the chiefs would be secure by remaining unknown to its ordinary members. That, Dupeyron maintained, he could achieve thanks to the spies he had in the Ministry of Police. He wanted 2,000 louis a month for the organisation, but as 2,000 louis were considered too much, his plan was dropped. He evolved another which promised to keep spies at police headquarters, daily receive all secret police reports, finding out when and where royalists would be arrested, in fact obtain the day before copies of every warrant issued against royalists, and have the enemies of the cause followed if the necessity were to arise. That plan was cheaper, therefore the émigrés in London accepted it. A little later Dupeyron could inform Hyde in England that through his agents in the ministry the police came to believe that the black flag on the belfry of the church of the Madeleine had been planted there by the Jacobins.

However, Fouché, the new police minister, was nobody's fool. He refused to believe that the Jacobins had been responsible for the black flag and similar manifestations. On January 7, 1800, Dupeyron received intelligence from the ministry that Fouché had announced to his collaborators that a royalist plot was imminent. Dupeyron was not frightened, and told his colleagues that Fouché had said that to impress his collaborators without "being the depository of any important secret". At the same time he warned them not to become foolhardy. If they remained cautious, then even with their bribery the police could not penetrate the organisation. The Chevalier de Coigny was suspected by the police of hatching some plot, and was followed everywhere; however, Dupeyron could report a week or so later that the police had stopped watching Coigny, consequently there was nothing more to fear.

Fouché paid some impoverished members of the nobility heavily to spy on their own caste. Dupeyron received a list of the noblemen who were in his pay, also the names of all police agents, including those who were received in society. Still, in London they were not too impressed. In a letter Hyde reproached Dupeyron for having been kept in the dark when several royalists were arrested. Dupeyron riposted, saying that the police had 6,000,000 francs and three hundred informers at their disposal; so how could he find out about every arrest with only eighty louis a month?

The counter-police were organised in sections, each consisting of two or three agents who were in touch with their section-chiefs, the chiefs having another chief above them who was in touch with Louis XVIII and the Princes. If an agent was arrested, his chief went straight into hiding. If the agent ratted on him he could not be found, thus the police could get no further since the agents only knew their own chief. All very clever; none the less the police did get on the organisation's track, the chiefs had to take refuge in England, and their correspondence was seized in Calais. Of course, somebody had been bought. Gold in Napoleonic times was the best and most reliable policeman, and Fouché's most trustworthy ally.

After a while the counter-police were again reorganised. One of their new tasks was to follow prominent men. The erstwhile Abbé Sieyès, now one of the three consuls, Bonaparte and Ducos being the other two, was chosen to be shadowed. While keeping on his tail the royalists discovered that Fouché, too, had Siéyès followed. Dupeyron wrote to England, asking for extra money to buy a horse for his agent, as Sieyès always went about in a carriage. One can almost see Sieyès riding in the carriage with Fouché's and the royalists' agents trotting side by side.

Dupeyron and his associates raised many false hopes among the émigrés: since Brumaire 18 everything had gone from bad to worse, the army grumbled; the soldiers loathed Bonaparte, who was an ambitious foreigner; half of the general staff was on the King's side; and if Louis XVIII or one of the Princes had ridden into Paris the town and the garrison would have risen for him. Bonaparte was preparing another *coup d'état;* the people hated him because he had deserted the war in Egypt; he would soon be out; the French were convinced that the war would go on till they got rid of the revolutionary government; and rumour had it that an entire regiment of dragoons had gone over to the enemy, and so on.

The royalists did not despise other folk's money. In a letter Dupeyron announced that a man who had acquired a lot of land that had belonged to the nobility or the Church would be attacked in his house which was three leagues from Paris. The man was robbed, and a few months later the royalist agents who had taken part in the armed robbery were caught by the police.

The counter-police continued to exist till the end of Napoleon's reign, though between 1800 and 1810 their activities consisted mainly of aiding and hiding agents coming from England.

III

Joseph Fouché

"Expressing my opinion of this famous man," wrote Edme-Théodore Bourg in 1829, "I formulate this sincere wish: let France never again produce a man who resembles him!" Amen, one could almost add.

Fouché is remembered as the clever, cunning, infinitely intelligent and suave police minister, the begetter of the modern police system, and the father of the Gestapo and the OGPU (though he would vehemently have contested that). The times in which he lived fitted him like a glove. The Napoleonic era was a continuous fiesta, the hangover was kept at arm's length till after Waterloo, everybody who could fished in the sunlit, brilliant troubled waters, and Fouché was a first-rate fisherman. It was a euphoric, corrupt, heroic and lying age. Nothing was true, albeit everything glittered. The great Napoleon, as a French saying has it, went from victory to victory so that the Cossacks should bivouac in the Champs-Elysées. Throughout the reign Fouché remained the bland police minister and intriguer when not in disgrace. But he did not begin like that. When he had reached the police ministry he wanted to erase his past: however it clung to him, though he tried hard to make the world forget that he had been one of the most monstrously cruel men of the Revolution, as bloodthirsty as any of the other beasts of the Terror that gorged on blood.

Joseph Fouché was the son of a captain in the French merchant navy. He was born in Pellerin, in the Loire-Inférieure (now Atlantique). His father wanted him to follow in his footsteps; the son did not care for the sea. He was educated by the Oratorians who were impressed by his excellent brain. He entered the Congregation of the Oratorians, never took vows, yet was known till the Revolution as Father Fouché. He was principal of the college in Nantes when the Revolution came. He had met Robespierre while he was teaching philosophy at Arras. The story has it that he lent money to the Incorruptible to make it possible for him to establish himself in Paris. Fouché wanted to marry his sister, but Charlotte Robespierre would not have him. It is not known when exactly he left the Oratorians to become deputy of the Loire-Inférieure to the Convention; in 1792 he was already one of the noisiest of them. If one looks at his career under the Consulate and the Empire one finds it inconceivable that so clever and cunning a man could have behaved with such utter lack of caution. He, who would be careful not to get entangled or show his true colours, was as foolhardy as any member of the mob of the Faubourg Saint-Antoine. In 1792 he was appointed to the Committee of Public Education.

Louis XVI was prisoner in the Temple, where he showed admirable dignity, tutoring his son, praying, meditating, and treating all who saw him with consideration. That became common knowledge, and the people of Paris no longer saw him as a despicable ogre and the enemy of the nation. As a prisoner the King was more dangerous than when he still reigned in Versailles.

In the Convention, the Girondins, whom Fouché had joined at the time, wanted the King declared "guilty of conspiring against the common safety of the State", yet allowed a national vote to confirm or reject this judgment. Fouché prepared a rough draft containing the rejection of the death sentence. When the death sentence was debated in the Convention the Girondins were convinced that Fouché would vote with them against it. After all he was the author of the draft.

The voting went on the whole night of January 20, 1793; one after the other the deputies mounted the tribune to call out their votes. *"La mort!"* echoed through the Convention. The Girondins' first shock came when their foremost member, Vergniaud, President of the Convention on that day, voted with the enemy. The deputies of the Loire-Inférieure were called to vote. Some expressed the opinion that the King should be kept a prisoner till the end of the war, then expelled from France. One deputy voted for his death, another against it. Then came Fouché's turn. As white as a sheet he shouted, *"La mort!"* He never lived that down.

For the moment Fouché had no regrets since he was swimming with the tide without asking himself how long the age of mass massacre would last. On March 9, 1793, the Convention sent him with Villers into the Loire-Inférieure and Mayenne to raise 300,000 men for the Armies; on June 24 of the same year he was sent into the Centre and the West "to invite and request the citizens to take arms against the rebels of the Vendée". He went to Troyes, where he assured the victory of the Jacobins, then to Nevers, giving himself the mission of destroying Christianity and founding the cult of Reason. He ordered that in all cemeteries a statue to Sleep should be erected, for death was eternal sleep. His fellow-representative was Chaumette, as bloodthirsty as he, and those in Nevers who did not agree with them were quickly put to death. Then on October 30 Fouché was given a new mission: he was sent with Collot d'Herbois to Lyons to superintend the massacres there. Lyons had risen against the Government, but was conquered by the revolutionary forces.

The citizens of Lyons were looked on as the enemies of the people, and as the number of Lyonnais was large it would have taken too long to have the condemned executed one by one. Soon after Fouché's arrival forty men were sentenced in one lot, all of them to death; the trial lasted only half an hour. On December 12, 1793, the mass executions began in the Place Brotteaux, where a platform was erected for the Representatives of the Convention. Fouché took his place, and watched the spectacle through his lorgnette. Two trenches awaited the corpses of the sixty-two young men condemned on that day; fastened together in pairs. They were mown down by cannons, a new manner of executing death sentences. After the cannon balls did their work the soldiers' sabres finished the condemned off. Collot d'Herbois reported that that was only the beginning. He did not exaggerate. When there were too many corpses they were thrown into the Rhône so that floating down the river they struck terror into other rebels. By April 1794 one thousand six hundred and sixty-seven persons had been executed in Lyons.

Even Paris thought that the Representatives had gone too far, and Collot was sent for. In the Jacobin Club he declared that to have two hundred men shot simultaneously could not be considered a crime. In fact, it was an act of mercy, a sign of commiseration. If twenty men were guillotined one after the other the twentieth died twenty times whereas the two hundred had died but once. Collot did not bother to disclose that looting had gone hand in hand with the massacres. "A bayonet piercing a human heart," said Fouché a year later, "makes me tremble. However, this bayonet is guiltless, and only a child would wish to break it."

The Convention did not blame Fouché, but Robespierre was far from satisfied with him, though not because of the organised killing but because he and his friends had lived too well in Lyons. The Representatives' fare was excellent and expensive; enormous bills were sent in; and they gorged on capons and pike which were washed down with gallons of choice wines. The Government was also charged with the price of clothes, shirts, frills and ruffles.

After his arduous work in Lyons Fouché was elected chairman of the Jacobin Club. Then soon after he fell out with Robespierre whom he had called a fool "possessed by the ridiculous idea of giving a public acknowledgment of the existence of a Supreme Being". Fouché nearly paid with his life when Robespierre had him expelled from the Jacobin Club. Only the amnesty of Brumaire 4 saved him.

Fouché fell on evil days. To begin with he was married to a woman who had no fortune, Bonne-Jeanne Coignaud of whom Paul Barras said, "she was terribly ugly and redheaded like her husband, even to eyebrows and lashes". They had married in September 1792 and had children but no money. For a while he associated with a pig-dealer. He maintained for the rest of his life that his fortune came from his business deals. His partner advanced the money to buy small pigs which Fouché fattened up then sold at double their cost. After a time the partners fell out, and Fouché, who had thought it all up, wanted the lion's share. The partner objected since he had put up the money. There would have been a lawsuit if Barras, who had befriended Fouché, had not intervened. Fouché also tried detective work when his financial troubles were over. In December 1795 he was banished from Paris by the Government. When he was able to return to Paris he started a company for the delivery of provisions to the troops in the north-east of France. That and the pigs, declared the man who would leave fourteen million francs in 1820, were the basis of his fortune. Posterity refuses to believe that.

In the year VI (1795) he joined Babeuf and his friends whom he denounced to the Directorate. Thanks to Barras, he was appointed envoy to Milan, where he immediately started intriguing against the Government of the Cisalpine Republic. He was expelled from the Republic. After a brief stay in Holland he was appointed minister of police. That was on July 20, 1799.

With that appointment began the remarkable career and tribulations of Joseph Fouché, who had sold himself too soon and for too low a price to the Jacobins. The reaction to the excesses of the Revolution was in full swing, and the reaction would mount with the Consulate and then with the Empire. He had to embrace it if he wanted to forge forward; yet he could not embrace it completely since he had belonged to the action itself. Hence his dilemma. He had to crush the Jacobins, stamp out all revolutionary movements in spite of having been an active revolutionary. On the other side were the royalists who would never trust the regicide and *mitrailleur* of Lyons. In the centre, so to speak, stood Napoleon who would be his master for most of his active life. Napoleon leaned more towards the royalists than the Jacobins. And it was Napoleon who seldom missed the occasion of reminding Fouché that he had voted for the death of Louis XVI, therefore could not turn to the royalists. But he could not turn to the revolutionaries either, because he had betrayed them. So Fouché had always to walk the tightrope, and betray both friend and foe whenever his interests demanded. "A monster brought forth in the revolutionary pond by the mating of anarchy and despotism," Chateaubriand was to say of him. And Talleyrand, who was no more above reproach than he, described him as "a heart of diamond, a stomach of iron and a tearless eye". It was also Talleyrand who said of him, "a man who must have a finger in everything that concerns him, and, above all, in what is no concern of his". But given his past Fouché could not do otherwise.

When he was made minister of police he closed the Jacobin Club, suppressed eleven newspapers, and became the terror of the left purely to show his new masters that he did not belong to it. Yet he could not break away from it completely. Anne-Jean-Marie-René Savary, later Duc de Rovigo, who was to succeed him in 1810 as minister of police, rightly spoke of him as one who belonged to every party of the Revolution only to desert every one of them to follow the most convenient cause of the moment. The most convenient cause was Napoleon's *coup d'état* of Brumaire 18 when Fouché, as police minister, gave him all the help he could to establish the rule which with one interruption, the short term on Elba, lasted till 1815.

Napoleon was no easy master; neither was Fouché the trustworthy servant. When Napoleon emphasised that Fouché had burnt his boats by voting for the King's death the master thought that the servant would have to remain faithful to him out of sheer necessity. On one such occasion, unperturbed, Fouché replied, "Yes, Sire, that was the first service I rendered your Majesty". None the less, he knew perfectly well how ambiguous his position was, and would remain to the end. As Emile Faguet observed, "Fouché looked at everything through the *lunette* of Louis XVI's scaffold". Because his position was ambiguous and as he could not afford direct action, the police of the Consulate and the Empire had to act as the minister was compelled by his past to behave.

Each phase of the Revolution had had its victims. Napoleon's *coup d'état* had plenty too, and they, who had known him in revolutionary times, turned to Fouché for help. He enrolled them, if he found them suitable, in his secret legion of spies and *agents provocateurs*. He used his fellow Jacobins to spy on Jacobins; down-and-out aristocrats to shadow the nobility. He found nothing degrading in tempting a poor man to betray his cause. After all, he had betrayed so many. He was such a cynic in matters of honour and decency that he never regretted any of his wicked actions. Undeniably he had a sense of humour. When a secret code of the royalists was discovered one of his henchmen suggested using it to lay a trap for another member of the same family, the one the police had caught being already executed. "One bereavement is enough in a family," replied Fouché.

Nobody knew better than Napoleon how morally depraved his police minister was and how scrupulously his police followed Fouché's example. One day the Emperor complained to Fouché of his police methods, reproaching him with watching and spying on his own courtiers. Fouché coolly answered that even his Majesty was not safe where police vigilance was concerned.

"That is all right," said Napoleon in an icy voice. "You do your job."

Napoleon could not have been shocked since he himself spied on Fouché's police in so far as Veyrat, Inspector-General of Police, sent without his chief's knowledge every night a secret report to Constant, the Emperor's valet.

Napoleon and Fouché were linked by their mutual distrust. Before the beginning of a campaign Napoleon asked Fouché what he would do if he were killed by a bullet or had an accident. "Sire," said Fouché, "I would assume as much power as I could so as to be able to dominate events and not be carried along by them."

The Emperor thought that over, then said, "À *la bonne heure,* that is the law of the game". He could have said that of the jungle.

It was always difficult for Fouché to fight simultaneously on three fronts against his three enemies, the Jacobins, the royalists and his master, the Emperor. In 1801, for instance, he felt compelled to stoop so low as to draw up a list of a hundred and thirty persons who ought to be deported, old terrorists who had done far less harm than he between 1792 and 1795, but he had to pacify reactionary opinion. On January 5, 1801, the Senate confirmed his proposal, and the men were expelled, many of them never to see France again. To those Jacobins with whom he was still in touch Fouché explained that it would have been worse for their cause if he had resigned and allowed a true reactionary to take his place. Fouché wanted to remain on good terms with all who were hounded by him, and in fact believed that he made no enemies. He would catch a group of royalists, have six executed, let the seventh go, convinced that with that act of mercy he had made friends among the royalists. Because of his equivocal position he was too much a manipulator, a puller of strings. Napoleon observed of him, "M. Fouché always wants to be my guide and at the head of all the columns; but as I never tell him anything he does not know which direction to take, and so loses his way". What Napoleon did not appreciate was that Fouché had lost his way during the Revolution, and now he badly needed to obliterate the landmarks and milestones.

In his position as police minister he succeeded in destroying practically all the papers and documents relating to his correspondence with the Committee of Public Safety while he was their representative in Lyons.

He was infinitely clever, and could turn any situation to his benefit. In November 1800 Lucien Bonaparte, the First Consul's brother and Minister of the Interior, sent to his subordinates throughout the country a pamphlet entitled, *A Comparison between*

Caesar, Cromwell, Monk and Bonaparte, in which he suggested that
the First Consul should be made dictator since he was as worthy
of the position as Caesar or Cromwell. Moreover, he represented
both the educated and the ordinary masses. Fouché saw his opportunity again to ingratiate himself with the First Consul and show
him how circumspect and what a deep thinker he was. In a report
he pointed out that the situation was fraught with danger as the
people were not yet prepared for such a change. The First Consul
saw his point, ordered Fouché to confiscate the pamphlet, and
forced Lucien to resign.

Fouché was minister of police on four different occasions. July
20, 1799, to September 15, 1802; July 10, 1804, to June 2, 1810;
March 21 to June 23, 1815; and from July 9 to September 25, 1815.

In 1802 Napoleon allowed all émigrés who had asked to return
to come back to France, even giving them back their property if
it had not been confiscated. The First Consul had a list made out
of the émigrés, and those whom he considered not dangerous
were eliminated from the list. He was at the time so enthusiastic
about the unity of Frenchmen, which he believed he had established, that he decided that there was no need left for a ministry of
police. Also by abolishing it he knew that his popularity would
increase. He attached the police to the Ministry of Justice, convinced
that with the gendarmerie and the tribunals order could easily be
maintained. Fouché thought that it was Talleyrand's doing. He
left the police and entered the Senate, but the ministry being re-
established in 1804, because of the plots against Napoleon and the
constant activities of the Chouans, Fouché was in the saddle again.

He had to intrigue continuously to cover up his traces and use
methods any honourable man would have shrunk from, because
under Napoleon he could never be totally master in his own house,
for Napoleon believed that he alone was entitled to absolute power.
The Police Minister had to share his authority with the Minister
of Justice in the control of local administration, and with the
Prefects, and the Minister of Public Worship in matters concerning
the clergy. In his own ministry he had to deal with the Prefect of

Police of Paris, Dubois,* who behind Fouché's back was constantly in touch with Napoleon. In 1804 a council was appointed consisting of three—for a brief period four—members responsible for different police districts, Dubois for Paris, Réal for the North and Western departments, and Pelet de la Lozère for the rest of France and parts of Italy. Pelet like Dubois was no friend of Fouché; however, in Councillor of State Réal, Fouché found his ideal henchman.

Pierre-François Comte Réal was born in Chaton in 1757. A lawyer by profession, he came first into public notice when in 1792 he took a delegation to the Convention, asking for the enormous, indisciplined mass of the *sans-culottes* to be sent to the frontiers to fight the enemy. That was the beginning of the *levée en masse* decreed on August 23, 1793. Réal was a friend of Danton, one of the editors of the *Journal des Patriotes*, Councillor of State in 1804, remaining the head of the first police department till the end of Napoleon's reign, and Prefect of Police during the Hundred Days. He was outstanding in making prisoners confess. Napoleon had a high opinion of his police tactics.

Charles Desmarets, Chief of Police throughout the Consulate and the Empire, was another outstanding member of Fouché's team, a true pillar of iniquity. Fouché called him an exceptionally supple man. Born in Compiègne in 1763, he was brought up at the College Duplessis, and like Fouché studied for the priesthood. The Revolution turned him into a ferocious Jacobin; he entered a department of the administration that sent him to Switzerland. On his return to France an army contractor recommended him to Fouché who found a kindred spirit in him, and took him into the Ministry of Police, soon promoting him to Chief of Division of the *Haute Police*. Desmarets suited Fouché to the ground, for Desmarets had tact, an engaging smile, and was a master of insidious questions. He had the gift of making the prisoners confess to him as he oozed goodwill and understanding. Probably he was the most sinister of the lot. Though he was daily in touch with Napoleon to whom he frequently betrayed Fouché, he saw him but once

* See C.

during his long service. There was no need for it, he explained in his Memoirs, since the Emperor and he understood each other perfectly, in fact he guessed his intentions before they were formulated. When in 1810 Fouché fell into disgrace, Desmarets gave the same sort of loyalty to Savary, the new Police Minister. "He turns instinctively towards the sun," was Fouché's comment.

While Fouché, Réal and Desmarets worked together most of their time was taken up by the Chouans, that constant thorn in Napoleon's flesh.

IV

Jean Chouan

"Qui a chouanné chouannera", was Fouché's dictum. He looked on the Chouans as criminals and mean rebels, a constant source of irritation. Their patriotism, love of the country's traditions, their loyalty to the Bourbon cause and their religious feelings were beneath his contempt. Now and then he was not far wrong; for Chouannerie, after the death of Jean Chouan whose real name was Jean Cottereau, took strange courses at times.

The rising of the Vendeé was an honest-to-God counter-revolution. The Vendéens had their own proper army, the Catholic and Royal Army, which had fought bravely in the open and was defeated in battle by the Republican forces. It was General Hoche who pacified the Vendée. In a public square in his native town of Versailles stands his statue. "The man who pacified the Vendée", reads the inscription. In the year 1968, that is more than a century and a half after Hoche's death, some unknown person chalked the words, "Six hundred thousand dead", under the inscription. Roughly speaking that was how the Vendée was pacified by Hoche, who, had he not died young (1768-97), would have been a serious competitor with Bonaparte for absolute power.

The rising of the Vendée was a military matter with which the police had little to do. With the Chouans it was altogether different: for within that movement not only exalted patriots plotted and schemed to rid France of Napoleon, but they were joined by adventurers and gaol birds. The Chouans operated in Normandy, Brittany, Anjou and Maine. They were always in need of money. You cannot conspire efficiently if you are penniless. There were only two means of getting hold of money. The first, to take it from the English Government whose end the Chouans served; the second, by stealing it whenever the opportunity presented itself. Holding up mail coaches was the Chouans' favourite means of solving their financial problems. Of course, there were many who participated in those attacks purely for patriotic reasons, but there also were a number who acted with the sole intention of putting the money into their own pockets. Most of the Chouans were poor outlaws. The man whose name they took was a poor outlaw himself, yet he never thought of his personal advantage. He fought only for God and King.

Jean Cottereau was born in the year 1757 in the forest of Concise near Saint-Berthevin, not far from the town of Laval. His father was a wood-cutter and sabot-maker. The large family lived in a hut and were as poor as church mice. It was the father who was nicknamed Chouan because he beautifully imitated the screech of the owl. Around 1760 the family settled at the Poiriers, a smallholding Jean's mother inherited. It was in the vicinity of the village of Saint-Ouën-des-Toits. The father died in 1778, and Pierre, the eldest son, took over his work as wood-cutter and makers of sabots. His three brothers, Jean, François and René, became smugglers.

King Louis XII exempted Brittany from paying tax on salt. The Chouan brothers smuggled salt from Brittany into the province of Maine, where salt cost ten times more. The brothers were daring smugglers, took countless risks, and were now and then caught. The penalty was death, but each time they were released, thanks to the intervention of the great noblemen of the district who admired their courage.

According to local legend, his mother went on one occasion to Versailles to ask for the King's pardon, which was granted, and Jean, the illiterate smuggler, never forgot that he owed his life to the King's mercy. When the Revolution came there was no more fervent supporter of the King than Jean Chouan.

On August 15, 1792, all people in the neighbourhood were summoned to Saint-Ouën-des-Toits, where in the church, now turned into a public meeting place, they were harangued by revolutionary orators, sent by the Government with the intention of raising a battalion or so. The local people hissed and booed them. The Government men ordered the gendarmes to arrest the lot; however, the peasants stood their ground, and their attitude became so aggressive that the orators took to their heels. Jean Chouan addressed the young men of the village, asking them to swear a solemn oath that they would only serve God and the King.

Thus was Chouannerie born.

The first Chouans had only long poles, but in time they acquired rifles, that is they took them from the gendarmes and Government soldiers after having killed them. The Chouans lived in the forest, assembled when Jean decided on an attack, and dispersed when the job was done. For the authorities they became an invisible festering sore. The Republicans kept away from the forest of Misedon, where Jean had his headquarters. Local people called it the Place Royale, and those who wanted to join his band came into the forest and waited for him in the glade. When Jean was notified that a stranger had arrived, unseen by the person he observed him from behind a tree, and if he thought that the man looked trustworthy he came out to speak to him.

One day he and his men attacked a detachment of the National Guard. The battle was fought near the marsh of La Chaîne, and ended with the Chouans' victory. The National Guardsmen who managed to escape raised the alarm in the town of Bourgneuf. Jean remained near the marsh, waiting for the enemy. And the enemy came. Though the new force was much stronger than the one he had defeated he immediately gave battle. The National

Guard's superiority, also the two cannons they had brought with them, forced Jean to abandon the terrain and vanish with his men. He was sentenced to death in his absence. Now it was up to the authorities to catch him.

They tried everything, including sending spies who pretended they were faithful royalists, but Jean did not fall into the trap. He stayed in the forest till his mother sent for him because she had nobody to till the land. He came out, and once the work was done returned to the forest of Misedon. He left it only for foraging. After one of those brief expeditions he found his camp demolished and his provisions stolen. The blacksmiths of Port-Brillet, who had turned into fanatic revolutionaries, were responsible. Jean sallied forth with three companions. On reaching the wayside inn where the blacksmiths were celebrating their victory he shot dead the look-out man they had posted, then burst into the inn. There were twenty-six blacksmiths inside. When they saw the four men, first they barricaded themselves in the back room, then ran for dear life. Jean and his companions took the firearms they left behind in their hurry, and sped back into the forest.

The blacksmiths were ashamed of their cowardice and went to occupy Jean's mother's smallholding. Jean did not hesitate: he gathered thirty Chouans and attacked the blacksmiths, whom he smartly defeated. Frightened, the republicans of the neighbourhood left their villages and took refuge in the town of Laval, leaving the whole district in the hands of the Chouans, whose lightning attacks on the Government forces became more and more frequent.

In the summer of 1793 Jean suspended all operations so as to give his men leave to gather in the harvest. The Blues, as the soldiers of the Republic were known, took advantage of the lull by arresting the wives and children of several of his companions, imprisoning them in Laval. The Chouans took to fighting again. They fought intrepidly, had real panache, spared women and children, but were merciless to their foes. They did not pillage, had no other motive than fighting the Revolution, and after each fight they disappeared only to reassemble at a given moment at some distant spot. They also came to the aid of the Catholic and Royal Army led by the Prince de Talmont, and fought like lions.

Of course, they could not last. After the defeat of the Catholic and Royal Army the Chouans withdrew into the forest, where Jean, to his delight, was reunited with his two brothers who had been captured by the Blues, but had managed to escape from imminent death. The Blues shot or hanged all their prisoners.

The Government decided to exterminate them. Under the command of General Beaufort six thousand Blues entered the forest. They advanced with rolling drums. The search was pretty inefficient, for the Blues had not the courage to enter the darkest parts of the forest where the Chouans were hiding. None the less, it was touch and go, and when the Blues marched out empty-handed from the forest the Chouans fell on their knees to thank God for their deliverance.

Jean's brother François was wounded by his own rifle while cleaning it. In order not to compromise his mother and sisters, he had himself carried into the forest of Misedon, where he died of his wound. His mother had followed the Catholic and Royal Army against her sons' advice. After the rout of the army at Le Mans she was run over by a cart and died two days later. The Blues came to the smallholding, took Jean's two sisters and carried them away. Through his spies Jean found out that the Blues had taken the road to Bourgneuf and from Bourgneuf would proceed along the road to Ernée. Jean decided to save his sisters, that is ambush the column when they passed through the forest of Durandais. He and his companions waited for long hours in the pelting rain, waited in vain, for the column had reached Ernée on its way to Laval. Both the young girls were sentenced to death. The elder girl asked to be executed last so that her younger sister should be spared the awful sight of seeing her sister's head roll into the basket. When her turn came her last words were, "Long live the King!"

Meanwhile the Blues caught Jean's brother Pierre. They tore his clothes, marched him through the streets of Laval, then he was taken to prison, sentenced to death and guillotined the next day, June 11, 1794.

In his distress Jean seemed to have lost his dash, whereas his remaining brother René thought only of revenge. Jean held him back till the day a delegation of peasants arrived in the forest, seeking Jean's help because the Blues had dragged of several peasants from their village. Immediately Jean put himself at the head of his men, charged the Blues, liberated the prisoners and chased the Republican soldiers out of the district. That was Jean's last triumph.

On Sunday, July 27, 1794, Jean ventured out of the forest. His spies had told him that there were no Blues in the neighbourhood. He was accompanied by his brother René, René's pregnant wife and a few Chouans, their intention to find food and clothing. They came to a farm on the road to Saint-Ouën-des-Toits. The farmer recognised Jean and invited them in. The small party went to rest in the orchard. Jean left a look-out on the road, but after a while the man came into the orchard to join the party. Somebody ratted on them, and soon a detachment of Blues was approaching the farm.

The Chouans decided to hurry back to the forest, but René's pregnant wife lagged behind. When the men were already at a considerable distance she shouted for help. Jean turned back at once. The Blues had reached the scene, and as Jean dragged the woman along they opened fire, a bullet hitting him in the abdomen. He managed to crawl behind a chestnut tree. Unseen by the Blues his companions returned, carried him into the forest of Misedon and laid him on the ground. His agony lasted the whole night. He asked his friends to find him a priest, but it was too late, and he died without the last rites. He was buried in the forest, and his friends swore never to divulge where his grave was. Nobody ever found it. His brother René survived, and after the Restoration King Louis XVIII gave him a pension of four hundred francs. René was twice married, had seventeen children, and died at the age of eighty-three.

This then was the story of Jean Chouan, a brave guerilla leader, his exploits worthy of anyone's admiration. Precisely because of the admiration and respect the royalists had for him, all who in Western France sided with the Bourbons began to call themselves Chouans. As time progressed so the name Chouan lost its purity. When Fouché said *qui a chouanné chouannera* he meant once a thief always a thief, in his bland manner overlooking the fact that he too was responsible for Chouannerie sinking so low.

The many martyrs of the movement did not interest him apart from catching them and making martyrs of them. What did interest him, however, was to bribe Chouans to give their friends away. There was some competition in so far as the English Government were also willing to use the Chouans. England could offer them money and eventual refuge; Fouché could offer the Emperor's pardon, though that promise was seldom kept. Thus the movement which started with the pure, patriotic dash of Jean Chouan became at times but a business venture with England and Fouché bidding against each other.

Almost every Chouan plot against Napoleon was discovered by Fouché and his stalwarts, Réal and Desmarets. All attempts on the Emperor's life were frustrated; the guillotine worked overtime; none the less Chouannerie outlived the Empire. You squashed one group only for another to arise; for, fundamentally, the west of France, especially Brittany, Normandy, Anjou and Mayenne, hated Napoleon and considered him a usurper. Though some could not resist the temptation of badly needed money, or collapsed in the shadow of the guillotine, the great majority remained faithful to God and King, hence the survival of the movement. And it should not be forgotten that the examples of Georges Cadoudal, Comte Louis de Frotté, and Charette who had fought Napoleon, only added to their fervour and resolve to continue to plot and fight against the Usurper.

In 1801, when the Chouans still fought in the open, the First Consul signed a concordat with the Chouan leaders, and a general amnesty was granted. However, only a few Chouans kept the

First Consul's peace. The movement went underground, remaining a festering sore and Fouché's constant nightmare. The security of the State depended on him, and there could be no security while the Chouans existed. To the Chouans he added the army of deserters and brigands who operated in bands; and over there in London one plot after another was hatched by the émigrés and escaped or visiting Chouans.

V

Georges Cadoudal—the First Phase

Georges Cadoudal was born on January 1, 1771, at Kerléano in the Morbihan, son of the plough and not of the mill, as his nephew Georges did not fail to point out in his life of his uncle whom a Paris newspaper referred to as a miller's son. In fact, Cadoudal's father was an agricultural labourer. Kerléano is in the Brech, and the King himself was the local landlord. "We were," boasted the Cadoudals, "direct subjects of the King." Already as a baby the man who was to be known all over France as General Georges or simply Georges was inordinately fat.

At an early age Georges was sent to a school in Auray, where he received an elementary education and was taught a little Latin. His teachers noticed his courage coupled with an even temper, and found him the outstandingly typical Breton boy in the midst of dozens of other Breton boys. His curls were fair; however, as regulations forced him to have his hair frequently cut, and as in any case peasant boys had their hair cropped short, his hair soon turned brown. Yet he remained the Breton giant with golden locks in the legend that grew with him. Besides, he did not mature into a giant in the physical sense: he was a squat, broad-shouldered, corpulent person.

From the elementary school he moved to the College of Vannes, run by Jesuits and organised like an English public school. He became a school prefect. In the college they studied mathematics, rhetoric, Latin and philosophy. These were not arduous studies, and in later life Georges referred to himself as half-educated. The college became a hotbed of the Chouannerie of Morbihan, though with a strong inclination for reforms. Most of the pupils were preparing to enter the Society of Jesus. Not so Georges, who left college in 1791 to work in a notary's office.

The Bretons were and still are deeply religious people. When the Revolution turned on the Church they turned against it in spite of the reforms they longed for. "Our churches are attacked and sacrilegious hands are laid on our altars," the ordinary folk of Morbihan cried with some justice. One has only to quote Hippolyte Taine who said of the Act of the Civil Constitution of the Clergy, "An admirable law that under the pretext of reforming ecclesiastical abuses outlaws all the faithful, whether priests or laymen". Only three of the bishops of France, one of them Talleyrand, Bishop of Autun, swore allegiance to the Constitution. One hundred and thirty-four archbishops, bishops and coadjutors abstained. The peasants of Morbihan and all Brittany rose for their bishops and priests. Thus came about the resistance of the Bretons whose guiding spirit Georges would become.

Vannes, the capital of the province which was dotted with Jacobin clubs, was the scene of the start of the revolt. On March 14 1793, large crowds of peasants gathered there. The garrison consisted of a battalion of volunteers from Maine-et-Loire, men of the 109th Regiment of the National Guard, and a few brigades of gendarmes. Deployed in platoons, the Government troops went to meet the insurgents who had entered the town and carrying only sticks shouted in loud voices for their priests to be given back to them. Some of the municipal representatives of the Revolution spoke to the crowd; when they saw that their words were of no avail the troops opened fire. Fearlessly the swelling crowd surged forward, so the troops got ready to fire grape-shot into their ranks.

The peasants did not flinch. It often rains in Vannes; that day was no exception, and as the matches could not be lit the people thought that they were witnesses to a miracle, and shouted in unison, "Long live St Anne!"

When another column of peasants forged its way into the town the municipal representatives asked them what they wanted. "To die for our religion", was the answer a young peasant gave as he stepped forward unarmed. The Government troops unfurled the red flag and fired into the crowd. The peasants had to retreat, one hundred and fifty prisoners were taken who, being questioned by the justice of the peace, declared to the magistrates, "We have no longer a King and have lost our priests".

The events of Vannes persuaded Georges to leave the notary's office and make common cause with his people.

Eight to ten thousand peasants were soon marching against the Blues. As in the Vendée, it was an explosion of the people. The year 1793 was the great year of the Civil War in the west. Georges marched with the peasants, their aim to join up with the Catholic and Royal Army of the Vendée. His first martial action took place in an inn. When he reached it he found the landlord and his wife sobbing their hearts out because in one of the rooms four Blues were raping their daughter. Georges entered the inn, shot dead two of the soldiers, then, reloading, he killed the other two. Of course, with that action he became an outlaw barred from mercy. He fought the whole war, was at Laval, Pontorson and in all the other battles. He took part in the defeat at Le Mans, by then with the rank of major, and with his Bretons fought a rearguard action as the Catholic and Royal Army retreated. The Government troops took no prisoners, that is anybody they caught was either guillotined or, if there was not time enough, shot.

The battle of Savenay saw the end of the rising of the Vendée. Stofflet, under whom Georges had served during the campaign, observed of him that if a cannon ball did not hit his huge head Georges would go a long way. Georges had already become a legend, his exploits were related as one tells fairy-stories. He stalked the Republicans, shot them dead, then vanished, and was always followed by a mysterious dog which carried the correspondence of the Chouans in his collar. His emissaries covered great distances recruiting army deserters, hiding émigrés and peasants. In some localities he took by force all unmarried males over fifteen to serve in the Chouan forces; gave them strict military discipline; forbade them to marry, declaring to them that he would not marry before the King was in his kingdom again. He had artillery, cavalry, even a medical corps. His men robbed the mail coaches transporting moneys collected in taxes or soldiers' pay, he had a general staff, the chief of which was Mercier La Vendée, brother of Lucrèce whom he intended to wed after the final victory, and his intelligence was so excellent (not difficult when operating on his own territory) that he knew of every movement the Blues planned against him. He had a spy in every village, and when the Government troops appeared the women shrieked, "The pigs are in the cabbages!' and the men of the village vanished.

After the defeat of the Vendée rising, Georges returned to Kerléano only to hear that his entire family had been arrested and locked up in prison at Brest. They would have been exterminated had Robespierre not fallen at the time. Georges himself was caught and put into prison, where he struck up friendship with the royalist prisoners, all of them members of the high nobility who were in touch with Louis XVIII, the Comte d'Artois and the Princes, and which turned him from the simple leader of the Breton peasants into an important link in the royalist chain. He helped them to escape.

Georges was a man of incredible courage and loyal to the core. One day while he was in conference with the Rector of Ploemel, the Abbé Lomenech, news was brought that the Blues were approaching. The Abbé hid Georges in a cellar in spite of Georges's protests. When the Blues arrived they immediately seized the old priest whom they wanted to take to Auray, then to Lorient to be guillotined. Georges was told of it as he emerged from his hiding-place. At once he went in pursuit of the Blues, and though they outnumbered his few men he succeeded in freeing the Abbé. "You are too good, General," said the priest. "You should not have courted danger for my sake. I only did my duty when I hid you." By then Georges was known even to the enemy as General Georges.

When General Hoche marched against the Chouans, whom his army enormously outnumbered, Hoche himself expressed his admiration for Georges's strategy, for not only did he fight a splendid rearguard action but succeeded in breaking through the enemy lines, thus saving his men.

Already Georges was in touch with England; he went there first in 1797; then returned there every year, meeting General Pichegru, with whom his fate would be linked in several ventures.

Charles Pichegru, born in 1761, took part in the American War, in 1791 became president of the Jacobins in Besançon, promoted general by 1793, and as commander-in-chief of the Army of the Rhine the conqueror of the Low Countries in 1795; in short, one of the outstanding military lights of the Revolution. He took Mannheim in the same year.

The Prince de Condé, who commanded the Royal Army in Germany, sent an emissary to him in the person of Fauche-Borel, of whom much more will be heard in this book. Pichegru's correspondence with the Prince fell into the hands of General Moreau due to the capture of an Austrian general. Moreau did not give him away, for Moreau too had ideas of his own which would take more positive shape as his dislike of Bonaparte grew. None the less, the Directory suspected Pichegru of treason. He resigned, was elected to the Council of the Five Hundred in 1797, chosen as president of the royalist majority, and on September 4 in the same year was arrested and deported to Guyanne, but escaped, reaching London in June 1798.

In 1800 Georges and Pichegru planned a descent on Brest with the help of the Royal Navy, taking the Comte d'Artois and the Prince de Berry with them, to proclaim Louis XVIII king, bribe General Brun of the Blues or smash his army, then march on Paris.

If the Parisians saw any of the royal princes they would rise for their king. Such was the plan which remained but a daydream.

Meanwhile the First Consul decided either to buy Georges or have him killed. He said to Fouché on June 4, 1800, "I am assured that Georges is back from England. It is indispensable to have him arrested, also the brother of Frotté who is in the Orne. Use all means to catch these men dead or alive."

The army of General Brun was ordered to march on Morbihan. The Chouans put up a fine show at Pont-du-Loc, yet were roundly defeated. The First Consul's offer of amnesty followed on January 18, 1801, Suzannet, d'Antichamps, Chatillon and several other royalist leaders accepting it, and making peace with Napoleon. Georges was given a safe conduct to Paris as the First Consul wanted to win him over. Napoleon rightly believed in his personal charm and gift of persuasion. Moreover, he liked exercising both, and he admired courage. Their first meeting came to nothing. "I saw Georges today," said Napoleon. "He seemed to me a fat Breton who might be used in the interests of the country." Georges had already contacted Hyde and other royalists in Paris.

At the second meeting Napoleon used all his charm, urging Georges to give up the cause of the Bourbons. He spoke of *la patrie* and *la gloire*, spoke of them with his usual eloquence; but *la patrie* and *la gloire*, as Georges afterwards said, had a different meaning to each of them. During the interview Georges never changed his expression.

"I need men full of energy like you," Napoleon said. "I offer you the rank of divisional general in General Moreau's Army." Though in one sense Georges would have loved to be a general he felt compelled to refuse it as his sense of honour would not let him accept. Then Napoleon offered him a yearly income of one hundred thousand livres on the condition that he led a quiet life and abstained from politics. Since money meant even less to Georges than the rank of general in the First Consul's armies, he promptly turned that offer down.

Hardly had Georges left Napoleon than the order for his arrest was issued, his safe conduct notwithstanding. Luckily a member of the royalist counter-police informed Georges. He did not lose his head: he went into a restaurant, where he ordered a dinner for twenty persons for the same evening, then took a fiacre, and though he was followed by the police he managed in an alleyway to hop from one fiacre into another in which Hyde de Neuville and another royalist were waiting for him. At the same time three faithful friends left Paris in a chaise, and the counter-police spread the rumour that Georges and his two companions were on their way to Orleans. Georges and Hyde safely reached Boulogne, where they embarked on a fishing-smack which took them to London.

Had Georges accepted Napoleon's offer, Napoleon would have kept his word, but as he did not the First Consul considered the safe conduct as just a scrap of paper, and if caught Georges would have been executed.

In London the Treasury paid Georges a guinea a day, and from far-away Mittau Louis XVIII wrote to congratulate him on having escaped from the tyrant. When General Bernadotte marched against the Chouans of Morbihan after replacing General Brun, Georges came back from England in a brig. His brother Julien, who accepted the amnesty as genuine, in February 1801 returned to the family home. He was immediately arrested, taken to prison at Auray; then special orders arrived from Fouché, and Julien was told that he would be transferred to prison at Lorient. On the pretext that his brother might try to free him, the escort shot him dead on the road.

Georges's presence in Morbihan became known to Fouché, who wrote to Véret, one of his secret agents, "Georges is in Morbihan, chase him, pursue him with all your strength. The First Consul has won in Italy, he must win everywhere. Spare no single one of the chiefs of the rising. Shoot them without pity. Our agents are becoming known, so I will send you new and better ones, noblemen whose names and titles are respected by all the Chouans. They will easily obtain their trust, and will deliver the Chouan chiefs at the right moment." Fouché was too optimistic; the Chouans were on

their guard; so Fouché changed tactics, browbeating two unfortunate captured Chouans into returning to Morbihan to poison
Georges. The men duly got in touch with Georges, who had them
searched, the poison was found on them and they were both shot.
Napoleon continued to urge Fouché to catch Georges dead or alive.

During one of his trips to England Georges observed to Hyde de
Neuville who accompanied him, "If the King mounts the throne
he ought to have both of us shot. We shall always remain, you and
I, nothing but a couple of conspirators."

VI

Two Plots against the First Consul

Already in the days of the Directory the High Police's main task was to unravel plots and catch the plotters. Everybody in power was, to coin a word, plotminded, and few more than Louis Gohier who in 1799 became a member of the Directory. He nagged the police, expecting them to catch conspirators day in, day out. He insisted on a continuous flow of reports, so one day Fouché, who was tired of having to send him about two hundred unimportant reports a day, took Réal with him to Gohier, observing that it was time to do something stupid to damp the man's ardour. Stupid yet not too stupid, he added. They laid before Gohier the report of an agent who affirmed that one night he had seen only a league and half from Paris about six hundred men together, conspiring in low voices. The agent carefully approached, but they spoke in whispers, and he could not make out a word they said. Gohier took the report seriously, scolding Réal for not having followed it up. Réal sent an intelligent man who reported the next day, "Monsieur, I caught them out".

"Is there any truth in it?" asked Réal.

"As much truth as one finds in any police report, a quarter or one fifth. In this case one sixth."

"Speak clearly."

"Here it is, monsieur. The garden in question belongs to a hat manufacturer, and at night if the weather is fine—the first agent forgot to tell you that the conspirators met only on fine nights —the manufacturer puts all the felt hats on hop poles to dry. There is a hedge as high as the poles, and if anyone approaches the hedge one sees only the hats. Now an agent is entitled to believe that those hats are on the heads of men, and often the wind whispers."

After Brumaire 18 the High Police had no time left to joke or follow up clues like hats in a hatmaker's garden, for the First Consul was not only hated by Chouans and royalists: Jacobins and even moderates considered that he had betrayed all that was worth while in the Revolution. One such moderate was Joseph-Antoine Aréna, a Corsican officer who had been a member of the Council of the Five Hundred, and who believed that only with the elimination of Bonaparte could liberty be saved, or rather re-established. The plot he hatched became known as the Opera House Plot.

One of its interesting features was that Fouché was caught napping, though not the First Consul; in fact the plot was to be referred to by wags as Napoleon's own plot against himself, for in a sense it was he who directed it. In any case he had the gift of laying traps for his enemies, and often even for his faithful followers. With Aréna his task was not unduly difficult: Aréna's conspiracy, as Desmarets observed, was typically French inasmuch as everybody knew of it. To begin with the First Consul hated Aréna, not an unusual sentiment among Corsicans. Aréna reciprocated his hatred. Aréna contacted Demerville, Céracchi, Diana and Topino Lebrun, all of them the First Consul's enemies, each of them ready and willing to eliminate him.

One of the First Consul's own secret agents got in touch with Jacobin circles, also with a captain of the 45th Half-Brigade who, because he was unemployed, nursed a grievance against Bonaparte. The secret agent's name was Harel, and when he heard of what was afoot he did not go to Fouché but to Barère who, instead of informing the Police Minister went straight to General Lannes, commanding the Consular Bodyguard. The general reported to Bourrienne, the First Consul's secretary, who at last informed Fouché. None the less, Harel remained directly under Napoleon's orders as the First Consul loved showing Fouché that he knew more of police matters than Fouché himself.

Aware now that Aréna was behind the conspiracy Harel saw his friend Demerville who had been a member of the Committee of General Security of The Convention. Posing as an enemy of the new regime Harel made Demerville unburden himself, declaring that soon something would happen that would favour the true patriots. Harel continued to visit Demerville, and in time Demerville told him that the only way out was to kill Bonaparte. Harel thought that that was a difficult proposition. Not at all, answered Demerville, he could easily be killed at the Opera House while watching a performance. Harel considered that a capital idea, then introduced another police agent, Lefèvre, who, averred Harel, could enormously help the conspirators. Demerville now had complete confidence in the two agents who continued to encourage him. The trouble was, Demerville said, that he, Aréna and the other conspirators needed a goodish number of men to overpower the First Consul's bodyguard before he reached his box. Harel promised to find him a hundred trustworthy men, and Demerville handed him a sum of money to recruit the hundred. Daily Harel reported to Dubois, the Prefect of Police, who kept the First Consul informed.

Harel returned again to Demerville's house, where he met Céracchi, a distinguished sculptor whom many compared favourably with Canova, and who had sculpted a bust of Bonaparte. Harel asked for more money, which he received from Demerville and Céracchi. They told Harel that *Les Horaces* would be played at the Opera House on October 10 (the year was 1800) and they would strike on that night, so Harel should get his men ready. Harel promised to bring his resolute men to the Opera House.

Bonaparte, Demerville said, was a second Caesar and had, therefore, to perish like Caesar. Then Demerville warned Aréna, Diana and Topino Lebrun to be present at the Opera House on the night of October 10.

According to Réal, Demerville became suddenly frightened and spoke to Barère, giving him the date and place of the attempt. Immediately Barère informed General Lannes who told Bourrienne who contacted Fouché. That sounds unlikely since Harel was daily in touch with his superiors, giving them every detail of the conspirators' plans. But, of course, Réal wanted to give the High Police the kudos. The truth probably was that Demerville, who for a long time had had friendly relations with Barère, did confide in him without giving the date and place away. In any case Harel was in the secret which was sufficient for Bonaparte.

On the 10th Harel met four of his men in the Tuileries Gardens, then dined with them in a nearby inn. After dinner they went to fetch daggers, gunpowder a .d pistols, and Harel posted them at different doors of the Opera House. He assured them that Demerville would be at the Palais-Egalité with a large number of men who would hurry to the Opera House to cover their escape once Bonaparte was killed. The four men, who believed that Harel was Demerville's fellow conspirator, took themselves to the Opera House, then Harel posted Demerville in the Palais-Egalité, Céracchi in the passage leading to the First Consul's box, and Aréna went to the public foyer shortly after Bonaparte's arrival.

When Harel gave the signal the police agents who were hidden all over the Opera House arrested the conspirators, Céracchi in the passage, Demerville who had managed to escape in the house of a friend, and Aréna in his own home, Diana and Topino Lebrun inside the Opera House. What became of the four men Harel had dined with and armed remains a mystery; consequently one can but surmise that they too were police agents. All was done so swiftly in the Opera House that the audience noticed nothing.

Neither Napoleon nor Fouché was ever in a hurry to bring before the tribunals men whose abortive plots filled them with no fear. Aréna and his fellow conspirators would probably have saved their heads if the far more dangerous and spectacular attempt on the First Consul's life had not followed three months later. The new attempt is known to history as the Attempt of Nivôse 3.

In the summer of 1800 Georges Cadoudal summoned four trusted Chouans, telling them that he needed a man to go to Paris on a secret mission. Pierre Robinault de Saint-Régent (or Saint-Réjant), who had commanded a division in the Catholic and Royal Army, was chosen, as he was the senior officer present. Georges said to him, "I give you the means to reach the capital, where you will get in touch with people whose names and addresses I will give you; with them you will arrange to buy a number of horses, clothes and arms which I shall be needing later on". That was Saint-Régent's mission. On July 7 in Paris he received a letter from Georges, signing himself Gédéon, in which, in answer to Saint-Régent's message that he was contemplating vigorous action, he said he would soon have good news for him. That letter is proof that Georges had nothing to do with the plot Saint-Régent evolved in Paris and put into execution.

With hindsight that never failed them the High Police declared after the event that they, that is Fouché, Réal and Desmarets, knew of Saint-Régent's arrival in Paris. If they did, then why did they not arrest him, thus nipping in the bud the attempt which, but for Napoleon's guardian angel this time disguised as a drunken coachman, would have been successful?

Saint-Régent got in touch with M. de Limoëlan, a leading royalist through whom he met an engineer called Chevalier, an expert at making bombs. The usual idea of liquidating Napoleon was either to attack him, say, on the road to Saint-Cloud or when out hunting, or shoot him while reviewing troops, or stab him to death as Demerville had planned; but to kill him with a bomb was certainly a new departure, and would never have occurred to Saint-Régent if he had not come into contact with Chevalier. It should be added that the same Saint-Régent had protested in Rennes against the assassination of General Hoche when Hoche was "pacifying" the Vendée and Brittany. Yet now he opted for finishing Napoleon off with a bomb.

On Christmas Eve 1800 the First Consul was going to hear Haydn's Oratorio *Saul*. In the evening a horse-drawn cart appeared in the rue Saint-Nicaise in front of the rue de Malte, the horse led by de Limoëlan and Saint-Régent, assisted by one Carbon, the three of them dressed as carters. Saint-Régent alone remained beside the cart, which was pulled across the street so as to hinder the traffic, both in the rue Saint-Nicaise and in the rue de Malte. At the time the rue Saint-Nicaise reached as far as the Carrousel. The accomplices, four in all, were posted at vantage points in order to be able to signal to Saint-Régent when the First Consul's carriage left the Tuileries. Saint-Régent, who had been a naval officer under the old regime, had made calculations with great precision, working out exactly how long it would take the consular carriage to reach the cart, that is the corner of the rue de Malte. The conspirators had drawn lots on who should remain with the cart and ignite the bomb. Saint-Régent was the one assigned by the luck of the draw. First they had been convinced that whoever stayed with the cart would perish in the explosion; but then they worked out that he had a fair chance of escaping. The bomb was to be exploded with tinder, and Saint-Régent even calculated how long it would take the tinder to explode the bomb.

Bonaparte's favourite coachman, who had been with him in Egypt, was generally drunk. Since it happened to be Christmas Eve he happened to be drunker than usual, and instead of taking the rue Saint-Nicaise in its length he turned into the rue de Malte, whipping the horses smartly along. Thus the carriage was already out of the way when the explosion occurred; for by turning into the rue de Malte Bonaparte's carriage was not impeded by the cart obstructing the road. The consular carriage had reached the rue de Rohan as the burning tinder reached the gunpowder. Yet the explosion was of such force that the carriage windows were shattered, and the mounted escort felt as though lifted out of their saddles. Tiles dropped from roofs, doors were smashed, and General Lannes, who sat beside the First Consul, thought for a moment that the entire neighbourhood had been blown up.

Four people were killed in the rue Saint-Nicaise, dozens were wounded, including people inside houses. A fair number of the injured either died of their wounds or were mutilated for life. If the explosion had occurred a few seconds earlier and if the drunken coachman had not turned into the rue de Malte, Napoleon's career would have ceased then, and more than a million French soldiers would not have perished in his wars. Inside the *Café d'Apollon*, at the corner of the rues Saint-Nicaise and de Malte, thirteen clients were badly wounded. The consular carriage and its occupants would have gone up in smoke.

Napoleon stopped the carriage to inquire whether any member of the bodyguard was wounded; then without showing any emotion he drove on, and listened to Haydn's *Saul* till the end. He received several reports in his box, yet remained calm till his return to the Tuileries, where he gave vent to his fury, at once accusing the Jacobins of this heinous crime. "Those men of mud and blood," he thundered. He did not suspect the royalists as he was still convinced that they could be no enemies of him who had in no way soiled his hands with their blood during the Revolution. On the other hand, Fouché, who knew that all Royalist doors were closed to him, the regicide, and who had not yet discovered that a subtle, well-placed man like himself could deal with anybody and any party, straightway suspected the Royalists, or rather the Chouans. And in Morbihan Georges, when he first heard of the explosion, also thought that it was the work of the Jacobins.

Saint-Régent and his accomplices vanished from the scene. Later it was rumoured that he had asked a little girl to hold the horse's head which, of course, would have meant inevitable death for her. Even to the last Saint-Régent hotly denied that. He sent a report to Georges. "A person should have warned the assassin of the First Consul's departure, but he did not. The assassin had been assured that the carriage would be preceded by a mounted guard, which was not the case. He alone, and without the warning he should have received, saw the carriage only when it reached the spot. At once he wanted to put his plan into execution; however the horse of a mounted grenadier pushed him against the wall. None the less, he returned to the cart and ignited the tinder, but the gunpowder was not as good as it should have been, therefore the explosion took place two or three seconds later than estimated. If not, the First Consul would certainly have been killed. The fault lies with the gunpowder and not the assassin. If fate allows me to see you again I want to have it out with my associates in front of you and your comrades. It is here that I am waiting for them."

Georges was horrified. He was a soldier and not a murderer. He remained convinced that the idea emanated from the Jacobins who had put Saint-Régent in touch with Chevalier. Georges's own idea was to find an opportunity to attack the First Consul with the same number of men as the consular guard. He had sent Saint-Régent to Paris to find the horses and arms he and his Chouans needed to attack Bonaparte in open combat. He continued to maintain that the Jacobins had led Saint-Régent and his associates astray. In any case Chevalier was an old Jacobin.

When the bomb exploded the blast threw Saint-Régent over, then he staggered to his feet, and, as he told a friend, he suddenly found himself without knowing how under the entrance gates of the Louvre, where the fresh air revived him. Then he swiftly crossed the Pont-Royal. He went home in great pain, spitting blood and blood trickling from his ears. Limoëlan rushed out to find a priest as he thought that his end was near, coming back with his own uncle, Father Picot de Clos-Rivière. Later a young royalist doctor was summoned. Only after he had revived did Saint-Régent learn that the attempt had failed. Saint-Régent put the blame on the tinder, adding, "I would have set fire to the gunpowder with a fire-brand, remaining beside the cart".

Meanwhile, the police got busy. The horse like the cart had been blown to pieces, but one horseshoe remained intact. The police visited every blacksmith in the capital and the outlying villages, trying to find who had shod the horse. Fouché, who because of his Jacobin past was also under suspicion from the First Consul, immediately published the names of M. de Limoëlan, Saint-Régent, La Haye-Saint-Hilaire, Joyaux and Carbon, ordering their arrest. Neither the gendarmerie nor the prefects listened to him, since they had it on the highest authority that the explosion had been caused by the Jacobins. Fouché remained alone with his conviction while notorious Jacobins were arrested by the score, and dozens deported. Everybody produced his list of the conspirators according to his ideas. Desmarets was present when an amnestied Chouan chief brought his own list of revolutionaries responsible for the attempt. Fouché said, "Then why are M. de Limoëlan and Saint-Régent in hiding? If it was the Jacobins then why have they vanished ever since that day? They are your friends, bring them to me to justify themselves. I am ready to give them a safe conduct."

The First Consul was still unwilling to believe him. However, the police, taking the horseshoe from one blacksmith to the other, eventually found one who recognised it. The blacksmith gave the description of the man who had brought the horse along, five feet, one inch tall, a scar above the left eye. The description tallied with the police's own description of Carbon. The man who sold the cart and the one from whom the barrel was purchased gave the same picture of the buyer. Carbon was a well known Chouan. A number of witnesses who had seen the conspirators were summoned to police headquarters. Two hundred and twenty-three persons who had been arrested straight after the attempt were set free, and the hunt for Carbon and his accomplices began in earnest. Every possible means was employed to catch them, such as bullying and torturing Royalists already in the hands of the police.

In an outlying suburb Carbon's sister and her two daughters were run to earth. The girls were questioned, and they remembered, if that is the right word, that Limoëlan had shown them some barrels, observing, "Mesdemoiselles, this is the sort of timber that costs a lot". When the house was searched twelve pounds of gunpowder of foreign origin were found, also four carters' blouses. The sister or the daughters must have given Carbon's hiding place away because fifteen days after the explosion the police discovered that he was in a convent, where he took part in all the services offered up for the miraculous escape of the First Consul. He was caught and imprisoned, and Desmarets got working on him. Carbon spilled the beans, averring that he had been only the lackey of the conspiracy, had been used only to buy horse, gunpowder and the cart. He gave the names of Saint-Régent, Limoëlan and the others who took part in the attempt.

Now the hunt turned against the Chouans who were arrested practically in batches. Everybody known for royalist sympathies was taken for Saint-Régent or Limoëlan. Fouché once more had to tone down the zeal of his men. A stockbroker, a M. Nolin, was arrested in Montpellier, dragged to Paris because police agents in Montpellier thought that he might be either Saint-Régent or Limoëlan. M. Nolin spent some time in prison before being set free.

Saint-Régent remained in Paris, still not strong enough to escape; by the time he had recovered the roads out of town were so carefully guarded that it was impossible to leave. In the end Carbon gave the police his address, and he was caught, tried and executed. So was Carbon. Only Limoëlan escaped. He found his way to Saint-Malo, where he embarked as an ordinary seaman and reaching America entered a monastery. Others say he became a priest. Anyway, he took no more part in royalist activities, writing only to his sister in France. He wrote on the top of one of his letters that was bound to be intercepted by the Royal Navy, "Oh, *Anglais*! Let this letter through! It is from a man who did a lot and suffered much in your cause!"

The letter reached its destination.

The plot of Nivôse 3 had many repercussions. The First Consul ordered that Aréna, Demerville, Topino Lebrun, Céracchi and Diana be tried at once, for attempts on his life could no longer be looked on as jokes. All of them were executed. Fouché, because he had not prevented the attempt of Nivôse 3, lost his master's confidence, and he got rid of him on September 15, 1802, by abolishing the Ministry of Police. He made him a senator. However, on July 10, 1804, the Ministry was re-established, and Fouché recalled.

Georges left Morbihan and sailed to Jersey, where he was detained for the time being as the English Government wanted him out of the way during the peace negotiations in Amiens. Later he was allowed into England.

The remaining conspirators, Joyaux and La Haye-Saint-Hilaire, had made good their escape from Paris during the hue and cry against the Jacobins. They reached England undaunted, their only thought to continue the fight for the King against the Usurper. Joyaux returned to Paris in 1804 with Georges, and was executed with him. La Haye-Saint-Hilaire, as will be seen, continued his Chouan activities, and was caught in September 1807 in a pitched battle with gendarmes, heavily wounding one of them before being captured. Then he suffered the same fate as the others who had taken part in the bomb plot on Nivôse 3.

VII

Georges Cadoudal—The Last Phase

In 1801 the First Consul signed a Concordat with Pope Pius VII, for not only did he want to cement his relations with the right, but he also was not altogether void of religion. Besides, Joséphine, his wife, was all for it. "One should swear on nothing," he observed drily when Gaspard Monge, the mathematician, expressed his hope that the confessional would not be re-introduced into France.

One of the results of the Concordat was the cooling off of many of his followers who had belonged to the Revolution; and the hatred of those, who had already resented his betrayal of their principles, rose like a flame, General Moreau the first among them. The military men who had won their spurs in the war of the Revolution thought the moment had come to get rid of Bonaparte. One plot was hatched after the other. Pull him off his horse during a review and then trample on him was one of the more moderate schemes to liquidate him. However, plans and plots came swiftly to the attention of the police as soldiers were not too good at keeping secrets. Bonaparte had most of the plotters removed from Paris; there was plenty of scope for their bellicose spirit in Italy or Germany. Anyway, the Consular Guard under General Lannes knew how to look after the First Consul's safety.

None the less, part of the army remained disgruntled. General Bernadotte commanded the Army of the West. He was in Paris at the time of the signing of the Concordat, but at his headquarters in Rennes three pamphlets attacking Bonaparte were printed under the title of *Adresse aux armées françaises*. The first pamphlet called the Corsican tyrant, the second the Usurper, and the third the Deserter and Murderer of Kleber. Those pamphlets were sent by post to all serving generals, and were intercepted by the police, thus never reaching their destination, except for one sent in a basket containing butter in the Rennes-Paris mail coach to M. Rapatel, aide-de-camp to General Moreau. When Fouché informed Bonaparte of the arrival of the butter basket he sent Fouché to see Moreau, and ask for an explanation. Moreau told Fouché that he considered it a huge joke, referring to it as the conspiracy of a slab of butter. His cook, he added, had a "casserole of honour" and his dog a "collar of honour".

Fouché reported their conversation to Bonaparte who said, "This battle must finish. France does not deserve to suffer torn between two opponents. . . . Were I in his position and he in mine I should willingly be his first aide-de-camp. If he feels capable of governing then let him! Tomorrow at four in the morning he should come to the Bois de Boulogne. His and my sword will decide the issue. I will be expecting him. Do not fail, Fouché, to let him know." (Those words of the First Consul were on the same day repeated by Fouché to Desmarets.)

It was nearly midnight as Fouché left the Tuileries, and taking Desmarets along, summoned Moreau to the Ministry of Police. As M. Devilliers, Fouché's personal secretary, was away in Lyons, where he was getting married, M. Lombard Taradeau went to fetch the general. Moreau arrived and Fouché was in his element, succeeding in persuading Moreau to be present in the morning at the First Consul's levé in the Tuileries. He had not been there for a long time. Fouché let Napoleon know before he went to bed. The First Consul received Moreau with great signs of friendliness; everybody present was much impressed, though not one of those present had the faintest inkling that the two men nearly fought a duel a few hours earlier. In spite of all the smiles and expressions of goodwill the two men remained steadfast enemies.

General Pichegru was still living in London, and in 1803 he received the unexpected visit of General Lajolais, who had secretly crossed the Channel. Lajolais had once served as Chief of Staff to Moreau. He told Pichegru that Moreau too was up in arms against Bonaparte because he had hushed up the reports of Moreau's outstanding victories, depriving him of the honour and glory that were his due. Pichegru, who had been deported from France in 1797, could not know that Lajolais was not so much sent by Moreau, fundamentally not an intriguer or conspirator, but by Moreau's mother-in-law, Mme Hulot, a sworn enemy of the First Consul, who wanted her son-in-law to take his place. Lajolais assured Pichegru that Moreau would help him to overthrow Bonaparte and restore the Bourbons. Pichegru was delighted. Though in constant touch with Georges Cadoudal in England, as a professional soldier he needed more assurance than the Chouans, those irregulars, could provide. Now Lajolais had given it. So Pichegru was ready to throw in his lot with the Chouans since at the other end General Moreau was waiting for him.

It was already 1803 when Georges finally decided on his *coup de main* against Napoleon with a battalion of his best Chouans. He liked to remind his friends of Hannibal whose conviction was that the Romans could be defeated only in Rome. Bonaparte could be beaten only in Paris. Ever since the Vendée chiefs had accepted the amnesty and made their uneasy peace with Bonaparte, he believed that there was no other way of pulling down the First Consul and re-establishing the Bourbons. The Revolution had to be strangled in Paris.

The omens, he thought, were all in his favour. Pichegru too was in favour of it, especially since Lajolais's visit. Besides, Moreau's and Napoleon's mutual hatred was common knowledge in London. Both the Comte d'Artois, brother and heir to Louis XVIII, and the English Government encouraged Georges. News reached London that Moreau had declined to be present at a military review held by Napoleon who, never slow in repaying a slight, refused to invite Moreau to a feast he gave on the anniversary of the Republic. On the same day Moreau, who was not slow either, went dressed as an ordinary citizen to a restaurant, where everybody could see him, in the company of other disgruntled citizens. In short, fair stood the wind to France.

"If Moreau and Pichegru agree I will soon be back in France," said the Comte d'Artois, and it was decided to send an advance-guard to France to prepare the great attack, Pichegru to contact Moreau, and Georges to organise his Chouans. Pichegru was warned to keep away from Georges after reaching Paris, not to write to him, and not to send him any messenger, so that if all failed he could say that he had been kept in the dark. In fact, according to the Baron de Guilhermy, Pichegru did not know Georges's ultimate plan.

On August 21, 1803, Georges left London in the company of Hermely, La Haye-Saint-Hilaire, Joyaux (both wanted as accomplices in the bomb plot of Nivôse 3), Brèche, under the name of Kirch, Querelle, an officer from Morbihan, Troche, and Louis Picot, who was Georges's servant. In his belt Georges carried one million francs in bills from the English Treasury. Pitt had made it clear to him that England was ready to help and finance him only on the understanding that Bonaparte would not be killed, but taken prisoner, and sent to England to be transported to St Helena. (So St Helena had already been thought of in 1803.)

Georges left for Hastings to meet his fellow conspirators who had departed from London separately; however they were arrested before his arrival on the denunciation of an Englishman with whom they had had an altercation. Georges got them out of prison. When they were ready to sail Georges had such an awful toothache that the departure had to be postponed till a dentist could attend to him. A dentist was called, a poor man in a threadbare suit, inspiring little confidence. None the less, he extracted the tooth with praiseworthy dexterity, and Georges was so pleased with him that he presented him with twenty-five guineas, a king's ransom at the time. But Joyaux, the expedition's treasurer, thought that five guineas were more than plenty, which the dentist gladly accepted, and before they sailed he came in a new suit to thank Georges again.

At the foot of the cliff of Biville, four leagues to the north of Dieppe, near the village of Penli, the conspirators were to disembark. They sailed in H.M.S. *Vincego*, commanded by Captain Wright, and once on land a lantern would show them which direction to go. After the landing, which was more difficult than had been expected, a Chouan called Raoul Gaillard, who was well acquainted with the countryside, led the small column towards Aumale, eventually reaching Saint-Leu-Taverny. Two more Chouans, Charles d'Hozier and De Sol de Grisolles, came there to meet Georges in d'Hozier's carriage. Georges entered the carriage, but before leaving he said to his companions, "I do not know the sort of fate that is awaiting us, yet I am sure that if any of us falls into the hands of the Usurper he will acccept his fate with courage and give no one away".

D'Hozier was disguised as a coachman, De Sol and Joyaux sat in the coupé with Georges, and they reached Paris without incident. In one of the suburbs a small lodging was prepared for Georges. The plan was simple enough: Napoleon would be seized, and once out of harm's way Moreau would go to Boulogne, put himself at the head of the army and bring back Louis XVIII.

The first setback was the meeting in January 1804 between Pichegru and Moreau, a total disappointment for the cause as Moreau at once declared that in spite of his dislike of Bonaparte and his enmity to everything that upstart stood for, he was and would always remain a Republican, and under no condition whatsoever would he take part in reinstating the monarchy. Moreover, he would have no dealings with Georges and his Chouans.

Georges lay low in Paris for eight months. With Moreau unwilling to play, the whole scheme had to be changed and new plans worked out. Pichegru, who also remained in Paris, seemed to be of no help since the misunderstanding over Moreau had taken the wind out of his sails. Georges was perfectly aware that there could be no worthwhile rising without the Comte d'Artois or one of the Princes taking the risk of appearing on French soil. Not one of them seemed willing to take it. One cannot help wondering why Georges, who had promised Pitt not to murder Bonaparte or have him murdered, did not call it a day and return to England as he had done several times. He doggedly remained and so did his companions. Yet there came the day when both Georges and Pichegru agreed that if soon nothing new turned up they would withdraw. Alas, such decisions are always taken too late.

In the beginning all the police knew was that a number of Chouans had landed from England near Dieppe. As there was a continuous coming and going between the French coast and England the police did not at first attach too much importance to it. Eventually it was decided to keep a stricter watch on the Normandy coast. By then there were over two hundred and fifty conspirators hiding in Paris. In the Prison of the Temple a number of Chouans and other royalists were held. They were questioned: they swore they knew nothing. Though some of them had five louis or more sent in monthly the police did not bother unduly.

Then Napoleon, who was a man of intuition, had a sudden inspiration. He felt that something was very wrong somewhere. Strangely enough the inspiration came to him on the night of January 25, 1804, while Moreau had a meeting with Pichegru and Georges. Napoleon ordered five of the detainees in the Temple to be tried immediately. Without him knowing it all five were Georges's men. Two were acquitted, three sentenced to death. Two of the convicted were executed without revealing anything. But there remained the third who was to be guillotined on the following day.

Napoleon was at the Tuileries, chatting with Réal and some other Councillors of State when General Murat, Military Governor of Paris, was announced. Murat brought a letter from the third condemned man who wanted to reveal all he knew. Having read the letter Napoleon observed, "The poor devil wants to gain an hour. Hope, as you can see, is the one thing that remains till the end.

His confession, I am sure, hardly warrants seeing him. Never mind, Réal, go and speak to him, but no stay of proceedings. I don't want that."

Napoleon often declared that every time he pardoned a condemned man he had to regret it. Réal drove to the Prison of the Abbaye to which the third man had been transferred. The firing squad had arrived before him. The condemned man was in a downstairs cell, and thus could see the preparations. One of the gendarmes belonging to the firing squad had tied his horse to a bar of the cell. Réal found the prisoner trembling with fear, pale as death, and hardly able to speak. He repeated that he had a lot to reveal, then pointed at the awful sight on the other side of the window. Réal had him transferred to another cell, gave him a drink, put the prisoner at his ease, in short obtained his confidence. He asked him to speak up. The man said that it was in the First Consul's interest to know the truth. He, the trembling prisoner, had been condemned by a military tribunal, though in one sense he was completely innocent. However, in another sense he was guilty indeed, for he had taken part in Georges's conspiracy. He had been present when the conspirators disembarked near Dieppe, came to Paris with them and they, Georges included, were still hiding in Paris.

What a windfall for Réal! At once he issued orders for all the city gates to be closed, then hurried back to the Tuileries. He repeated to Napoleon everything the man had said. Napoleon asked whether the man had been executed, Réal said no, Napoleon at once signed the stay of execution. Then he ordered Réal to find Georges and his accomplices without delay. Réal pointed out that the situation was fraught with danger since Georges and his cutthroats, now that they could not escape, would surely try to murder him. The Corsican fatalist shrugged his shoulders, observing that it was Réal's duty to watch over him while his own duty was to review the troops, which he would do the following day.

Réal returned to police headquarters, issued orders, then sent for the condemned man. The houses round the Carrousel were occupied by prostitutes. Réal despatched policemen to see to those women leaving the district before daybreak as the review would be held near the Carrousel, and the fewer present in the houses the better the First Consul could be guarded.

Questioning the prisoner again Réal discovered his real name. He was Querelle, a country surgeon, one who had travelled with Georges from London to Hastings, then embarked for France with him and his companions in the conspiracy. The descendants of the Chouans still curse his memory, yet it is possible that if he had not been sentenced by mistake he would not have ratted; and if arrested with his own party he might have died as bravely as the others. Anyway, he had no idea where Georges was hiding, and had no idea of Pichegru's presence in Paris. Escorted by the police Querelle returned to Dieppe, then took the police agents to all the farms where he had been hidden on his way to Paris. Several farmers were arrested, one of them hanged himself on the day he was locked up in a cell in the Temple. On February 8 Georges's servant Picot was caught. The net was closing.

"The air is full of daggers," Fouché wrote in a report to Napoleon, who again reminded the High Police that Georges had to be found. The police did not look or search beyond Georges; however another detainee came, as it were, to their rescue. A royalist officer, who had been imprisoned at the end of 1803, tried in a moment of despair to commit suicide in his cell. His name was Bouvet de Lozier, and when his warders had saved his life in his gratitude (so said Fouché, Réal and Desmarets) he mentioned Pichegru and Moreau, and asked to see Réal. Taken to Réal, his face swollen, and, as he put it, still in the shadow of death, bemoaning the sad fate of France because the nation did not stand completely by the First Consul, he revealed that Moreau and Pichegru were also conspiring against the great man, spoke of General Lajolais's mission to London, Pichegru's arrival in Paris and his meetings with Moreau "who had surrendered his principles to make common cause with the royalists".

Bouvet de Lozier's confession lasted till seven in the morning. Réal went to the Tuileries, where he found Napoleon with Constant, his valet. Napoleon said that Réal could speak before Constant (who received his nightly secret report from Desmarets and Veyrat without Fouché's and Réal's knowledge), but when he heard that Pichegru was in Paris he dressed speedily, dismissed Constant, and told Réal to take no action against Moreau till Pichegru's presence in Paris was definitely confirmed. Napoleon was no great believer in the confessions of prisoners; moreover the English newspapers continued to mention Pichegru's presence in London. The High Police questioned Roland, an old friend of Pichegru, also Lajolais for whom several traps were laid before the truth was torn from him. So on February 15, Moreau was brought to the Temple.

The Great Judge, accompanied by the secretary of the Council of State, went to the prison to question him, bringing a message from the First Consul. If Moreau wanted to speak to him in person he should at once be brought before him. Moreau refused to see him.

Pichegru was arrested on February 20, sleeping peacefully in the house of a M. Leblanc who had betrayed his presence to the police for a large sum of money. But where was Georges? The police were well aware that his Bretons would never betray their hero and general. There they were right.

Georges was staying with Joyaux, Burban and Raoul Gaillard in a small lodging on the Montagne Sainte-Geneviève. Georges wanted news from the companions who had not yet been arrested. He did not use d'Hozier who was in charge of the carriages, but applied to Louis Léridant, brother of one of his aides-de-camp. Léridant came often to see Georges, bringing him whatever news he could pick up of the other conspirators. He had observed suspicious figures who followed him on his errands. A council was held, and it was decided that Georges should move. Caron, a scent manufacturer and a staunch supporter, offered Georges asylum in his house in the rue du Four. Not wanting to use d'Hozier's carriage Georges instructed Léridant to find him a cabriolet to take him to the scent manufacturer. Léridant asked a Parisian friend, one Goujon, with whom he shared an apartment, to hire the cabriolet. Goujon promptly accepted the task, for Goujon was in Fouché's pay, one of the hundreds of royalists that had been blackmailed into spying for the police.

The next day, March 9, Léridant was waiting with the cabriolet Number 53, a public conveyance, in the Place Saint-Etienne-du-Mont. Accompanied by the three officers who had been lodging with him Georges came into the square, followed by a young girl, Denise Lemoine, carrying a large parcel containing 35,000 francs in foreign money, part of the English Treasury's gift. The moment Georges entered the fiacre two police inspectors, Petit and Destavigny, ran up, followed by two more, Buffet and Caniolle. Joyaux, Burban and Gaillard turned on them, Burban hitting (not stabbing) one of them on the shoulder with his dagger while the cabriolet went off at full speed without the girl having time to throw the parcel into it. She took it to the baker near her home, asking him to keep it for her. She returned a little later but, the baker, having opened the parcel, refused to part with the money. After the baker had tried to change some of the foreign gold, it was grabbed by the police, and the baker arrested.

The three policemen shouted their heads off while the three aides-de-camp tried to restrain them. The six of them had a running fight, and Georges, who saw them through the fiacre's back window, told Léridant to whip the horse into a faster gallop. The cab rattled down the rue Monsieur-le-Prince, and as it reached the Odéon Petit, Buffet and Caniolle came racing along, Buffet throwing himself in front of the cab, trying to seize the reins. Georges shot him dead with a pistol shot, then jumped out of the cabriolet. Caniolle raised his heavy stick, Georges fired again, wounding him in the side. In spite of his wound Caniolle got to his feet, and as Georges entered the rue de l'Observance he hit him hard on the head. A hatter called Thomas and the two brothers Delamotte, clerks in a lottery office, some passersby too, all of them believing that the police were chasing a criminal, threw themselves on Georges who because of their number could no longer defend himself. Tied with a rope they dragged him to the Préfecture de

Police, where Dubois, the Préfect, questioned him before handing him over to Judge Thuriot, an old Jacobin. Georges thought only of one thing, not to incriminate any of those who had helped him. He declared that he wanted to attack Bonaparte with as many men as protected him, take him prisoner, then proclaim Louis XVIII king.

"Where did you stay in Paris?" the judge asked.

"Nowhere."

"Was Pichegru one of the conspirators?"

"I have no idea."

"Moreau?"

"Don't know him, never met him."

"Was Louis Picot not your servant?"

"I have no servant."

"Where were you lodging when you were arrested?"

"In a cabriolet."

"What prompted you to fire at a policeman?"

"The necessity to repulse force by force."

"Are you aware that you killed a family man?"

"You should have had me arrested by bachelors."

"When did you come to Paris?"

"I think five months ago, but I did not stay all the time in Paris. I moved about, but I will not tell you where I went. Anyway, you have me, and there are enough victims without adding to their number."

Georges was taken to the Temple, and, of course, his fate was sealed. Yet he continued to behave with the courage that still gives the Bretons and all the descendants of the Chouans an inner glow that time will not dim.

One of the smaller fry in the conspiracy was Louis Bayard, apparently an Englishman, who came to France in 1801, declaring that he hated his native country, and settled down in Paris as a cartographer, swearing eternal loyalty to the First Consul. When Georges was arrested he vanished, leaving his furniture behind. His brother Charles, who had worked with him and voiced similar sentiments, killed himself after Georges's condemnation. The police put his death down to gaming losses. Fouché was to discover in 1806 that Louis Bayard was living in Plymouth, receiving a pension from the English Government.

By far the largest fish caught in the net was General Moreau. From prison he wrote a dignified letter to Napoleon, reminding him of his feats of arms, his victories and success, then pointing out that he never thought of or wanted to bring back the Bourbons, which the joint efforts of all the European powers were unable to do. Napoleon, who had always seen a competitor in him, did not reply, but sent Régnier, the Great Judge, to speak to Moreau on his behalf.

"Citizen General Moreau, today at eleven o'clock I put your letter before the First Consul," said Régnier. "He was deeply moved by the measures adopted against you because the security of the state demands them."

Then the Great Judge went on to say that it was Moreau who had refused to see Bonaparte when his life was still in danger, and he could have helped him. (That was a reference to Moreau having been arrested while both Pichegru and Cadoudal were still at large.) "Before taking further action," the Great Judge continued, "I wanted, by questioning you a second time, to discover whether a possibility existed of separating your name from this odious business. You did not give me the chance."

At his trial Moreau was given only a two years' sentence. "The same as one gives a handkerchief thief," was Napoleon's comment.

Among Georges's accomplices were the two Polignac brothers, Armand and Jules, who was to be Charles X's leading light. Armand de Polignac was sentenced to death, Jules to two years. When Jules offered to be executed in his brother's place Napoleon commuted Armand's sentence to life imprisonment.

General Pichegru's death remains anybody's guess. He was kept in a cell at the Prison of the Temple. There he died of "self-inflicted strangulation" as five judges, the attorney-general, his assistant and six surgeons and physicians confirmed. All who loathed Napoleon said that he was strangled by the police on Napoleon's orders. That belief still seems to persist. But if one examines the matter impartially one can find no valid reason why Napoleon should have chosen Pichegru as his personal victim. If there was a general he resented, and resent him he did, that was Moreau; yet he pardoned Moreau shortly after the two years' sentence was passed on him and let him leave for the United States. Pichegru had been out of France since 1797; consequently he was no competitor like Moreau. Besides, Pichegru would in any case have been sentenced to death at his trial. It should not be overlooked either that Napoleon and the High Police were eagerly awaiting the trial, hoping and expecting that Pichegru would reveal far more than they knew at the time, such as his relations with the English Government and their plans for future action against the First Consul.

Pichegru was of a sullen and harsh temper. The Marquis de Rivière, a royalist friend of his, strolled one night in the streets of Paris with Pichegru. That was shortly before his arrest. Suddenly, Pichegru whipped out a pistol, saying he could not tolerate his clandestine existence any longer, and would do away with himself. M. de Rivière succeeded in calming him, afterwards taking him to a lady in the rue des Noyers, where he found refuge for the night. "One more night like this," said Pichegru, "and that will be the end." The woman in question confirmed this to Réal and Demarets. She believed that he was referring to Napoleon's end, not his.

Pichegru would not have left England if Lajolais had not assured him of Moreau's collaboration. He was a soldier and not a plotter. Yet after Moreau had made it clear that he would not lift a finger to help the royalists he became as much a conspirator as any of the ordinary Chouans. Then came his humiliating arrest, for nothing humiliates one more than being betrayed by a person one trusted. It is like losing faith in oneself. He was asleep when twelve police agents pounced on him. He tried to grab his pistol which was under his pillow, but it was too late, and naked as he was he fought till he was overpowered. In prison he was kept in a cell on the ground floor, his window giving on to the courtyard. To the left was

Bouvet de Lozier's cell. Bouvet de Lozier, having attempted to kill himself, was guarded day and night. To the right was the cell where Georges was held with two gendarmes and a non-commissioned officer keeping a constant watch on him. Was that the place where the High Police wanted to keep the man they intended to murder? asks Desmarets in his Memoirs, and for once one feels like agreeing with him.

Of course, they might have poisoned him, and then strangled him. But why get rid of the one man who could have incriminated Moreau? When Réal heard of Pichegru's death he was so upset that Napoleon could not resist observing, "That is because he was the best piece of evidence against Moreau".

From the moment of Pichegru's arrest Réal did not stop questioning him, then reporting all he said to the First Consul. "Tell Pichegru," Napoleon said according to Réal and Desmarets, "that before his blunders he served and honoured his country with victories . . . tell him that this was but a lost battle . . . I do not thirst for his blood, but he cannot remain in France. Talk to him of Cayenne; is there anything to be done in that colony?" Then Napoleon added, "But promise him nothing". Réal returned to the Temple, and with Desmarets continued the questioning. At the end of it Réal mentioned Cayenne which Pichegru came to know well after he had been transported there. Always according to Réal, Pichegru expressed the opinion that given thirty thousand men and thirty million francs Cayenne could be turned into the best colony France possessed. Then Pichegru told them that while he was in England some English officers wanted to show him round a military establishment, which he refused, saying, that one day he might return to his country and fight against England. Therefore he could not take advantage of their hospitality. (That sounds quite untrue since being a Royalist he would consider England only as a staunch ally.) Réal asked him whether he wanted books. Pichegru said he had Seneca and that sufficed. He wanted a portrait he was attached to; however it was refused as it was already in the inventory of the tribunal. That grieved him, and he said to the prison's concierge that M. Réal mocked him when he brought up the subject of Cayenne.

He complained of the two gendarmes who were present day and night in his cell. He asked for their removal. His request was referred to Napoleon who said, "Why tire him unnecessarily? A man, whatever one does to him, remains the master of his life." The gendarmes were removed, and Pichegru was found dead two days later.

Of course, say Napoleon's enemies, they were removed so as not to witness the murder.

The book lay beside the corpse, open on the page where Seneca described Cato's death. Napoleon's comment was, "What a fine end for the conquerer of Holland".

All that talk about Cayenne and the First Consul's mercy may sound pretty unconvincing, especially as Réal, as well as Desmarets, wrote, or found someone to write, his memoirs well after the Restoration, whitewashing himself and oozing belated bonhomie, but one is practically forced to believe them when they say that Pichegru killed himself. Some witty woman, possibly Mme de Staël, observed, "Bonaparte is unlucky with his enemies: they die on him".

With Georges and his fellow Chouans all was plain sailing. They behaved before their judges with reckless courage. Coster de Saint-Victor said to Thuriot, one of the four judges who tried them, "Hold your tongue, regicide, the blood of Louis XVI streams from your eyes".

Mme Récamier watched the trial, and was impressed by Georges's stoic dignity. "One contemplated this intrepid Georges," she wrote in her memoirs, "thinking that the head of one who was so wholeheartedly devoted would soon drop on the scaffold." After he was sentenced to death the judges asked him whether he would seek the First Consul's pardon.

"Could he promise me a finer occasion to die?" Georges answered.

In St Helena Napoleon strongly denied that he ever thought of pardoning Georges who was "a wild beast and I had to get rid of him".

With the exception of Moreau, Jules de Polignac, Louis Léridant, Roland and Marie Hizay who all received two years, the other members of the conspiracy were condemned to death. Charles d'Hozier, Rusillon, Rochelle, Armand de Polignac, Lajolais and Armand Gaillard had their sentences commuted to four years' transportation and detention in a State Prison. They were all members of the old nobility whom Napoleon was still courting, whereas with Georges, the son of the plough, no such consideration was needed.

Yet, so Chouan tradition remains, on July 25, 1804, the day of his execution, Georges was offered the First Consul's pardon which he refused as his companions were not included.

Georges arrived in the Place de Grève at eleven in the morning. The guillotine was waiting for him, Louis Du Corps, Louis Picot, Michel Roger, J. B. Coster-Saint-Victor, Alexis Joyaux, Louis Burban, Guillaume Lermercier, P. J. Cadoudal, Jean Le Lan and Jean Merille. Georges was assisted by the Abbé de Kéravenan, who after the Restoration became the parish priest of Saint-Germain-des-Prés. Reciting the Hail Mary Georges stopped after "Holy Mary, Mother of God, pray for us sinners now. . . ."

"Go on," said the Abbé, "and in the hour of death."

"Unnecessary," Georges replied, "this is the hour of death."

He stepped on the scaffold, and the large curly head that would bow only before God and King dropped into the basket.

As an epitaph to Georges the present writer considers it worth relating that in 1969 he heard an altercation in the Boulevard Saint-Germain between a Breton newsvendor and a client. The newsvendor pulled himself up to his full height which was just over five feet as he said in a dignified voice, "Be careful, you are speaking to one of Georges Cadoudal's Chouans."

VIII

The Duc d'Enghien

Cadoudal's last conspiracy had a deep, almost traumatic, effect on the First Consul, who previously had believed that basically he had nothing to fear from the Bourbons. He had offered to return them all their property if they renounced the throne. After consulting his brother and the Princes, Louis XVIII refused the offer. In his letter he spoke of his duty to his ancestors, mentioning St Louis and François I. When he read the letter Napoleon remarked that he had done more in the Holy Land than St Louis and far more in Italy than François I. So far so good; however now the same Bourbons whom he wanted to treat so generously allied themselves with wild beasts like Georges and his rabble of Chouans to assassinate him. In vain Georges insisted at his trial that he wanted only to capture the First Consul. Napoleon remained convinced that they intended to murder him. He thirsted for revenge.

Querelle, the most loquacious among the arrested Chouans, named all who had been present at a meeting in a cul-de-sac near the church of Saint-Roch except one whom all present had treated with conspicuous respect and deference but whose name was not even whispered. Querelle gave a description of him which did not help the High Police to identify the man. When reported to

Napoleon he immediately decided that the man treated with such respect could only be a Bourbon. Régnier, the Great Judge, excelled in taking any myth for truth and Cambacérès, the Second Consul, ably assisted by Fouché, liked playing on Napoleon's fears, at times succeeding, as he was wont to boast, literally in petrifying him. It was decided that one of the Princes had come to Paris at the time of the conspiracy in the hope of taking over in Louis XVIII's name after the assassination of the First Consul.

As a matter of fact, the man treated with such deference was Pichegru, but before that transpired Napoleon besmirched his name for ever with the blood of an innocent man.

Napoleon, Régnier, Cambacérès and the heads of the High Police asked themselves who the prince in question could be. One knew where the Comte d'Artois, the Ducs d'Angoulême and de Berry lived. They were not suspected. However, the Duc d'Enghien usually lived at Ettenheim in the States of Baden, near enough the French frontier to be able to pay quick, furtive visits to Paris. The High Police knew of several meetings of émigrés in Ettenheim, and a secret police agent reported that General Dumouriez, the traitor of the Revolution who had gone over to the enemy and now lived in England, had arrived in Ettenheim to see the Duc d'Enghien. A few days later Dumouriez left for Berlin. Secret agents then as now liked to make their reports sensational for obvious reasons. In his zeal the agent did not take the trouble to check. If he had he would have discovered that the person was not Dumouriez but a harmless émigré, the Sieur Desmoutier. The fact, as was believed in Paris, that Dumouriez had seen Enghien was further proof that that Prince was in the thick of evil plots against the First Consul. Therefore, Enghien had undoubtedly been the man at the meeting in the cul-de-sac near Saint-Roch.

General Moncey commanded the gendarmerie. He had a high opinion of his own powers of detection. He promised the First Consul to find out whether Enghien had really been in Paris during the Georges-Pichegru conspiracy, that is to say give proof to men who were already convinced, and, therefore, needed only confirmation instead of proof. One of Moncey's sergeants had been employed in the House of Condé before the Revolution, and knew every member of that household. Moncey sent him to Ettenheim to find out whether Enghien had absented himself from that town while Georges was still free. The sergeant brought back the news that Enghien had undertaken a mysterious journey at the time of the meeting of which Querelle had spoken. The report was true but once again the basis was wrong, for the journey the Prince had embarked on was to visit Mlle de Rohan to whom he was secretly engaged.

Immediately Bonaparte took measures to seize the person of Enghien who had conspired with Georges and was now hatching some awful plot with hated Dumouriez. To kidnap Enghien in the States of Baden meant violating foreign territory. The Duke of Dalberg was the Minister of the Grand Duke in Paris, a man who was completely on Bonaparte's side, in fact made his fortune through him, and whose uncle, the Prince Archbishop and last Elector of Mainz, was one of the First Consul's chief supporters in Germany, so the Minister was not unduly upset when he heard that the territory of his country would be violated by the First Consul's troops.

Two expeditions were sent to Germany, one under General Ordoner, the other under General Caulaincourt. Caulaincourt was specially trusted by Napoleon, yet in spite of that he was not told by his master why he wanted the person of the Duc d'Enghien. The First Consul never put his faith entirely in any of his followers, therefore one can believe Caulaincourt when he declared after the Restoration that he had at the time no idea of the fate awaiting the poor Prince. If he had, he swore, he would have disobeyed the First Consul. Since Caulaincourt's career was an honourable one his words deserve credence.

Enghien behaved quite foolishly. He was warned of troops assembling on the frontier, he also was, so the story has it, in possession of a message from one of Caulaincourt's officers with royalist sympathies, letting him know that he would be kidnapped, so the quicker he removed himself from Ettenheim the better for his safety. Enghien did not heed the warning, went shooting on the following day, and when the French surrounded his house in the middle of the night he first threatened to shoot, then let them take him away in a coach. His dog ran behind the carriage the whole way to the dungeon of Vincennes, to which Enghien was brought on Bonaparte's orders. Not for a moment did he appreciate the danger: he was convinced that he had been kidnapped because Bonaparte wanted to see him and probably keep him as a hostage or use him as an instrument in negotiations with Louis XVIII, which in any case he would refuse. He told this to the officers who accompanied him in the coach and with whom he took his meals in different inns.

On the day the semaphore brought the news of Enghien's capture there was a ball in the evening in the mansion of M. de Luynes. Talleyrand was present, and asked by another guest what would happen to the Prince, the Limping Devil calmly answered, "He will be shot". The next day his reply was repeated to Pasquier, future Prefect of Police, and Pasquier thought that Talleyrand had been misunderstood.

When Bonaparte received the news of Enghien being on French soil he held a meeting with his most intimate counsellors, having already had one with his brother Joseph, Cambacérès and Talleyrand. Joseph Bonaparte strongly advised his brother to do Enghien no harm as he had not been caught on French territory. On March 9 the council consisted of the Great Judge, Talleyrand and Fouché who at the time was no longer minister of police, only a senator, yet was always needed when there was trouble or a complicated problem had to be solved. Talleyrand, it was reported to Pasquier, urged Bonaparte to use the utmost rigour in his treatment of Enghien. Lebrun, the Third Consul, said that it would make a terrible impression all over the world if the Prince were executed. Cambacérès wanted to keep Enghien as hostage, and would have him shot only if another royalist attempt was made on the First Consul's life. Talleyrand, who wanted him shot without further ado, had his way. Of course all this was only hearsay; after the

Restoration every one present at the meeting loudly proclaimed his innocence.

When the meeting was over Cambacérès followed Bonaparte into his study and warned him of the consequences of his decision, telling him with more vigour than those that knew him would have credited him with that if Enghien's blood were shed the whole of Europe might rise against France, and pointed out to him that he, Napoleon Bonaparte, who had been innocent of the crimes of the Revolution, would by executing Enghien join the ranks of the criminals. His words fell on deaf ears. The First Consul wanted the Prince's blood because, as he said, those people had tried to kill him. The death of Enghien would prove to the world that Bonaparte was no weakling. Let the House of Bourbon understand that it was preferable not to conspire against him. That was the only fashion to stop them plotting against him. He told Cambacérès too that he wanted his own followers to see that a rapprochement between him and the Bourbons was an impossibility. Then losing his temper he shouted at Cambacérès, "It suits you who voted for the death of Louis XVI to be so scrupulous and so miserly with royal blood".

"It has nothing to do with it," Cambacérès answered. In any case he had tried to save the King's life with a rather complicated manœuvre during the voting. (When Louis XVIII returned to France Cambacérès's name was taken off the list of regicides.)

Savary here enters the picture. At the time of Enghien's kidnapping he commanded the Gendarmerie d'Elite. Born on April 26, 1774, he had been aide-de-camp to Desaix, later to Bonaparte, and was the First Consul's most devoted follower, a soldier, not considered too intelligent, despised by Fouché, but of complete loyalty to his master. Napoleon knew that he could use him in any capacity not so much for his talent as for his blind obedience.

Savary had been sent to the coast of Normandy because a landing of Chouans led by the Duc de Berry was expected. The landing did not take place, though an attempt was made, but the wind made it impossible for the vessel to approach the coast. Savary arrived back in Paris twenty-four hours before Enghien was brought to Vincennes. He went straight to Malmaison, where the First Consul, whose aide-de-camp he still was, resided at the moment with Joséphine, his wife. Bonaparte was closeted with Talleyrand, so Savary had to wait. When Bonaparte came out he ordered him to go with a detachment of the Gendarmerie d'Elite to Vincennes and put himself at the head of the troops that had already been sent there. On his way he should stop at General Murat's residence and hand him a sealed letter. Murat, who commanded the garrison of Paris, would give him the final instructions. Savary maintained for the rest of his life that the First Consul gave him no precise orders concerning Enghien.

Savary got on his horse and rode to Murat's house, arriving exactly at the moment Talleyrand was leaving the general. Murat told Savary that a military tribunal would judge Enghien, and he, Savary, was to guard the Prince, and see to the judgment being executed without delay. Savary arrived in Vincennes shortly after the members of the military tribunal. The tribunal consisted of officers who, with the exception of the president and the *rapporteur*, a captain, learnt only on the spot why they had been summoned. The president swore in later years that he was unaware of the prisoner's name. Little credence can be attached to that. Except for the one captain all the members were colonels.

Now let Savary speak for himself.:

". . . The Prince was conducted to Strasbourg, and then to Paris. The Colonel of the Grenadiers and aide-de-camp of Napoleon arrived separately and not with the escort, as has been said. He did not enter the house of the Duc d'Enghien but surrounded it with the troops that he had. It was the Gendarmerie who proceeded within and made the arrest. The Colonel of the Grenadiers did nothing but protect them."

What Savary here means is that a brother officer would do nothing as degrading as kidnapping a person in a foreign country. Let the blame rest on the shoulders of the uncouth gendarmes.

"I had just arrived from a mission which had taken nearly two months," Savary continues, "and during which I had learned the apprehension of Moreau, Georges and Pichegru. . . . If I had been absent two days longer I should now have nothing to say upon the death of the Duc d'Enghien, and it would be absurd to suppose that it depended upon my return. Thus far I had remained a stranger to everything that had just taken place, when, being on duty at Malmaison, I was at five o'clock in the evening called into the Cabinet of Napoleon who gave me a sealed letter to General Murat, Governor of Paris. I set out on horseback and arrived at his house at about six o'clock. At the door I passed the Minister for Foreign Affairs. As I had seen him at Malmaison in the morning, and knew that Murat was confined to his room by indisposition, I soon dismissed the reflection that this was not the Minister's usual hour, and put the visit to the account of the Governor's indisposition. Murat took the letter, read it and told me that he would communicate to me the orders which concerned myself.

"I here declare, in all the sincerity of my heart, and upon the assurance of military honour that I was totally ignorant that the Duc d'Enghien was in question. Not a word had been said to me at the Malmaison, unless it was vaguely at the moment of my departure, because the telegraphic dispatch, which announced his departure from Strasbourg, had just arrived, and it was whispered in the guard-room."

So far there is one important passage to retain from Savary's apologia, namely his running into Talleyrand in Murat's house. That was corroborated by several of their contemporaries.

Murat gave Savary his orders to take under his command a brigade of infantry which occupied the extremities of the Faubourg Saint-Antoine, and which was to be at Vincennes at ten o'clock at night. As his own legion of the Gendarmerie d'Elite was in the neighbourhood of the brigade, occupying the Arsenal, "I had been charged to watch whether any endeavours were employed to make it swerve from its duties. When I said I had been charged, I meant my legion, for I was generally absent." Now according to Réal, who unfortunately missed his part in this tragic affair, the Gendarmerie d'Elite had already taken over in Vincennes from the troops who usually guarded the fortress, and Savary was simply sent to command them since he was their colonel, an unimportant detail, though further proof that all concerned had a slightly different axe to grind when defending themselves after the Restoration, the one exception being Talleyrand who ensured that all documents concerning Enghien disappeared long before the return of the Bourbons. He was a truly farsighted man.

"About eight o'clock in the evening," says Savary, "I was engaged in disposing the brigade and the Gendarmerie at all the avenues of the place, when I beheld the approach of the Members of the Court Martial. Until the moment of my learning at Vincennes that the Duc d'Enghien had arrived there at four o'clock in the afternoon from Strasbourg, I believed that he had been found in Paris, as the companion of Georges."

Savary was, so he says, impatient to know the details. The Court Martial was composed of the colonels of the different regiments forming the garrison of Paris, decent officers who had "no extravagant opinion", yet "as well as all France were indignant at a project to assassinate the First Consul, and were persuaded that Georges acted under the direction of the Duc d'Enghien". That disposes of the President's statement that the Court Martial was unaware of the name of the man they were trying.

The court assembled in the great hall of the inhabited part of the castle. Savary maintained that its meeting was not secret, whereas Pasquier, who later had the opportunity of questioning the colonels, said that it certainly was. Since only the judgment survives, all minutes of the trial having vanished, this point is of no importance, but nobody could deny that Enghien was given no time to prepare his defence. Colonels Bazancourt and Barrois, members of the tribunal, told Pasquier, that the *rapporteur* questioned Enghien while he was still resting, Enghien demanding to be taken to Bonaparte, and asking the captain that the trial should not begin before he saw the First Consul. The captain reported back to the colonels, but Savary who was present (he later denied that) expressed the opinion that such a request would only infuriate Bonaparte, therefore should not be granted. In any case, he said, the tribunal had to do its duty and not act as an intermediary.

The Duc d'Enghien was brought before the tribunal, and the colonels, or so they told Pasquier, begged the Prince to deny all the charges brought against him, especially not to repeat that it was his wish to fight against France and serve under the English flag. But Enghien refused to retract. He would, if he had the chance, fight against the present Government of France because he owed that to his family, and repeated that he had asked the English Government to enlist him in the army, which had been refused. However, he indignantly denied that he had any dealings with Georges or that he ever thought of having Bonaparte assassinated. He repeated his demand to be taken before Bonaparte. That was again refused, and he was escorted back to his cell, where he was offered a meal. He asked that the meal should be given to his dog.

"I arrived too late to see the Prince enter," wrote Savary. "He repelled with indignation the imputations brought against him. The court allowed him to say what he pleased. . . . I wrote down immediately the reply of the Prince, 'Sir, I understand you perfectly; it was not my intention to remain indifferent to it. I had requested from England a commission in her army, and received for answer that she could not grant it, but that I should remain on the Rhine, where I should shortly have a part to play. . . .' The Court closed the proceedings, and had the hall cleared to deliberate in secret." Savary rejoined the troops on the esplanade of the Castle. Two hours after the court had been cleared he was told of the sentence. The officer who commanded the infantry of the Gendarmerie d'Elite came up to him and said that a picket had been demanded from him to execute the sentence.

"Give it," Savary answered.

"But where should I station it?"

"Where you cannot wound anyone," said Savary, thinking of "the inhabitants of the populous environs of Paris who were already on the road going to the different markets."

When the court had been cleared the president, so Colonels Barrois and Bazancourt related to Pasquier, asked the members of the tribunal for their opinion. Barrois and Bazancourt suggested imprisonment, the others too, but after two hours of deliberation they unanimously decided on the death sentence because of the Prince's declaration that it was his duty to his rank and blood to serve against the French Government. It did not occur to a single member of the Court Martial that they were not competent to judge a man brought by force from a foreign country.

There was a certain amount of quibbling about the execution of the sentence. In the official newspaper *Le Moniteur* of March 22, 1804, the Court Martial's judgment appeared. There the usual paragraph concerning death sentences by court martial was given, namely that the sentence would be executed within twenty-four hours. Now Savary maintained all his life that the judgment said, "The execution will take place at once". Here one can almost believe Savary who would never have given a firing squad if the judgment had said twenty-four hours. He was too much a martinet for that. Yet there are several witnesses against him, one of them General Hulin who was then still a colonel, though the president of the tribunal. He swore to Pasquier that the insertion in the *Moniteur* was the correct one, and, in fact, Hulin, after reading out the sentence to the Prince, had sat down to write a letter to the First Consul, imploring him to have mercy on Enghien but suddenly Savary burst in, tore the pen from him and shouted, "Messieurs, your business is over, mine begins". Then he stormed out, banging the door behind him.

Hulin immediately called for his carriage, his intention to go to Malmaison and intercede with Bonaparte. As he came out he saw Savary escorting the Duc d'Enghien down the stairs. Hulin thought that Savary was taking him to the tribunal to hear the sentence. Hulin hurried to call the other members of the tribunal, but on his way heard firing. A few minutes later Savary reappeared, looking pale, and saying, "One has to admit that he died bravely, but why was he against us?"

To return to Savary's own story, "After having examined the ground the officer selected the moat, as the most certain place for not wounding anyone; there was no other motive for the preference. The Prince was conducted there by the tower stairs at the entrance next the park, and heard his sentence which was executed. (Between the sentence and its execution a grave had been dug, which gave occasion to the rumour that it had been dug previous to the sentence being pronounced.) What trials are sometimes heaped upon us by fortune, whether we command or whether we obey. The most infamous reports have been made about me."

In his apologia Savary denied that he had a lantern attached to the breast of Enghien, or that he had kept his gold watch and took pleasure in showing it to his friends. He was never in the moat, but remained with his troops on the esplanade. He also refutes the accusation that he refused to let a priest come to the Prince. "No one ever spoke of it to me." He adds that at that period ecclesiastics were still very scarce, and probably it was impossible to find a priest in Vincennes.

To complicate matters, that is to find the one responsible for the murder of Enghien, it transpired afterwards that Hulin signed the death sentence at ten o'clock, four hours after the execution of the Prince. Pasquier, who had spoken to everyone connected with the ghastly business, though he put to paper his findings but long after the Restoration, reached the personal conclusion that in his zeal and deep attachment to the First Consul Savary exceeded his instructions. But then who gave him those instructions? Murat whom Talley-rand had just visited? The Court Martial? But every member of the Court Martial maintained that the sentence was not yet signed when the Prince was shot.

After Enghien was put into the hurriedly dug grave Savary mounted his horse, and set out for Malmaison to report to Bona-parte. He had on him the Prince's farewell letter to Mlle de Rohan and his watch. Approaching the barrier of Paris he met Réal, who dressed in his robe of counsellor of state, was driving to Vincennes. Réal told him that he was going to the Castle of Vincennes to question the Duc d'Enghien. He had the First Consul's order to do so. Savary replied that Enghien had been shot at six in the morning. Thunderstruck, Réal ordered his coachman to drive him back to Malmaison, where Napoleon had a fit of temper on hearing the news. "There is something here that I do not understand," he shouted. "That the court should have pronounced on the avowal of the Duc does not surprise me, but, in short, this avowal was only obtained by beginning the trial, and it ought not to have taken place till after Réal had interrogated him respecting a point on which it was important that some light should be thrown. There is something that exceeds my comprehension. Here is a crime which leads to nothing, and only tends to render me odious."

The meeting between Savary and Réal was a fact. Both of them spoke of it to their acquaintances long before the shadow of the Restoration began to make Napoleon's stalwarts fidgety and resort to lies. When Réal drove to Vincennes he was convinced that he would make Enghien speak, in fact expected him to confess to being Cadoudal's chief. After he heard that the Court Martial had already sat and Enghien was sentenced to death and executed, he became convinced that Talleyrand was behind it, that is he had persuaded Murat to order both the Court Martial and the immediate execution of the Prince, thus giving the First Consul no time to change his mind. No one knew better than Talleyrand, who had been present at the meetings, that the other two Consuls, Cambacérès and Lebrun, were definitely against the killing of the Prince; one more reason to hurry. Talleyrand wanted to make all reconciliation between Bonaparte and the Bourbons impossible; with Enghien's death the First Consul would join the ranks of the other guilty men, Talleyrand included; hence his leaving Malmaison precipitately and Savary finding him on Murat's doorstep when he arrived to take the sealed letter. However, it should not be forgotten that Réal was Fouché's right-hand man, and Fouché and Talleyrand hated each other. "This is worse than a crime," Fouché is supposed to have observed when he heard of Enghien's death, "it is a blunder."

The truth will never come to light. Bonaparte locked himself up in his study the day Enghien was brought to Paris because he wanted nobody to try to sway him. Joséphine, according to M. de Rémusat, the chamberlain, forced her way into his presence, begging him to be lenient with the Prince. "Go away," Napoleon said, "you are a child, you understand nothing of the duties of politics." And always, according to M. de Rémusat, he woke up at five in the morning, and said to Joséphine, "At this hour the Duc d'Enghien is no longer alive." She burst into tears and shrieked loudly "Come," he said, "try to sleep. You are only a child."

Then what was Réal doing in the morning on the road to Vincennes?

The murder of the Duc d'Enghien was the result of one blunder heaped on top of the other. Napoleon was incapable of ever admitting that he could make mistakes or cause them. In his will he said, "I had the Duc d'Enghien arrested and judged because it was necessary for the security and the interests of the French people at the time when the Comte d'Artois, as he admitted himself, had sixty assassins trained in Paris; in similar circumstances I would do the same". Yet when he was on the Island of Elba he blamed Talleyrand in front of an Englishman as having been the one who had influenced him at the time; and even before that, namely in 1809 when he practically kicked Talleyrand out, he shouted at him before witnesses that the Duc d'Enghien had to die because of Talleyrand's perfidy, for the whole kidnapping and execution had been instigated by him. In any case it was Talleyrand who, as Minister for Foreign Affairs, wrote at the time to the Envoy of Baden, informing him that the person of Enghien would be seized in the Grand Duchy. After the execution he pooh-poohed the whole business, observing to friends that all that happened was that a traitor was caught near the frontier and executed.

Though in 1823 the Duc de Rovigo, as Savary then was, published his apologia under the title of *Extrait des Mémoires concernant la catastrophe du duc d'Enghien* from which extracts were quoted in this chapter, he showed no remorse for the part he played in

Enghien's execution. In July 1807 he was sent as Ambassador to Russia, where he used to say, "Everybody is mistaken. It was Caulaincourt who kidnapped him, Murat who had him judged and I had him executed". Because of his part in the murder he was declared *persona non grata* in Russia, and Napoleon had to recall him.

When Caulaincourt was created Duc de Vicence the printer of the *Gazette de France* indulged in a little joke: Duc de Vincennes, he printed.

IX

The Kidnapping of a Senator

Touraine had stayed out of the wars of the Vendée and the Chouans, probably because it was too close to Paris. Yet it was, so to speak, feudal land with its many châteaux, *gentilhommières* and large properties, most of which, however, had been confiscated by the Revolution. Senator Clément de Ris, born in Paris in 1750, and belonging to the nobility of the robe, possessed a country mansion in Touraine. In 1791 he had been Administrator of Indre-et-Loire, a department the Convention had carved out of old Touraine. He was imprisoned under the Terror as a moderate, escaped death, and was named senator under the Consulate. He was a quiet man, virtually lacking enemies.

On September 23, 1800 (Vendémiaire 1, Year IX) four men arrived on horseback in the village of Saint-Avertin near Tours. They were mounted on cart horses. They took a meal in an inn, the innkeeper remembering that the eldest of them could not be more than thirty years old. They left around three in the afternoon, taking the road to Larçay. As they emerged from Saint-Avertin they were joined by two ill-clad fellows without mounts. A few minutes later a farmer was heard complaining that he had been robbed and one of his horses led away. His loud protestations caused a number of peasants to assemble on his farm, and led by the farmer they went in pursuit of the six men who, entering the woods of Larçay, opened fire on the pursuers, making them withdraw in a hurry. Coming out of the woods the six men stole another horse. Now they were all mounted. They rode through the village of Véretz at the end of which they ran into the band of peasants. The mounted, armed men forced them to go along with them, but one of their prisoners succeeded in escaping. A little farther on they grabbed M. Boissy, a health officer of the district. Near Azay-sur-Cher they reined in on the drive leading to the Château of Beauvais, the country residence of Senator Clément de Ris and his wife. Beauvais, once a feudal property which had belonged to Miron, François I's physician, had been the Senator's home since 1791.

Then the horsemen and their prisoners went into a small wood where the horsemen opened their luggage, took out hussar uniforms, and arms, donned the uniforms, and as the newfangled hussars rode out of the wood the Senator's carriage appeared, bringing Mme Bruley, a friend of Mme de Ris. The hussars surrounded the carriage which they accompanied to the *cour d'honneur*. There they dismounted and entered the mansion with Mme Bruley.

Clément de Ris was in his wife's bedroom. She had been unwell for a time and was still in bed. The hussars burst into the bedroom, laid hands on jewels and eighteen hundred francs of cash, then forced Ris to go with them, promising that no harm would come to him. The petrified wife jumped out of bed, dressed, and drove straight to M. Graham, the new Prefect of Indre-et-Loire, who was not unduly perturbed (politically speaking) since they were not in Normandy, Vendée or Brittany, but in peaceful Touraine far from the tentacles of the Chouans. It was ten at night when Mme de Ris reached the Préfecture. Immediately the Prefect sent out several brigades of gendarmes to search the countryside; moreover, he sent messengers to Police Minister Fouché and General Radet, Inspector General of the Gendarmerie, letting them know that the bandits with their captive had ridden to the Forest of Loches, taking the Senator in his own coach.

At the edge of the forest the sham hussars told the Senator to get out of his carriage, and mount one of his carriage horses. Then the coachman was sent back to Tours with the carriage. On their way to the forest the bandits had made prisoner of a surgeon called Petit whom they forced to guide them. The eight men now vanished into the thick forest.

When news of the kidnapping reached Fouché he at once suspected the Chouans who in their need of money were apt to kidnap people and hold them to ransom. He ordered the arrest of several well-known royalists in Touraine. His police watched de Ris's town house in Paris in case the kidnappers brought a letter from the Senator, asking his friends or servants to pay the ransom. Fouché got in touch with Comte Louis de Bourmont, a leading royalist, who on frequent occasions had acted as intermediary between him and the Chouans. When Bonaparte heard of the kidnapping he reacted to it in his own special fashion: Fouché was a born double crosser, therefore faithful Savary should go at once to Touraine. With his customary sabre-rattling and convinced that he would be one up on hated Fouché, Savary rode into Tours.

Savary learned what everybody already knew. Petit, the surgeon, on his way home from a sick person, had been seized by the bandits and forced to go with them. Savary had arrived three days after the Senator was taken.

The night before Petit had turned up at the Château of Beauvais, bringing a letter from the kidnappers, asking Mme de Ris for fifty thousand francs of ransom money which she should bring in a week's time to the Hôtel des Trois-Marchands in Blois. When he heard of the letter Savary sent for Petit whom he questioned at length. Petit could give little information because his eyes had been bandaged, and the bandits took him too far from their hiding place to be able to find it again. The gendarmes had found a hat near Montresor; Mme de Ris recognised it as her husband's; however Petit assured them that the Senator lost it at a goodish distance

from the bandits' lair. He remembered hearing the church bells of
Montresor ringing somewhere to his left when they halted for the
first time. Savary sent out the gendarmerie brigades of Loches and
Chinon to beat the countryside near Montresor.

Shortly after a blacksmith came to tell him that he thought that
he had found the house that corresponded to the surgeon's description of the building where they spent the first night. It had three
steps leading to the front door, a room beside the staircase, and old
leaves of artichokes were found inside, also some bits of ham. Petit
was given a meal by his captors consisting of pâté, ham and artichokes. The gendarmes drew a blank.

Savary (laterg lossing over the matter because it did not succeed)
advised Mme de Ris to pay the ransom money, but in gold pieces
so as to give the gendarmes time to arrest the man who would
come to fetch it. In her carriage Mme de Ris took fifty sacks, each
containing a thousand francs to the appointed place; however when
the bandits' emissary saw that huge quantity he vanished without
the hidden gendarmes ever seeing him. So nobody was arrested.
Savary was angry, and his anger rose when he heard that some
Chouans, who were in Fouché's pay, had reached the district and
brought back the Senator. Infuriated Savary rode home to Paris.
Not at all contented Savary reported to the First Consul that Fouché
had allied himself with the Chouans. Still the Senator was safely
back in his Château of Beauvais.

Near the Château de l'Ebeaupinais which belonged to a M.
Lacroix, an ardent royalist, the gendarmes found a dagger and a
pistol. Moreover, Lacroix had vanished when the Senator was
kidnapped. The gendarmes were convinced that they were on the
right track. On October 10 Lemaître, the Under-Prefect, accompanied by Lieutenant Paultron and several gendarmes searched the
Forest of Loches, then on their way home they ran into four horsemen. The gendarmes stopped them, the men showed their passports;
their names were Arthur Guillot de la Poterie, Robert Couteau,
Carlos Sourdat and Charles Salaberry. They declared that they were
merchants, their passports carried the visa of the Prefect of Indre-

et-Loire and they produced a letter from Fouché addressed to the Senator in which he recommended the four horsemen as reliable fellows who would save him, for they had the necessary courage to attack the brigands and liberate him. They would return him to his wife. "The moment you are set free and have seen your family come to Paris to give me all the details of your kidnapping." The so-called merchants also showed an order from Fouché which authorised them to find the brigands and conduct them to the prison of Tours. Impressed, the Under-Prefect let them continue on their errand. The men said they would spend the night in Loches and be in touch with Lemaître the next day.

Lemaître waited in vain for them, the men did not turn up, so he sent messengers all over the district to find out what became of them. One of the messengers returned announcing that in the village of Blère he had run into the men escorting Clément de Ris.

Lemaître at once sent Lieutenant Paultron to Azay-sur-Cher, where he was told that the Senator had already reached the château. Paultron saw Sourdat, Salaberry and Couteau, but Guillot was no longer with them. Paultron hurried to the Château of Beauvais, where he took down the Senator's statement whose captivity had lasted nineteen days.

After Petit's departure with the letter asking for the ransom the Senator was guarded day and night by a man wearing a black mask. He was dressed like a peasant though he wore riding boots. Another masked man brought him food three times a day. The Senator was kept in a cellar, and only once did he catch a glimpse of his guardian's face. He was a bearded peasant aged about forty. The man told him to be patient since his troubles would soon cease. The other man spoke in the same vein, adding, however, that if the ransom were not paid he would be put to death. The Senator signed the letter asking for the fifty thousand francs.

On the night of October 8 several masked men entered the cellar, bandaged his eyes, then dragged him through fields till they reached a forest. He could touch the trees as they marched him along. Three horsemen joined them in the forest. They all hurried

(RIGHT) Cadoudal (*Georges Cadoudal, The First Phase*)

(BELOW) Machine Infernale (*Two Plots Against the First Consul*)

A Chouan (*Georges Cadoudal, The Last Phase*)

La Mort du Duc d'Enghien (*The Duc d'Enghien*)

La Haye-Saint-Hilaire
(*The Bishop of Vannes*)

LE C.ᵗᵉ LOUIS-JOSEPH-BENIGNE DE LA HAYE-SAINT-HILAIRE (1

Dessiné au crayon à la prison de Rennes.

(L'original appartient à M. le Cᵗᵉ de Saint-Hilaire
château de Saint-Hilaire (Ille-et-Vilaine).

Savary (*The Ducs*
d'Otrante and de Rovigo)

Sujet Allegorique (*The Maubreuil Affair*)

on, holding de Ris by the arms. Nobody spoke. Suddenly a pistol shot was heard, and the brigands told the Senator that he was free. The brigands decamped, and the men Fouché had sent congratulated him on his safe escape. They were three leagues from Chavigny. The Senator rested for a while, then his deliverers took him home. All four of them were members of the royalist party, had been amnestied and were for the moment in Fouché's pay. Guillot had commanded a royalist division during the War of the Vendée, Sourdat had been aide-de-camp to Bourmont, the Comte de Salaberry had served in the Prince de Condé's army, and had been an officer in the Vendée's cavalry. Bourmont had put them at Fouché's disposal, and they had explained to the kidnappers that it was not the moment to exasperate Bonaparte.

So far so good; but then the case became complicated as inevitably happened whenever Fouché was involved. The liberation had been a sheer comedy, and Fouché knew how it would go before the four men were sent into Touraine. It was possibly Savary who suggested to the First Consul that Fouché was plotting with the Chouans, hence the speed with which the Senator had been freed. To show that he had nothing to fear Fouché turned on the men who surrendered the Senator, in fact saw to it that a special tribunal be appointed to try the kidnappers, the men who took him at his word when giving up de Ris.

Shortly after the Senator returned home two Touraine land-owners were arrested, Cazenac de Castres and Mounet. Though they could prove an alibi they were held for several months. Another royalist, Charles Gondé from Romorantin, was imprisoned, and he gave the names of several other royalists as having taken part in the kidnapping. Gondé was set free. The men whom he betrayed were the Marquis Dumoustier, his father-in-law the Comte de Mauduisson, a retired officer called Renard, and Gaudin, known as Monte-au-Ciel, a highwayman. They, according to Gondé's statement, had put the names of several rich landowners into a hat, and Clément de Ris's name was drawn; and before embarking on the kidnapping they came to Azay-sur-Cher on the pretext of

wanting to have a swim in the river, but actually to reconnoitre the
land. Pierre Aubereau from Orleans and Mme Lacroix, of the
Château de l'Ebeaupinais, were also named as accomplices. They
were all arrested with the exception of Renard. Then followed the
arrest of a physician, Dr Leménager, and of Charles-Marie Leclerc
from Néac in the Gironde. Leménager had been recognised by one
of the Ris servants, his passport was not in order, and, on top of it,
a hussar uniform was found in his suitcase. Mme Bruley thought
that he was one of the kidnappers. Jourgeron and his wife confirmed
that he guarded the Senator on Lacroix's order, and Mme Lacroix
came daily to the farm to bring food for the prisoner. Mme
Lacroix was taken to Paris and locked up in the Temple. Fouché
questioned her in person. Lacroix, who had been in hiding, went
to the police to find out what became of his wife. So he was arrested
too.

Both of them escaped the death penalty, were set free after a time,
and the only conclusion one can draw is that they helped Fouché
to get the others condemned.

The Marquis de Canchy and the Comte de Mauduisson were
sent to the Temple. They were joined in prison by Lacaille,
Jacquet and Guéry, a pork butcher's assistant, because they were
friends of Leménager. One Dubois-Papon was also wanted
because he was blind in one eye, and the mayor of Véretz swore
that one of the bandits had only one eye. Besides, the evening before
the kidnapping he had been to Tours, where he bought an English
saddle. The prisoners were all brought to Tours, only Lacroix
and Jourgeron, the farmer, remaining in Paris. The arrested men
declared themselves innocent; and stuck to that throughout the trial.
Petit, the surgeon, did not recognise any of them. At least so he
said. The four men, who had freed the Senator, had vanished
completely.

Fouché warned the tribunal to show no mercy as the lot of them
were in touch with the émigrés in England, and quite recently the
police had caught forty-two émigrés who had returned to France
without a permit. The public prosecutor asked for the death sen-

tence against Canchy, Mauduisson, Gaudin and Lacroix, twenty-four years for Mme Lacroix and six years for Jourgeron and his wife. The tribunal's sentence was thrown out by the Court of Appeal, and a fresh investigation and trial was ordered. At the second trial Canchy, Mauduisson and Gaudin were sentenced to death, Lacroixs received six years, but they were soon pardoned. The others were acquitted. The Marquise de Canchy wanted to kill herself; Chauveau-Lagarde, her husband's lawyer, knocked the pistol out of her hand. He was convinced that Bonaparte would have mercy on the sentenced men.

A Captain Virot, attached to the headquarters of the 22nd Division, refused to sign the death sentences, declaring that the condemned men were not the ones who kidnapped the Senator. (Neither Ris nor his wife put in an appearance during the trial. As senator he was entitled to refuse to give evidence.) The guilty men were police agents, and he, Virot, had given them visas when they came to Touraine. He was so certain of that that on the same day he hurried to Paris to speak to the First Consul. Bonaparte was absent, so he saw Joséphine who said she could not get mixed up in such matters, and in any case could do nothing. Virot went to the Ministry of Justice, where he heard that the death sentences had been carried out.

The four deliverers were by then in London. Fouché arranged their departure from France. Thus he had kept one half of his promise to Bourmont who could no longer protest because he was under arrest. The men who had surrendered the Senator had been promised that they would go scot-free if they gave up Ris without trouble. They kept their side of the bargain, not Fouché.

X

The Bishop of Vannes

The Comte d'Artois, the future Charles X, was not a man of much courage. He declared to the Chouans before every Chouan descent on France that he would go over in person and fight for his brother's crown. Convinced that his appearance on French soil would rally the people to the royalist side the Chouans went to France only to perish for the cause while Artois remained in England. But not for a moment did Artois's zeal desert him. He sent one party after the other into Brittany or the Côtes-du-Nord. He had a high opinion of himself and his position as heir to the throne. In 1802 when he was in Holyrood he behaved so pompously and had such a royal bearing that a Scotsman observed, "One could say it is he who is at home and we were the émigrés". It was reported to the First Consul that Artois turned up at a ball wearing so many crosses and ribbons that some of the Englishmen present took a very poor view of him.

But the First Consul was no less ridiculous in matters of orders and decorations. On November 17, 1802, he wrote to the Courts of Naples, Spain and Florence, asking them to forbid the wearing of decorations bestowed by the old regime. When he heard that they were tolerated in Warsaw, which then was under Prussian rule, he addressed himself to the King of Prussia, insisting that those orders be not worn again. At the time of the Peace of Amiens Talleyrand brought up the subject with the English plenipotentiaries.

After the raising of the Camp of Boulogne in 1805 the Comte d'Artois, ablaze with his crosses and ribbons, reached the conclusion that the moment was ripe for the overthrow of Napoleon. Naturally, he counted on the Chouans to achieve this.

After the execution of Georges Cadoudal, Guillemot, known as the King of Bignan, became the Chouans' leader. However, he was caught and executed in Vannes on January 4, 1805. He too had been waiting for Artois. Now the mantle fell on Louis-Joseph-Benigne de La Haye-Saint-Hilaire, who had been with General Georges in Paris at the time Georges was arrested, but managed to escape and reach England with the police still looking for him in Paris.

La Haye, as he was usually known, was an intrepid man, as brave if not braver than Georges, and dearly loved in Brittany. In the campaign of 1798 he commanded a division under Georges, and was suspected of having had a share in the murder of Andrein, Constitutional Bishop of Quimper. When Georges went to Paris to meet Bonaparte La Haye accompanied him, and on reaching the Tuileries he offered Georges to blow out the First Consul's brains while the two men had their talk. Georges turned down the suggestion.

After La Haye's return to England Fouché's police considered him their arch-enemy, and to catch him became practically an obsession with Fouché and his men. The French spies in England reported his movements whenever they had a chance.

On June 10, 1806, a French agent reported to the Senator-Minister, that is to Fouché. "All I told you of the intentions of Windham (risings inside France) has now been confirmed. He remains in favour of that project, and it appears that he has persuaded the other ministers; there are serious preparations. As I signalled before, Debar and Penanster have come here in view of a rising in Brittany. Jersey and Guernsey will be the jumping-off points; no action has yet been taken; all our friends are still quiet; but, I imagine, the matter will be handled by the many underlings who are in the islands. La Haye-Saint-Hilaire, Bruslart, Durand and other *businessmen* are always here."

The correspondent, as French spies styled themselves, went on to say that a Frenchman had arrived in London who was very well received, and he thought it was a M. Dandigné who had gone to live in Hamburg six months before. Fouché wrote to Bourrienne, Napoleon's ex-secretary, who because of a financial scandal had lost his position and was now French envoy in Hamburg, but Bourrienne assured him that Dandigné had not left. None the less, the correspondent maintained that Dandigné was in London and something was afoot. The same spy had written on May 8 and 23, to the effect that La Haye was keeping aloof from all activity. But already in May La Haye had crossed over to Brittany.

In England on Artois's recommendation La Haye received a monthly pension of fifteen pounds. Before leaving for Brittany in May Artois promised La Haye to come to France the moment a rising was prepared. Despite La Haye's care in his secret journeys, the Prefect of Vannes got wind of his presence in Brittany, only six weeks after his arrival. At once Fouché was informed; as La Haye could not be traced, the High Police began to think that the Prefect had been misinformed.

Since the Concordat Monseigneur Antoine-Xavier Mayneaud de Pancemont was the Bishop of Vannes. He had been the parish priest of Saint-Sulpice in Paris, had hidden during the Terror, and soon after Brumaire 18 was presented to Bonaparte, probably by Joséphine, and made Bishop of Vannes when the Concordat was signed. There was one snag, namely there was another Bishop of Vannes, Monseigneur Amelot, who had been nominated by the King of France, but now lived in London as an émigré, and had not the slightest intention of resigning his see. In vain the Pope asked him to. Pancemont arrived in Vannes only to discover that many of the faithful would have no dealings with him, and continued to consider Amelot their Bishop. Of course, those who refused to accept him were Chouans or their partisans. He was insulted in the streets and even in the cathedral.

His flock accused him of having betrayed the King, of making common cause with the Usurper who dared to call himself Emperor; and suggested that he had embezzled the twenty-four thousand francs he had been given by the Princes while he was abroad to be distributed among the Chouans on his return to France. The opposition to the new Bishop was led by the Abbé Guillevic, who had been Prior of Ploemeur, a friend and counsellor of Georges.

A Police Bulletin dated March 24, 1806, reported, "The Abbé Guillevic is a member of the Council of the Chouans of Morbihan. He is a ferocious, bloodthirsty man who constantly opposes the re-establishment of order in his part of the world. The Senator-Minister has asked for information on the present doings of this priest in the place to which he has retired." The Prefect of Morbihan gave the High Police the following information, "The Abbé Guillevic has always been considered as one of the most dangerous priests in the Department. After the Concordat he was banished from the diocese of Vannes because he showed his opposition too arrogantly. He was received by the Bishop of Rennes to whom he submitted, and though his submission was not considered sincere he was allowed to exercise his ministry at Redon. The Parish Priest of that town had little faith in him, therefore did not employ him in his church, but allowed him to say Mass at the hospital. He led a retired life there. The Sub-Prefect, who is acquainted with his opinions and past behaviour, has him continuously watched, always ready to arrest him if there is the slightest trouble in the district. He left for Nantes on March 11; the reason for his journey is not known."

The Prefect was convinced that the Abbé had made other secret journeys, including one to Plumergat and Auray, where he met Le Leuch, a priest who was the English Government's secret agent, from whom he obtained a few guineas. Le Leuch had returned to England. The Commissioner of Police in Nantes was ordered to find Guillevic and keep an eye on him.

What the High Police did not know was that Guillevic had remained in touch with La Haye, and in March La Haye had let him know that he was returning to Brittany. The Abbé left Nantes, hurried back to Morbihan, where he met La Haye on June 27. Among the Chouans the English had landed with La Haye were two of Georges's officers, Jean-Louis Pourchasse and Jean Billy. Soon they were joined by the Chevalier Scecilion, De Bar, Polcarro, Maurice Legoff, Bertin and others. La Haye's first task, as he saw it, was to make the Bishop of Vannes's life impossible. He visited farms, entered peasants' cottages, spoke to them in the fields, telling them what a traitor Pancemont was, who had embezzled twenty-four thousand francs of royalist money.

Pancemont saw the mounting wave of hatred, complained to the authorities, but what could they do since it was impossible to find La Haye and his Chouans?

Then one day Pancemont received a letter from La Haye. "General Georges had asked for the twenty-four thousand francs, but you did not reply. If you do the same to me there will be trouble." Pancemont left it unanswered, so one night during a reception in the bishop's palace La Haye appeared in person. The servants did not know him, nobody present recognised him, and on the pretext that he had urgent business with the Bishop he succeeded in seeing him in his study. Details of their meeting never transpired, yet the local tradition has it that Pancemont had to lie down on the floor, and not budge before La Haye made his get-away. The Bishop did not pay the twenty-thousand francs, however.

On July 23 or 24 two of La Haye's Chouans, Pourchasse and Bertin, were involved in an affray in a tavern in the Sulniac district using their firearms without hitting anybody. The gendarmes who came on the scene arrested them, and took them to prison in Vannes. When he heard of their arrest La Haye decided to strike. He was not the man to leave his companions in the lurch.

He let a month pass before taking action. On August 23 at seven in the morning Pancemont left in his coach for Monterblanc, to confirm children there. The coachman was on the box, and inside the carriage sat the Bishop with the Abbé Allain, his vicar-general, his secretary, the Abbé Jarry, while Thetiot, a footman, followed on horseback. At nine o'clock as the coach reached the Parc Carré, three-quarters of a league away from Monterblanc, five armed horsemen surrounded the coach. The coachman was forced to pull up, then La Haye opened the door, and showed Pancemont a piece of paper on which was written, "If the arrested men are not freed within eight hours beginning this moment the bishop and all who accompany him will be shot". When Pancemont had read it La Haye said, "You have read it, monsieur, get out".

La Haye pulled him out of the carriage, then the two abbés. Holding a pistol to the bishop's chest La Haye ordered his companions to tear off his cassock, take off his hat, and told the coachman to undress as he wanted the bishop to put on his livery. At that moment the mayor of Monterblanc appeared with some of the leading figures of the village. The mayor was forced to surrender his hat and waistcoat. The Abbé Jarry declared that on no condition would he desert his bishop, so he had to take off his cassock too and put on the coachman's livery. The Abbé Allain was told that if he wanted to save the bishop he should go to the Prefect of Vannes, or the hostages would be killed. The Abbé Allain went off, Pancemont was hoisted on a horse, but then La Haye noticed that he was still wearing his violet stockings. He sent a man to buy white stockings which were pulled on the bishop's legs: the stockings were so thick that he could not get his shoes back on.

Till mid-afternoon the small cavalcade rode around in the country near Vannes, stopping from time to time in unfrequented lanes. Suddenly gendarmes appeared, sent by the mayor of Monterblanc. The bishop offered to go up to them, thus giving the others time to escape. La Haye would not hear of it; the bishop had to gallop off with them, La Haye and the Abbé Jarry holding him in the saddle. They stopped after half an hour near the village of Lange, where the distressed bishop, who was at the end of his tether, was lifted off his horse, laid down in the grass, and given a saddle to support his head. Then they all lay down to sleep, and were still asleep when towards three o'clock Pourchasse and Bertin turned up. As La Haye had expected, General Jullien, Prefect of Morbihan, had freed the men to save the Bishop's life. Thus for the moment La Haye was completely the master of the situation. The gendarmerie under Marshal Moncey did not dare to take action, for La Haye was known as one who kept his word. In short, nothing could be done before Pancemont returned to Vannes. They were soon to discover that even the Bishop's return would still leave them powerless.

La Haye was not yet satisfied. "You will be taken to the high road," he told the Bishop, "by one of my men. Before permitting you to go I want you to swear on your honour to let me have tomorrow before midday the letter I sent with your vicar-general, your gold episcopal ring, your Cross of the Legion of Honour, and twenty-four thousand francs in gold. I am keeping your secretary as hostage. Whom will you send with the money and the other things?"

Pancemont said he would send the parish priest of Saint-Avé. "Suits me," said La Haye. "Here is a piece of wood; I am keeping one that is similar. Your man will show your piece of wood to my emissary when he brings the money and the objects. Otherwise your secretary will be shot."

Pancemont embraced his secretary, then left with Pourchasse. He reached Vannes in the evening, and though feeling sick and dead to the world he at once complied with La Haye's instructions. The great difficulty was to find the large sum of twenty-four thousand francs in time. The Superior of the Seminary was asked to help. Thirty-six thousand francs were collected within an hour, twelve thousand more than were needed. To the twenty-four thousand francs the Bishop added the Cross of the Legion of Honour, but had the presence of mind to substitute an imitation for his episcopal ring, which had been a present from Napoleon. The parish priest of Saint-Avé handed it all to La Haye's emissary, and the Abbé Jarry was allowed back to Vannes. He brought a letter to the Prefect in which La Haye said, "Monsieur you served the King in this instance. Would you not prefer to serve under his authority than Bonaparte's?"

Now at last the High Police could act.

"An awful event has once more disgraced the Department," wrote the Prefect to the Senator-Minister. "Yesterday the Bishop, on his way to Monterblanc for a confirmation, was stopped on the road at nine in the morning by six armed men, who sent M. Allain, the Vicar-General, to tell me that if by four in the afternoon the two arrested Chouans were not set free and sent to Saint-Jean-Brévelay, the Bishop and M. Jarry, his secretary, would be executed. If I sent out the gendarmes the first shots would be for them.

"I did not hesitate for a second: I set the two men free.

"The Bishop and his secretary were robbed of their ecclesiastical robes, forced to dress as peasants and dragged to a forest three miles away. The moment Pourchasse appeared the Bishop was led to the Sominé road leading to Vannes, mounted on a bad horse, then abandoned. He fell off the horse, and peasants who came to his aid brought him back to Vannes at ten at night.

"The Chouans kept his secretary, and made the Bishop swear that he would send them a substantial sum, otherwise M. Jarry would be shot. The sum has gone to them this morning; it is three thirty in the afternoon, and M. Jarry has not yet arrived. The instant he arrives the gendarmerie of Vannes and the district will leave at full gallop for the spot where he has been set free; the tocsin will be rung in all villages; a proclamation I have just written will be distributed; and I will organise a general search with all the population against those monsters."

The Prefect either did not know the sum the Bishop had to pay, or feared Fouché's anger if he found out how large it was. However, His Excellency the Senator-Minister had his own special agents in Vannes, from whom he quickly learnt that the sum was twenty-four thousand francs.

The High Police believed that the Prefect and the gendarmerie had not attached enough importance to the two arrested Chouans. After they found out that Bertin was not La Haye-Saint-Hilaire, but a carpenter who had escaped from the prison of Brest, where he was serving a sentence for highway robbery. He should immediately have been taken back to Brest. The other man, Pourchasse, could easily have been La Haye, though he too maintained that he was a carpenter. They could not both have been just ordinary carpenters. The High Police had a report from a Frenchman who had recently left Guernsey which made it most probable that Pourchasse was no other than La Haye.

La Haye had been in London five months ago, but later went to Guernsey, an English frigate eventually bringing him over to France. Therefore Pourchasse could easily have been La Haye.

The Senator-Minister gave orders to the Prefect to catch the brigands by any possible means at his disposal so as to repair the damage the kidnapping of the bishop had done to public morale in Brittany.

In his next report, dated August 27, the Prefect advised Fouché that M. Jarry had returned to Vannes on the 24th at eight in the evening, after the ransom money had been paid. The Prefect also wrote to Champagny, the Minister of the Interior, and the Bishop to Portalis, Minister of Public Worship, and both letters were shown to Napoleon, whose anger was immense. He wrote to Portalis on August 31, "I read with distress the news from Vannes. The Prefect's behaviour is unforgivable. As regards the Bishop of Vannes I am told that he sent the brigands who captured him the ring I gave him and the decoration of the Legion of Honour. I cannot believe in such cowardice. None the less, I want you to let me have a report. The bishop, as any other man, should have preferred to die than commit such a contemptible action. . . ."

At the same time Fouché received a report from Morlaix in which the Government Delegate, referring to the abduction of the Bishop of Vannes, observed that in the Côtes-du-Nord the Chouans were becoming excessively active; expropriated landowners threatened the new proprietors; mayors neglected their jobs, not bothering to ask travellers for their passports; and the gendarmes stopped only ill-clad poor peasants, and in the town of Morlaix itself the Sub-Prefect and the magistrates criticised the Government Delegate.

On September 3 the Gendarmerie gave the results to date of their pursuit of the kidnappers. The parish priest of Saint-Avé handed the twenty-four thousand francs to an amnestied Chouan called Martin. The moment that came to light the gendarmes arrested Martin, Jean Marie Leray, Martin's brother-in-law, and Le May, a dissident priest and trouble maker. It was expected that they would give useful information. The gendarmerie added that the chief of the band had written to the Prefect, asking him to dismiss the mayor of Sulniac, where the two Chouans were arrested after the affray, and change the parish priest too. (The Prefect had not written to Paris since his second letter.)

On the same date the busybody Delegate of Morlaix wrote to the Senator-Minister, "The kidnapping of the Bishop of Vannes produced deep consternation in Morlaix. Noblemen and amnestied Chouans fear that they will be more strictly watched; proprietors fear that the success of the brigands will embolden them to blackmail; and the number of criminals will rise in proportion to the increase in the ranks of beggars and unemployed workmen." He suggested that troops should be sent to Morbihan and Finistère.

The Bishop of Vannes must have recovered from his shock because in a letter to the Minister of Public Worship, which the High Police found quite inadequate and hazy in detail, he practically accused the mayor of Monterblanc of having taken part in the plot since he had suddenly turned up while the brigands were undressing him, and even lent a waistcoat to help the brigands disguise him. He also described the arrival of gendarmes on the scene while the brigands were waiting for their two accomplices to arrive from Vannes prison. That too the High Police took with a pinch of salt. Who sent the gendarmes? Was it the mayor of Monterblanc? How was it possible that the gendarmerie did not corroborate it? One had only the bishop's and the Prefect's word for that. And far more important: how could the two detainees find the brigands so easily when, according to the bishop, they had been moving round the countryside? Everybody, Fouché and his collaborators were convinced, had something to hide. He sent thirty-eight questions to the Prefect.

The answers to those questions, it was hoped in the Ministry of Police, would shed light on obscure details. Through which places did the brigands take their prisoners; where did they find food and the white stockings; who received the bishop's cassock and vestments; what became of his coach and who guided the cavalcade round the countryside? The High Police suspected that in the bishop's circle there were persons favourably inclined to the brigands and the Chouans. In spite of their noisy emnity to the bishop, sentenced Chouans often were recommended by the bishop for mercy. Martin, who had fetched the ransom money, had been amnestied eighteen months ago because of the bishop's intervention. He had done the same for Leroy in whose house Guillemot was arrested; in short the bishop courted popularity among his sworn enemies.

The Prefect of Morbihan was out of favour also. To make his part less shameful in the affair he now suggested that the brigands were ordinary highwaymen, and Bertin and Pourchasse just common thieves. However, through their spies among the Chouans, the High Police had received information according to which Bertin had been one of Georges's men, and belonged to Guillemot's last band. They were truly shocked in the Ministry when the Prefect wrote to say he had withdrawn the gendarmes and called off the hunt.

Fouché ordered him to continue the search for the brigands. The High Police found it regrettable that so little energy was shown by a man who had been appointed Prefect of Morbihan.

The next word from the Prefect was about the leader of the gang. He had it on good authority that he was a young man of twenty-five whose description tallied with none of the Chouan chiefs, but was, in fact, a nobleman from Picardy or Normandy. The Prefect's informer was a deserter who had surrendered.

"A sergeant-major, two sergeants and one gendarme from Vannes," went on the Prefect, "disguised as Chouans went to the mayor of Plaudren. According to their report he was absent, but they were very well received by his wife who, treating them as Chouans, gave them shelter, food and all the information they asked for. She told them that her husband had always protected the Chouans; they were safe in his house because he was the mayor. She showed them the hiding place in case the gendarmes came. She told them too that she had hidden Gambert for whom the police was looking, also many of his comrades and priests. Her husband had gone to Vannes to ask the authorities to set Martin free." The Prefect added that he had reasons not yet to arrest the mayor of Plaudren. Then he spoke of the general misery of Morbihan, and his fear of salt smuggling starting again on a large scale.

"I confess," the Prefect ended his report, "that I cannot understand the obstinacy of that handful of brigands who want only to rob so as to be able to expatriate themselves when peace is signed."

The Police Commissioner of Brest reported on September 9 that the kidnapping of the Bishop of Vannes had upset the people of Brest who saw in this act the resurgence of the Chouans. If a rich proprietor was threatened he paid up if the threat came from the Chouans; they called in the police only if they were hounded by the riff-raff. The person mostly to be blamed was the Prefect of Morbihan who treated the Chouans too leniently. The peasants would not denounce them fearing the Chouans' vengeance. And since everyone in the glorious Empire plotted to his heart's content, the Commissioner informed Fouché that he had seen a letter written by the Captain of Gendarmes of Morbihan in which he bitterly complained of the Prefect's lack of zeal and his taking no precautions against the brigands who might attempt to embark for England. (The word brigand during the Empire meant anybody opposed to the Emperor.)

The Prefect of Finistère was more zealous. He reported that on August 23 at eight in the evening a man between twenty-six and thirty, unable to speak Breton, but speaking French with a perfect accent, and giving the impression of having had a good education, appeared at Laniron, a country house near Quimper, spoke to the servants, asking them to direct him to Quimper, which he had left at three in the afternoon to go to Bénodet or Plumelin, but lost his way. The servants told him to leave the house, and refused to have anything more to do with him. The Prefect of Finistère alerted both the gendarmes and the customs men. The High Police dismissed the matter since the kidnapping of the Bishop of Vannes took place precisely on the 23rd.

The Prefect of Morbihan received a second letter from the chief of the brigands, dated September 9, explaining that the reason he had detained the bishop was because he wanted to make sure that his companions were released. "We are French, monsieur," he went on, "and we love our country. The many governments and rulers that have followed one another have not convinced us that they were stable or legally entitled to govern us. If any of us fall into your hands it is because we have different opinions and not because we are criminals. We are the agents of no faction, or of any foreign power; but whatever sort of government unhappy France has, we cannot make friends before the King is back on the throne." Then he insisted again on the dismissal of the mayor of Sulniac and his deputy. They should leave the Department, one being an artisan, the other a young man who could make a living anywhere. The brigand chief called that a moderate request, and ended his letter with these words, "I cannot finish this letter without assuring you that the great moment of our lives will be the day when all parties will unite to salute Louis XVIII".

On the night of September 8 the gendarmerie of Vannes went in full force to the village of Kmane. Brigands were supposed to be hiding in the house of Khero, a farmer. The Captain of Gendarmerie, who had received the information, himself led the operation. He ordered Khero to open his door: the farmer refused. They heard a lot of coming and going inside the house: the door was opened only after Khero had kept them waiting for three-quarters of an hour. The Captain summoned Khero to declare whether anyone was hidden in his house. The farmer refused to answer. The house was searched but nothing was found. However, the gendarmes discovered a large stone in the stable which seemed to hide some secret hollow. The farmer was again summoned: once more he refused to answer. So the stone was moved, and in fact there was a deep hole beneath. The gendarmes pointed their rifles into the hole, shouting they would open fire. Then a voice cried, "Don't shoot, I surrender," and a man climbed out, wearing only a shirt, Guihuv by name, a non-amnestied Chouan who, till the arrival of the gendarmes, had been sleeping in the best bed in the house. Questioned he told the Captain that when the armistice was signed with the Chouan leaders he had surrendered his arms to Hervé, chief of the canton, and had simply forgotten to ask to be amnestied. The reason he had hidden was because he feared that the gendarmes might not know that he had submitted to the Government. He denied that he had anything to do with the kidnapping of the bishop. Both he and Khero were taken to the prison of Vannes.

When he was confronted with the Abbé Jarry the Abbé declared that he was not one of the kidnappers. Instead of being released Guihuv was clapped in irons because by his own admission he had not been amnestied.

On September 22 the Prefect of Morbihan informed the Senator-Minister that he had received an anonymous letter, telling him that one Baudeloque of the 4th Colonial Battalion knew all who had taken part in the bishop's abduction. Baudeloque corresponded with them, and if arrested one could make him disclose the truth. After investigation the Prefect discovered that Baudeloque himself had penned the anonymous letter. He was handed over to the military authorities.

Mahev of Monterblanc was arrested on the same day for having given refuge to the brigands; the mayor of Plaudren and his wife were also under lock and key; and Lebaron, Léo and the brothers Bourdiec, who had been arrested a little earlier, refused to confess. The same went for Mignotte in whose house ammunition was found. "What am I to do with all these detainees?" the Prefect inquired.

The last thing the High Police and their chief worried about was the large number of people in prison, for once inside they were out of mischief.

At the beginning of October it was decided to bring in the army. Under the command of General Boyer galloping columns were to operate in Morbihan and Finistère. Fifteen hundred men were allocated to the general who on October 10 had a long meeting with the bishop without discovering more than already was public knowledge. The bishop could give no accurate description of the five brigands.

"I wait," wrote the General to Comte Dejean, Minister of War, "for a company of Grenadiers and one of Voltigeurs whom I need to intercept communications between Morbihan and the Côtes-du-Nord. I expect to begin on the 8th of this month."

Meanwhile Pancemont wanted to send out a pastoral letter in order to obtain information from his clergy on the five brigands and their accomplices. The Prefect considered that measure dangerous as it might set alight the fanaticism of the peasants and strengthen the influence of the dissident priests. The Bishop wrote to the Minister of Public Worship, who replied that His Majesty the Emperor had agreed, on condition that the Great Judge and the Prefect approved the text. The Bishop published it with no results whatever.

General Boyer instructed the Prefect to forbid all shooting of game in the districts where his columns would operate. The Prefect found that embarrassing, as he already had issued shooting permits which had been paid for. Boyer reported to Fouché that the mayor of Moncontour had notified him that two dangerous Chouans, Debar and Dujardin, had lunched in September in Boscuy with the previous cook of Duval le Gris, another wanted brigand. The general immediately sent an agent to arrest them. As it was a month later Debar and Dujardin were no longer in Boscuy. The General's plan was to go to Orient to mount an expedition against the Isles of Houat and Hoëdic, where three brigands were reported to be hiding. Fouché strongly advised him to do so as it was possible that the five kidnappers were also on the islands.

His Excellency the Minister of Public Worship, whose domain

was strictly religious matters, took a hand in the chase too. On October 14 he sent His Excellency the Senator-Minister information he had been supplied with by a private person whose name he could not divulge, but who was doing detective work on his own, aiming to catch the five brigands. The private person had discovered that after the abduction the brigands had spent the first night with Madec, a fisherman, near Tanay in Morbihan. Madec was now in the prison of Vannes. He had come in 1803 from England with Georges, Mercier, Saint-Régent and the Abbé Guillot, all of them in possession of passports given them by the English Government. The Prefect of Morbihan was trying to find out whether the fisherman was the same Madec.

The wife of Leguevel, former mayor of Monterblanc, had declared in an inn called le Chapeau Rouge on the Elven-Vannes road that she knew of the kidnapping before it had taken place because a Chouan called Gambert had confided in her. Leguevel and his wife were in communication with the brigands, moved about a lot, and spent much money, though they had no visible means of existence. Leguevel received a letter from Strasbourg from Tossène of Plaudren, a former Chouan who was probably serving in an army corps in spite of having deserted several times. Believing that Leguevel was still mayor of Monterblanc he asked him to give his regards to Gambert and his friends. As Gambert, according to secret agents' report, was in Guernsey in June it stood to reason that he had since come to Morbihan. It was known that the mayor of Plaudren had also hidden Gambert and his accomplices.

On receipt of the Minister of Public Worship's letter Fouché instructed the Prefect of Morbihan to question Leguevel and his wife in detail. He should find out in which corps Tossène served and where Gambert was hiding at the present time.

As far back as June 3 the Prefect of Morbihan had signalled to the Ministry of Police that the Chouan chiefs, Thiesse and Pourchasse, were seen near Saint-Jean de Brévelay, both laden with English gold, and saying they were on a mission which would take about six weeks to complete. On October 14 Thiesse, a miller, was arrested at Sérent in Morbihan, and Brulé, a former Chouan, at Ploërmel. The gendarmerie was interrogating them to find out whether Thiesse was the Chouan chief and Brulé the ferocious Chouan who went under the name of *Brule-amorce*. The gendarmerie also signalled that some English vessels had been sighted near the promontory of Rubis, probably waiting to embark the brigands. The gendarmerie's report was addressed to General Boyer who had gone into action on October 9, dividing up his troops into seventy-five squads, each guided by gendarmes. The operation was intended to last for a week. The General felt certain of success. So did the Prefect who gave him a list of one hundred and fifty farms and houses that were suspect.

On the same night a fishmonger from Napoleonville was attacked on the highway by seven brigands who explained to him that they had fired on him thinking he was a gendarme. They spoke to him first in Breton, then in French. The General detached three squads and sent them in pursuit of the seven brigands. They were not caught however.

On the 17th the gendarmerie reported that a well-mounted stranger rode to the house of the mayor of Plemy in Côtes-du-Nord, and inquired whether he knew any Chouans. The mayor said he did not. "You will soon see fifty and shortly three or four hundred; I am their leader," said the stranger, and galloped away. The General received intelligence that a few Chouans had landed at Saint-Briac near Saint-Malo. So he left for the Côtes-du-Nord, intimating to Fouché that the Chouans chased by his troops in Morbihan had sought refuge near Dinan.

The troops led by the gendarmes were not very successful. They arrested two Chouans and a fisherman supposed to be in league with the enemy. A captain of the Voltigeurs caught a deserter in his father's house in Plougomelen near the sea. As he marched away he tried to escape; on a corporal's order the soldiers opened fire. The deserter was killed. In his report the captain said that the corporal would be punished. Even though the great search did not achieve its aim the prison in Vannes was filling up nicely. The detainees were questioned day and night, the Emperor's pardon was promised to anyone who showed where La Haye and his companions were hiding. The prisoners kept silent. Martin, who had collected the twenty-four thousand francs ransom, was brought before a military tribunal. Of the four witnesses produced only one recognised him.

The Bishop of Vannes now came forward accusing several priests in his diocese, declaring to the authorities that the English were behind them. He had been watching two priests in the seminary who, when they returned from England, promised to behave themselves. He formally charged them before the Prefect of conspiring to escape back to England. The Prefect put them in prison. The Bishop was convinced that under the ordeal of being questioned they would give useful information. The brave prelate also denounced the Abbés Guillevic and Le Franc. Guillevic, he announced, had been the instigator of all Chouan activities, the kidnapping included; Le Franc, a master at the College of Vannes, had signed the Concordat, and the Bishop offered him a parish, which he refused because he had, so he said, always been a teacher. He was sent to Redon, where Guillevic lived. The Bishop believed that he was the second priest whom the police suspected of acting as messenger between the Chouans of Morbihan and those of the Côtes-du-Nord. Guillevic could not be found, so, on the Bishop's advice, Le Franc was apprehended and brought to Vannes, where he was held in the seminary where he could do some useful teaching while waiting questioning by the police.

The village of Plaudren was known as a refuge of the Chouans, and Fouché instructed Boyer to search seven houses there, giving the names and condition of their proprietors. Fouché sent out similar lists concerning other villages. He sent these out almost daily, thus continuing the best Revolutionary tradition of using the military as a branch of the police.

On November 11 General Boyer reported to Fouché that in the Côtes-du-Nord near Loudéac his troops had run into seven strangers who could easily have been the five kidnappers plus two accomplices. The soldiers went in pursuit of them, but the brigands vanished. Unruffled the General sent a spy after them: the spy did not return, which made the General think that the brigands had forced the spy to join them.

In the same month of November the General sent three columns divided up in nine platoons to search two hundred and twenty houses and a number of woods. The only result of the operation was the arrest of fifty army deserters and conscripts without finding any trace of La Haye and his four men, though one thousand écus had been promised for information leading to their arrest. The peasants, the High Police in Paris was convinced, feared the Chouans too much to dare to come forward. Still, Boyer believed that even if he could not catch them La Haye and his brigands would be forced to leave the territory of the Empire as a result of the military operations.

At last good news reached the Senator-Minister.

La Haye had kidnapped the Bishop of Vannes in order to have Bertin and Pourchasse released, in which he was completely successful. After their release the two men had vanished like La Haye and the other four. Now on December 8 Bertin was caught during a search in the house of a tailor named Ledean. He was hiding naked under a bale of straw. The tailor was able to escape. Bertin was taken to the prison of Vannes, where the whole might of the police fell upon him. Where was La Haye? Where were Pourchasse and the others? Bertin held his ground; therefore different tactics were needed. The Bishop of Vannes was called in. He went to the prison, made long friendly speeches to Bertin, explaining to him that as a good Catholic he had to repent, and no repentance would be more pleasing to God than naming the kidnappers. He insinuated also that as he was the Emperor's bosom friend he would see to him being pardoned.

Bertin fell into the trap and named the five men as La Haye, Jean Billy, Thomas, Petit Vincent, and one whom he knew only as Louis or Jean. The Bishop reported Bertin's revelations to the authorities, and Bertin, who had the Bishop's promise of going scot-free, was brought before a military tribunal, was sentenced to death and execution the same afternoon. When Bertin discovered his mistake, putting his trust in the Bishop, he asked to be allowed to give the command to fire to the firing squad. His request was granted (was it on the Bishop's intervention?) and calmly Bertin gave the command—the last words he ever spoke. The tailor was caught two months later, and suffered the same fate.

While the police and General Boyer rejoiced, La Haye, Pourchasse and Billy remained together in hiding, waiting for help from London, for they were certain that the English and the Abbé Guillevic, who had made good his escape and reached London, would not abandon them. The three men were still in Morbihan. The police kept watch on La Haye's parents' house in Saint-Leu; in the Vallée de Montmorency which he had often visited in his youth; in Paris where Mlle Lacroix, a dressmaker who had been his mistress, lived; in Meaux at his brother-in-law's home; and at Rennes because his mother frequently went there. When one of his sisters, Mme de Saint-Thomas, made a journey to Paris she was shadowed by police agents, and in Rennes his brother, serving in the Spanish army, was arrested by mistake. Spain had to claim him to get him released.

The Abbé Guillevic worked hard for La Haye and his compaions. On January 11, 1807, La Haye received a letter from him. He had seen Windham, War and Colonial Secretary, sixteen times, Cockburn, Under-Secretary in the War Office, fourteen times, Sir Francis Vincent, Under-Secretary in the Foreign Office, eighteen times and the Comte d'Artois, nineteen times, but in spite of him having waited for him eighteen times he did not succeed in getting into Lord Howick's presence. None the less, the Government was willing to rescue La Haye and his men, wrote the Abbé, adding that the moment Napoleon suffered his first defeat forty thousand English troops would disembark with the Princes in Brittany.

In reply La Haye asked the Abbé to send him a number of émigrés while waiting for the British troops. The Abbé answered,

"Ah! my friend, you know not what you are asking when you request the return of your comrades. Sloth has conquered them . . . they cannot forgive you for having done so well for the cause without them." On the other hand, the Abbé had made arrangements for La Haye to be picked up by an English vessel and brought back to England. In fact the boat that brought the letter was waiting for him and his companions. La Haye refused to leave: his duty was to remain in Brittany to further the King's cause. And he remained for over a year in Brittany while Boyer's flying columns combed the countryside. Of course, it could not last. There were too many wretches whom the police could buy. Poverty and misery remained Fouché's best agents.

On September 23, 1807, General Paillard, commanding the troops in Morbihan, received information that La Haye was to meet Pourchasse and Billy in the house of a M. François le Hars in the vicinity of Vannes. The house was in the middle of a field.

At nightfall twenty-eight gendarmes, half of them mounted, the other half on foot, left Vannes under Captain Michelot. La Haye and his companions had just reached the house when the gendarmes arrived and surrounded it. La Haye, Pourchasse and Billy climbed to the garret, where they barricaded themselves in. The first summons was answered by shots from the garret, so the gendarmes opened fire, a bullet killed Pourchasse, and La Haye was wounded in the leg. In great pain and with only Billy at his side, La Haye continued the hopeless fight. Captain Michelot had ladders brought to the house, one of his sergeants placed a ladder against the wall, but a pistol shot hit him, and heavily wounded he was carried away. The battle continued, La Haye and Billy returning the fire in spite of La Haye losing blood and unable to move. They surrendered only when Michelot threatened to set the house on fire. The two prisoners were put in chains, thrown into a cart and taken to Vannes. The happy news was immediately communicated to Fouché who wasted no time in letting the Emperor know of the victory.

During their examination La Haye and Billy refused to answer the numberless questions put to them. No false promises could be made to them since they would have refused even real ones. On October 7 they appeared before a court martial, La Haye being carried in tied to a chair since he could not move on account of his leg wound. Rialan, their defence lawyer, tried hard to save them from the death sentence; La Haye's mother had already left for Paris to beg the Emperor for mercy. Neither La Haye nor Billy spoke a word before the court martial. For La Haye death meted out by the King's enemies would be the fulfilment of his mission. The death sentence was passed at nine in the morning, and by ten La Haye and Billy were in front of the firing squad in the Champs de Mars of Vannes, La Haye still tied to his chair, Billy standing beside him.

La Haye was thirty years old, Billy thirty-three.

Next to Georges Cadoudal La Haye-Saint-Hilaire remains the unforgettable hero of the Bretons and all who admire courage and devotion to a cause.

XI

1806

The year 1806 has been chosen because it was Napoleon's greatest year, with Ulm and Austerlitz and Trafalgar behind him and Jena before him. Never had the eagle soared so high, yet while he soared in his glorious flight the spirit of Cadoudal still brooded over the west of France; and as the Empire expanded so the work of the High Police became more arduous to preserve, as it were, all that glory safe inside the country that was conquering so many others.

The year of Napoleon's apotheosis is culled from the Police Reports (*Bulletins de Police*) for the year 1806.

The police had a finger in every pie. In reports to Fouché even necromancers, false prophets and seers had their niche. When in Marseilles a German priest of the seventeenth century, Keleviser by name, appeared before the Abbé Saint-Gaubert, rector of Saint-Lazare, and prophesied in Latin; the police questioned the rector, the prophecy was taken down in Latin and sent to the Senator-Minister. An orgy in an inn in the Landes was reported in detail. In most reports, dealings on the Bourse also played a large part. But the great were not spared either. Napoleon had defined the work of the police as watching everyone except him. The police watched him too.

The émigrés were not overlooked whether abroad or back home

in France. A number of them had accepted commissions in the Austrian army after the Prince de Condé's army was disbanded. If they were taken prisoner of war and expressed the desire to return home they were granted their request after the police satisfied themselves that they were not intriguers and had committed no other treason than fighting against Napoleon. But they had to go to the towns where they were born, report regularly to the police and not move from their address. Generally speaking, the Emperor bore no grudge against Frenchmen who had served in his enemies' armies. In that his outlook was still of the eighteenth century, that is pre-Revolutionary.

The police examined all petitions sent to the Emperor, regretting that it was so easy to get into his good graces. If a petitioner mentioned that while serving him, he or his son, or in a widow's case her husband, had a horse shot under him the request was granted; if two horses then the sum was doubled; if the two horses were shot under him at Austerlitz then trebled.

Priests loomed large and dark on the police horizon. In spite of Her Majesty the Empress's predilection for them and his Majesty's desire to live in peace with them, there was constant trouble with those bigots. One would refuse to countenance the marriage of a divorced person; another would preach against the constitutional bishops; a third object to burying the wife of a priest who had unfrocked himself during the Revolution and, to boot, became a greengrocer in Melun. Such reports went under the heading of "Intolerance". The High Police pretended not to interfere with these intolerant men; however in the case of the priest turned greengrocer the police were pleased to report to the Senator-Minister that in Melun there was such commotion that for the sake of law and order, the mayor found himself bound to persuade the intolerant priest to bury the lady.

Censorship was exercised by the police. In March, at Fouché's special order a new work by Kotzebüe, entitled *Souvenirs d'Italie*, was seized and destroyed because in some places the author did not speak respectfully enough of His Imperial Majesty.

Being acquitted by a court of law did not mean automatically regaining one's liberty if the High Police did not approve. An innkeeper in the Jura called Secretan and his son were charged with murdering a client at their inn. The tribunal acquitted them, but on instruction from the High Police they were kept in prison, charged with smuggling. They were not brought before a court of law; however after a long detention the police decided to let them go "as they will be wiser in future".

Gaming did not escape their vigilant eye. For instance on March 14 it was reported to Fouché that M. Longchamps, secretary of His Imperial Highness Prince Murat, had lost 1,200 francs in a gambling den after six coups at rouge et noir.

Deaf and dumb persons could be suspected, too. The day after M. Longchamps lost 1,200 francs Fouché was notified that a young man had gone through Saint-Claude in the Jura. Though the police stated that he was deaf and dumb the report added, "he said he was on his way to Zurich where he hoped to find his father, M. de Tavernay from Vincennes near Paris, of whom he had not heard for a long time". The deaf and dumb young man was brought up by the Abbé Sicard, looked intelligent and could write and read. He came, the police discovered, from Cortuatin, where he had spent several months with M. Desoteux who, as much in the Jura as in other departments, had the reputation of an intriguer ready to serve the enemy. The Commissioner of Police of Saint-Claude assured His Excellency the Senator-Minister that under the pretext of looking for his father the young man should not be able to act as Desoteux's secret messenger. So he was not allowed to proceed.

Deserters were another headache. As it was inadmissible to turn one's back on glory, the police often referred to them as brigands. Most of those deserter-brigands were conscripts who, afraid to go home, formed bands and lived in forests. Since they needed food they would raid villages; in short, their existence could not be tolerated. For example, a number of conscripts who had deserted formed a band in a forest in the department of Cher. The

Prefect sent out gendarmes, the band surrendered, and several non-conscripts were found among them. The Prefect let the civilians go, the conscripts were handed over to the military authorities who, after a short punishment, returned them to their respective brigades.

A soldier stationed in Boulogne had his arm broken by a bullet while on sentry duty. His story was that he had been attacked by brigands who then escaped. His colonel was willing to believe him but not the police, who had to be called in because of the brigands. The police investigation proved that the wound was self-inflicted: the soldier had wanted to go on leave.

In the department of Aude two brothers, whose sentence expired, would, according to the Prefect, have caused panic in their native village if allowed to return. On the High Police's suggestion they were allowed to join the army as an alternative to continued detention. The elder agreed, the younger refused; and on the High Police's instruction the younger remained in prison.

Escaped French prisoners, especially those who escaped from the English, were carefully watched even if to escape they had had to fight many hazards.

Affrays between soldiers and civilians were frequent, especially in Paris; in Italy insurrections, desertions and banditry were the order of the day; around the Bourbons police spies abounded, yet much of the information that reached Fouché was hearsay, or gossip or reports from double agents.

The police resented the judiciary, for in general judges preferred to acquit so as to show their independence and dislike of the police.

The police reports teem with names that crop up in one or two bulletins, then disappear from the sea of suspicion; the fate of many suspects and arrested persons cannot be followed; yet those reports remain fascinating because they show the other side of the medal on which the little hat, the green redingote, the eagle, the grognards, and the victories are engraved.

The year 1806 is taken in monthly order.

January

The year began with three fellows, Gaury, Bosselier and Taupin, causing scandal at Midnight Mass in the church of Saint-Médard. They were drunk, and behaved with great irreverence. Taupin, aged 19, asked to be enlisted, so was handed over to the gendarmerie to be taken to the army corps of his choice, the other two were sent to prison for a month.

On New Year's Day too the police dealt with one Ballereau, a priest who had refused to sign the Concordat. The man was truly a dangerous character from the security angle because he had been the parish priest of Hennenans in the Vendée before the Revolution. He came to Paris with a passport given him by the local Prefect who wanted to be rid of the turbulent priest. Now he lived in Paris without any visible means, kept by two nephews who were hardly able to make both ends meet, and yet he never ceased fulminating against the Concordat. The Senator-Minister ordered him to be sent to some village at least thirty leagues distant from the department of the Vendée and from any place where the Court might reside.

A coloured man called Joseph also chose January 1 to enter into police orbit. Aged about twenty-five, he was arrested for attempted robbery. He had already served six months for a previous attempt. The Secretary-General of the Ministry of War needed men for the battalion of coloured men stationed in Italy. Therefore, Joseph was to be sent there, "conducted from brigade to brigade" till he reached his destination.

On January 4 Comte Réal, Counsellor of State, received a report from St. Malo. The English sailors captured by a corsaire off St Malo, the *Vengeance*, had been transferred to the prison of Avranches where M. La Tour, the prison chaplain, had a long chat with the captain of the English schooner from whom he gathered that an expedition was being mounted in England to destroy the French fleet at Boulogne; that Sir Sydney Smith would command it; and those taking part in the raid would die happy if they achieved their aim before the Emperor's return. When M. La Tour observed that a disembarkation would certainly fail because the coast was too well guarded the captain replied, "It would be only a sea-raid. It is absolutely necessary to destroy the fleet".

Not only was the enemy, so to speak, on the police list; even the Emperor's brave generals did not escape their scrutiny. On January 8 a police spy let Fouché know that he could assure him in a most positive manner that General Macdonald, while dining at M. Destillières's a few days after the battle of Austerlitz when the bulletin of victory arrived, spoke with deep admiration of Napoleon and the army, going into detail of the Emperor's concept and execution, repeating several times, "*Voilà la guerre de génie*", proof that in spite of a certain amount of aloofness on the Emperor's side where the future marshal was concerned Macdonald could be relied on. The bulletin does not state in what capacity the police spy was present; though the most usual form was for servants in police pay to report direct to the police. If a man of Macdonald's standing went to dine anywhere the police considered it their duty to seek information from the servants immediately after his departure.

Of course, the police had to deal with the small fry too. Réal had to make a decision about forty-two men and three women arrested as vagrants. As there was not enough proof against them they were to be detained till further order. Schwester, a fiacre coachman, had used foul language in public, and spoken against the Government. He was sent to Bicêtre for a month.

Relations of Chouans and other royalists considered as suspects were kept under observation, and they had to show more zeal than Fouché expected from ordinary, unsuspected citizens. A M. Troche had been judged with Cadoudal, and though acquitted he and his son were sent to Vernon, where they had daily to report to the police, and were not allowed to leave. On December 27, 1805, Troche went to see the local commissioner of police to tell him that during a stroll he had been accosted by a total stranger who asked him whether he was M. Troche. When Troche answered in the affirmative the stranger said that Mrs Williams from Liverpool wished to have word with him. Troche replied that he did not know the lady in question, therefore refused to meet her. The stranger said he knew her perfectly well, they had often met five years before.

On receipt of the commissioner's report the High Police established that Mrs Williams was an English agent who went under the name of the Little Sailor because she would cross over from England and cross back dressed as a seaman. On July 15, 1800, a letter Hyde, the royalist leader, wrote to the Comte d'Artois had fallen into the hands of the police. "I have the honour," wrote Hyde, "to send you a letter with Mrs Williams who is returning to London and to whom I promised to give a despatch for your Highness." Hyde went on to praise her zeal and her devotion to the Bourbon cause. Mrs Williams, according to police files dating back to 1800, was about forty-two years old, and wore a lot of make-up when not dressed as a seaman. She had a son who was a colonel in the English army, she married at the age of fourteen; and the police believed was from Liverpool. Coming from England she had visited Dieppe, Tréport, Cayeux and Boulogne, making several trips each year. A French seaman from Rouen, who had since been caught and executed, had helped her across to England in 1805. She had spent a lot of time in Rouen.

The High Police were willing to believe Troche, though finding it regrettable that he did not follow the matter up. The Commissioner of Police of Vernon was instructed to tell Troche to do so if the opportunity presented itself again. It seemed quite probable that Mrs Williams wanted Troche and his son to join an insurrection. Only four days before Troche was accosted the stage-coach plying between Rouen and Vernon was robbed near Vernon. The Senator-Minister was assured that every effort was being made to find Mrs Williams. She is not mentioned again.

Plots against the Emperor, whether imaginary or not, had to be followed up. On January 4 the Prefect of Roër had received an anonymous denunciation written in bad German. A bomb was being constructed in Dusseldorf to kill the Emperor. The Commissioner of Police in Cologne was told to investigate, but the

Prefect found that Schoerning, the commissioner, showed little zeal. In the next anonymous letter the Prefect was informed that the bomb would be transported to a tavern called *Coq Rouge*, then to a place nearby. "When they are caught," said the letter, "I will come to Aix-la-Chapelle and introduce myself." Not trusting Schoerning the Prefect sent an intelligence agent to Dusseldorf, mainly to watch him. The affair ended with the agent reporting that the police of Dusseldorf had most zealously investigated, but found no trace of the bomb, the *Coq Rouge* did not exist, and in spite of enquiries in the village of Gerresheim, "the place nearby", nothing whatever was known of any stranger having recently come to the village. The handwriting of the anonymous letter writer was unknown to any of the police in the district, and the stamp was not from Dusseldorf. In short there was nothing more to be done. Such letters, the High Police believed, were written to frighten the authorities.

The police had continuously to investigate the rumour, usually spread by women, that Napoleon had been killed in battle or was taken prisoner.

On January 7 the High Police learnt that the wife of Hyde de Neuville had managed not only to reach Germany but to see the Emperor in person to beg him to pardon her husband who was still in exile. The Emperor gave the royalist leader permission to go to France, settle his family affairs, then withdraw to the United States. The High Police were not too pleased with the Emperor-King's generosity. The Prefect of Leman advised Fouché on February 11 that on the 2nd Hyde and his wife had passed through Geneva, and continued on their journey to France. Their permitted route was written into their passports. Hyde appeared to be in bad health. On the 28th of the same month Marshal Moncey, commander-in-chief of the gendarmerie, reported to Fouché that Hyde and his wife were in Lyons, and wished to stay there for two or three days. Moncey was incensed by the request since there was a warrant out against Hyde ever since the bomb plot of Nivôse 3, and now Hyde had the cheek to show himself publicly in Lyons.

He could not understand why the colonel of the 12th Legion had not arrested him. The High Police explained to the fulminating Marshal that the Emperor had permitted Hyde and his wife to pass through France on their way to Spain to embark for America, and the police would see to their keeping to the route.

In the Vendée the recent civil war was far from forgotten. In La Gaubretière a certain M. Vigueron fell ill at an inn. The innkeeper called in Deffaut, the local surgeon. On leaving the sick man the surgeon observed, "I know the fellow. With his brother he wanted to kill me during the war, but now I have him in my net." The next day the surgeon gave him medicine: the sick man died a few hours later, crying: "He poisoned me". The surgeon was arrested.

The High Police could become indignant too. On January 6 an English corvette was sighted by a M. Case on the Côtes-du-Nord. The corvette seemed to be asking for help, so a boat went out in answer, rowed by five seamen. When the boat reached the corvette she fired a gun, the seamen were taken prisoners, and she set sail "with the five unhappy victims of their generosity" on board. It did not occur to the High Police that the five seamen might have been disguised Chouans. However, the Prefect saw more clearly. He expected, he wrote to Fouché, to see those men back in a short time, saying they were released by the enemy, though, in fact, they would be returning on a secret mission paid for by the wicked English.

The police were in charge of conscription. To achieve his glorious aims Napoleon needed men. Either Moreau or Bernadotte —it had been attributed to both of them—had observed in Italy that General Bonaparte needed an income of ten thousand men a month. The Emperor Napoleon needed far more than a paltry ten thousand a month.

In the month of January the call-up at Aix-la-Chapelle was completed on the 8th, but then eight men deserted. They would be replaced within a few days, and in any case the contingent for the year was complete. Then twenty deserted on the eve of departure. The police got busy to find men to take their places.

In Melun the contingent consisted of five hundred and twenty men with only eight deserters; in Laval it was five hundred and seventy men; Le Mans owed not a single man; and Gap had already sent its conscripts two months before. And every town and department of France was continuously searched for more conscripts, and the number of deserters grew yearly. The same applied to the dead.

Things were not easy in the National Guard either. On January 16 the Commissioner of Police of Boulogne conveyed his displeasure to the Senator-Minister at the appointment of officers in the National Guard. He had not been consulted in spite of His Imperial Majesty having decreed it. The officers, he found, were mostly returned émigrés in whom one could have no confidence. The Prefect of the Pas-de-Calais favoured the members of the old nobility and the émigrés. Even if they were not dangerous their very presence and arrogant bearing disgusted the citizens whom they would command. A secret agent corroborated the Commissioner's statement. The Prefect had told those émigré officers that they should be happy at not having men of the Revolution in their midst. A Mme de Canettemont, aged twenty-two and born in Belgium, having failed to persuade her husband not to accept a commission in the National Guard, appeared in the Place d'Armes when her husband was reviewing his national guardsmen, shouting abuse and shrieking that he should be ashamed of himself for associating with brigands. Her arrest was ordered.

On January 24 the Commissioner of Police reported that the National Guard of the Pas-de-Calais was disbanded.

One could never be too careful. An English gentleman called Sloper, prisoner of war in Verdun since the beginning of hostilities between England and France, received Fouché's permission on January 17 to establish himself in Paris. Sloper had been known as one of Wickham's agents in Berne already in 1796, and had several times been sent to England on secret missions. "Watch him," wrote Fouché, "to find out whom he frequents; then arrest him." Sloper was brought before the Prefect of Police on January 21, but as nothing could be pinned on him he was allowed to stay on in Paris though kept under strict observation.

The Minister of War gave permission to d'Ambly, an émigré who had served in the Austrian army and who had been made prisoner at Geislingen, to spend a month in Paris. The Senator-Minister instructed the police to watch him carefully. D'Ambly duly arrived in Paris, where he took up residence with his uncle, the Sieur Chassel, who worked in the Ministry of War. He manifested no political opinions and spoke of His Imperial Majesty with the greatest respect.

On the 20th His Excellency M. Bourrienne advised the Senator-Minister from Hamburg that dreaded and hated General Dumouriez had disembarked in Stade, and that Saint-Martin, an émigré, who had reached Hamburg in secret, had bought two carriages with English gold, then taken them to Stade. Saint-Martin returned alone to Hamburg. Dumouriez took the road to Moravia, "some say he will be employed in the Russian army there, others that he will command the army coming from Warsaw". A member of the House of Orléans was supposed to be in his company. On the next day Bourrienne wrote again. Dumouriez had wanted to travel incognito, however his customary vanity had got the better of him. In Brunswick he boasted to the head waiter of the inn where he stayed of having come from London, sent by the Government, to replace General Mack. Though he had heard of the French troops entering Vienna he was not at all worried. Once he took command he would throw the French out; in any case he had promised the King of England to reconquer all the territory from Valenciennes to the Rhine; and he needed only forty thousand men to achieve that. The next day he left for Dresden on his way to Prague.

The Chouans were at it again. Marshal Moncey notified Fouché that a band of fifty Chouans was spreading panic in the department of Maine-et-Loire. Moncey could not find out who their leader was. (Reports of the gendarmerie were sneered at by the High Police who thoroughly despised the gendarmes and their simple methods.)

Nearer home a ball was given in the Faubourg Saint-Germain by M. de Marescalchi, a nobleman, which caused much whispering in the neighbourhood. It had been decided that straightforward loyal people would not attend the ball (Fouché himself continually frequented the Faubourg), so a number of guests did not turn up. Those who did would lose their reputation, the police having taken their names. However, what was remarkable was that news-vendors appeared in the rue de Bourgogne immediately after the ball selling a tract called *The Trial of Louis XVI* which included the names of the deputies who voted for his death. The High Police found it surprising that such old stuff was still printed and still sold well. The police were trying to find the printer.

Rightly Fouché attached immense importance to the mail. He had been appraised at the beginning of the month that a number of despatches brought by couriers from Italy were delayed in the districts of Montargis and Gien because of the negligence of the postilions attached to the postal service. It was even suggested that some of the despatches had been entrusted to ordinary stage-coach travellers. The Senator-Minister wrote to the Prefect of the Loiret who reported on January 24 that the courier service from Italy was diligently looked after by all the mayors. At every stage a mounted postilion waited to gallop off the moment the despatches arrived. The hour never changed except in case of accident, and never were the despatches given to ordinary travellers. Though it was true that at two relays there had been cause for anxiety (the Prefect did not name them) now the system was functioning perfectly.

Not being satisfied with the Prefect's answer Fouché made further enquiries. On May 10 the Director-General of the Post Office reported that the service of couriers between Milan and Paris had suffered considerable delay for some time. Some post-masters employed children, old men and old horses. Others had the despatches carried by stage-coaches, or expected the postilions to do the work for nothing though the postmasters received 30 sous for each postilion. It was impossible to discover the names of the erring postmasters. However, things had improved since then. Fouché instructed the police to control the postmasters more efficiently the whole way from Milan to Paris.

February

The month opened with the gendarmerie reporting the arrest of several brigands of Morbihan, one of them Sansquartier who had certainly taken part in the murder of the constitutional bishop of Quimper. He was caught in a mill in Finistère. According to High Police files he had been a trusted agent of Cadoudal who sent him into Finistère in 1799, with one Mercier and another nicknamed *Tappe à mort* shortly after the assassination of the bishop. Sansquartier was sentenced to death in his absence. Tavernier, his accomplice, had been amnestied at the time and retired to the outskirts of Rouen, yet shortly after he was pursued by the gendarmerie for robbing the Rouen-Rennes mail coach near Verneuil.

Now on February 8 Marshal Moncey announced to the Senator-Minister that the gendarmerie was in full pursuit of the brigands who last month had attacked the mail coach from Rennes and the stage coach from Rouen. In the Vendée another Chouan was arrested and immediately sent before a special tribunal. His name was Joussenet, and during the Chouan war he had served with Charette and Georges Cadoudal, and had since then refused to submit. He had escaped from Nantes prison, carried a false passport under the name of Louis Josse, and was caught on his way to St Malo to embark for England. The tribunal sentenced him only to hard labour as he was not implicated in the mail robbery. Meanwhile Tavernier, who had vanished from Brittany, was caught in Paris. His accomplices, nine in number, were already in gaol, and Tavernier should have appeared with them before the special tribunal, but he and the gendarmes who brought him along arrived after the nine were sentenced and summarily executed. Now there were no witnesses left to testify against Tavernier whom everybody suspected of having organised and led the mail robbery. He had to be acquitted for lack of proof, but as the High Police considered him an incorrigible Chouan he was sent to the colonial depot on Belle-Isle.

At the beginning of February the Prefect of Maine-et-Loire signalled the presence in the department of a band of deserters from the French navy, led by one Robin, known as La Demoiselle. The gendarmes were sent out against La Demoiselle and the other sailors. Before the gendarmes could go into action La Demoiselle came to the Prefect to surrender, bringing his mates with him. They promised to rejoin their ships and behave themselves.

Fouché sent two "faithful and intelligent" amnestied Chouans to Morbihan and Finistère to find out whether an army corps could be raised in those turbulent departments. They reported back to the Senator-Minister that a corps could be raised among the unmarried, unemployed young men, though there might be some in their midst who would at the first opportunity go over to the enemy. The useless lives they had hitherto led could become another handicap, and many of them had been in trouble before. On receipt of the report the Emperor ordered the raising of a corps in the West to be known as the Corps of the Chasseurs supérieurs, wearing the uniform of the rifle regiments, the corps to be complete before leaving the West, and the officers to be chosen among the men who cherished a military reputation. Truly Napoleon was in need of men.

On the 17th a man called Guillet, who had been in the service of the Princes, left Paris in secret and travelled to England, where he saw Charles James Fox, the Prime Minister. Guillet had let him know that he had something vitally important to communicate. When Fox agreed to listen to him he outlined a plan to assassinate Napoleon. A cannon should be hidden behind an iron railing on the Quai de Chaillot, and as the Emperor rode by in his carriage a cannon ball would kill him. Fox threw Guillet out, then on the 20th wrote to Talleyrand, Minister of Foreign Affairs, explaining that English law did not permit him to take action beyond having the man chased out of the country. However, he would keep Guillet in London for a few days in order to give the French Government time to take the necessary precautions. Arrested on his reaching Germany, Guillet admitted that he had been in England, but denied that he suggested the plan. He swore that the idea came from Fox, and he, Guillet, had refused English gold to kill the Emperor. Fouché put Desmarets in charge of the case who, after questioning him, reached the conclusion that Guillet, a poor old man aged seventy-two, was not right in his mind, and misery and poverty had prompted his futile action. He was locked up in Bicêtre, where he died three years later.

A brigadier of gendarmes brought sixteen English prisoners coming from Toulon to Cuges-les-Pins in the department of the Bouches-du-Rhône. The brigadier left the prisoners at an inn, and leaving them on their own rode to Auriol, where he asked the local brigadier to go to the inn, collect the prisoners, then take them to the next gendarmerie brigade. While they were left unguarded an English prisoner, d'Angelo, born in Civita-Vecchia, absconded with the belongings of another English prisoner. The brigadier of Cuges-les-Pins was put under arrest.

On the 21st the Senator-Minister wrote to his Imperial Majesty's Ambassador in the Hague, asking him to do something about the continuous coming and going between Holland and England. People travelled to and fro as they pleased. There seemed to be no obstacle to travel. In his reply the Ambassador pointed out that mighty little could be done as the fishermen went out unhindered both day and night. He explained that since the coast of Holland was guarded by French troops who were unacquainted with the sea, the Dutch could play any pranks they liked on them. It would be preferable if the responsibility for the coast were handed over to the Dutch Government, for at the present time the Government considered themselves in no way responsible for it. The answer to that was a fresh order to the French general commanding the coast to keep a more careful look-out; and the answer to that was that travellers continued to cross over and back.

The Continental Blockade was, or was supposed to be, in full swing. On the 22nd police agents notified the High Police that a large quantity of English merchandise was waiting in Dusseldorf to be smuggled into France. Fouché instructed the Prefect of the Roër to prevail on the President of the Regency to have the English goods seized. The President excused himself, saying he could take no action before receiving orders from the King of Bavaria. The

Prefect wrote to Fouché regretting the delay because it would give the smugglers time to take the merchandise into France. The King of Bavaria skilfully sidestepped the issue. His minister would confer with the Prefect of Roër on what action they could take together. If the English goods belonged to Frenchmen they would be seized once it was proved that they truly were French property, but if they were owned by foreigners then sheer respect for foreign property would never permit him to confiscate them.

Still, the Under-Prefect of Nogent-sur-Seine could joyfully report that a trunk was seized in the town, and on opening it he discovered that it contained English stockings sent from Lausanne.

On the 26th the Senator-Minister was informed that the rich English prisoners in Moulins behaved most ostentatiously by giving alms and presents to the Russian and Austrian prisoners. They gave each of them 5 soldes a day, and had daily food distributed among them. That generosity, thought the High Police, stemmed from the Englishmen's sense of gratitude to men who had fought for their country; also to persuade the prisoners not to enter French service.

The Rochefort squadron brought an English naval officer and seven women into La Rochelle. Fouché allowed them to stay in the town. The Minister of War countermanded Fouché's order, and the officer was sent to Verdun to join other English prisoners of war, the women had to leave too, taking up residence ten leagues from the coast.

Two French prisoners of the English escaped from Deal in a stolen boat, and disembarked between Boulogne and Calais. One was handed to M. de Launay, the captain of a corsair in which he had served, the other, a Negro, who had served in a corvette, was put at the disposal of the French navy. They reported much movement on the roads of Deal, where twelve to fifteen men of war were anchored. The Senator-Minister gave orders for the two courageous, escaped French prisoners to be shadowed.

March

On March 5 Senator Le Mercier reported that on February 26 the Abbé Raymond, a long-sought seditious priest, had been arrested, and the Senator-Minister ought to thank M. Janvier, registrar at Villiers, for the capture of this obstreperous ecclesiastic. For years Janvier had tried to catch him on his own initiative. He had persuaded the Prefect to offer 300 écus as a reward. As a result, two eager inhabitants of Saint-Paul succeeded after a fortnight in discovering where the Abbé Raymond was wont to say Mass, and they and two gendarmes in disguise seized him while he was confessing a believer. There were twenty people present yet not one of them made a move. Raymond was taken to Angers. Fouché immediately wrote to Janvier, expressing his satisfaction; and recommended him for an award.

The Abbé gave in. The Prefect of Maine-et-Loire informed Fouché that he had sworn on the gospel to be faithful and obedient to the Emperor and his Government, and if he heard anything that went against the interests of His Imperial Majesty he would notify the police at once. None the less Fouché sent him to be kept in prison till further order. Another recalcitrant priest, who praised the old régime, was sent to Bicêtre in spite of the protestations of the general commanding the 12th Division.

As far back as December 10 Fouché had received a letter from Hamburg in which it was disclosed that for the last eighteen months the writer had followed a man who had promised Mr Pitt of England, the Emperor's greatest enemy, to assassinate His Imperial Majesty. The author of the letter had already informed Bourrienne in Hamburg and they were waiting together to find his accomplices. The letter was signed Dranob, retired Captain of the Light Artillery.

Fouché sent it on to Bourrienne, asking him to collect all the information he could. Bourrienne replied at the end of February. Dranob was the anagram of Bonard which was the man's real name. He had been arrested in 1798 for forgery, but escaped from the Conciergerie disguised as a woman. The person he had denounced was called Le Simple, born in Paris and harried from the capital for embezzling. Bonard and Le Simple travelled together for years, apparently had gone to England, promising to work for the English Government, and received a few guineas' advance. On their arrival in Hamburg Bonard preferred denouncing his friend to undertaking the mission they were entrusted with. "He handed me," wrote Bourrienne, "several written notes of Le Simple which prove that they are both guilty of conspiracy." Le Simple had gone to Holland, but when he returned to Hamburg Bourrienne had him arrested.

Le Simple addressed a letter to Bourrienne from prison, "My arrest is a great honour to you. Keep to yourself the contents of the letter you sent about me till I can explain everything to you." Bonard was allowed to go to Paris to "develop his denunciation"; however, he disappeared on the way. The Prefect of Police issued orders to have him arrested if he turned up in Paris. "Thus," said the police bulletin of March 15th, "these two emissaries of the British Government are actually at the disposal of France."

Bonard was duly caught and locked up in the Temple. He confessed to having received, with Le Simple, 200 louis in London to make an attempt on the Emperor's life. They had arrived in London on April 11, 1804, were on the same day received by Mr Addington's secretary, and before they left Mr Addington put in an appearance. Bonard and Le Simple had promised to kill the Emperor, free General Moreau and take him to the army in Boulogne. They asked 200 louis for this. At ten at night Mr Addington let them know that their offer was accepted, all their expenses would be paid, they would be taken to Emden, and re-embarked if the attempt failed. The two men were taken to Norwich, where they were arrested because of a duel they had fought (as a matter of fact they had a row and fought each other with knives), then sent out of England with 132 louis, the balance of the 200. The High Police were not yet certain whether Bonard was telling the truth.

The Senator-Minister was relieved to hear from different Prefects that Hyde-de-Neuville and his wife had scrupulously kept to their route, reaching Perpignan on March 11, and Barcelona a week later. Hyde told the French Consul that he needed a few days rest before setting out for Cadiz to take a ship to America. His lungs were weak, and he needed asses' milk. The Consul explained to him that he could not authorise him to stay on for a few days in Barcelona without the Senator-Minister's approval. (It took the Consul's letter as many days as Hyde asked for to reach Paris.)

On the 27th the Prefect of the department of Vienna, and General Dufresse notified the Senator-Minister that David, a Chouan chief, had been arrested in Poitiers. David had been the cause of all insurrections and rebellions in the department of Deux-Sèvres. After the amnesty he had settled in Poitiers under the name of Alexandre. David was born in Grenoble, was 37 years old, and had deserted from a cavalry regiment during the Vendée war and gone over to the rebels. After the war he stayed on in the Vendée, stirred up trouble, was arrested, then escaped from the prison at Saumur. He went to Paris, where he begged the Abbé Bernier to find him work; as he was not received with open arms he returned to the Vendée, frequently visiting Poitiers. He had no obvious means of support, and was suspected of wanting to take up arms for the enemy. He was specially protected by the Demoiselles Gibos and Laroche-Jaquelin, and by the rebellious priests of the district of Bressuire.

Fouché gave orders that the two ladies, who were known to protect the turbulent elements in the West, including priests and Chouans, be sent under surveillance to the department of Isère. In a letter dated March 3 the Prefect of Deux-Sèvres announced that Mlle Gibos had gone to Niort, where she obtained a passport for Vienne (Isère) and had left on February 28. In a second letter the Prefect let Fouché know that Mlle Laroche had departed for Grenoble. Then Marshal Moncey informed Fouché that Mlle Gibos had stopped in Poitiers because of illness, and the doctor in the hospital declared that she needed treatment that would take twenty-five days. Finally, on March 28 the Marshal informed the Senator-Minister that the Captain of Gendarmes of Poitiers would conduct Mlle Gibos to her destination the moment she left hospital.

On the 28th too, the Minister of the Navy sent to the Senator-

Minister of Police several letters found on board *Le Bell* (*sic*), an English ship seized on her way to India. Only one was found worth the High Police's notice. It was written by Mme Guiche de Guilleford to Mrs Nightingale in Calcutta, "I hope the danger of invasion is over. The tyrant and usurper has found plenty to amuse him on the Continent, where all the Northern Powers are ready to attack him. . . ."

An émigré called de Vauban, who had lost his fortune before the Revolution, was in constant correspondence, as he himself admitted, with the Bourbons while he was away from France. He returned home in 1803. Now in 1806 the High Police received information that he kept up his links with the Bourbons and their courtiers, so his surveillance was ordered. The first reports were satisfactory: he lived quietly with his mother-in-law, Mme de Barbantane, praising the Emperor, and spoke of H.I.M. with respect. But in March he was arrested, his correspondence seized, and the High Police established that in his letter to his wife in Poland he used enigmatic language, and in her replies his wife did the same. She asked him to buy her dresses and other articles she needed, warning him to be careful when choosing them. She also gave him a list of people who would supply them. In one of her letters his wife congratulated him on not having to prostrate himself before the Emperor. She sent him money. The police found five notebooks in which he described his life till the pacification of the West, speaking frankly of his relations with the Princes, Georges and other Chouans. Questioned he admitted his past, but swore that he had no more dealings with the Emperor's enemies. He contradicted himself several times during his interrogation.

Two scribbled notes proved he had 411,654 florins in his possession. The explanation he gave was that the sum had been lent him by the sister of Prince Poniatowski whom he repaid in 1797 after his return to Poland from England. Eventually he admitted that since his homecoming he had received a number of letters from Louis XVIII and the Comte d'Artois. Fontbrune, known by the High Police as a confidential agent of the Princes, forwarded the letters from Warsaw. Fouché ordered de Vauban to be kept under lock and key.

On the last day of the month two tramps who looked suspiciously like Englishmen were arrested on the highway near Honfleur, and taken to the town. They said they were Americans, Patterson, twenty-nine years old, and Janson, thirty-five. They belonged to the crew of *John Jones*, Captain Clark, a merchant vessel from Wilmington. According to them the ship was seized by the Royal Navy, the two were taken to Guernsey, where they managed to get hold of a boat, escaped in her, and disembarked on the French coast. They were on their way to Le Havre to find a ship to take them back to America. They had no identity papers, and nobody knew them, consequently they could not be trusted. Hence they would remain in prison.

April

On the 4th the Great Judge sent to the Senator-Minister a letter he had received from the Magistrate of Security from Château Thierry. In Bezu near Charly lived a former timber merchant called Maugin who used "atrocious words" when speaking of his Majesty the Emperor-King. Arrested, he declared that he had used those atrocious words in connection with a man named Bonaparte who lived in the district and owed him money. That explanation might have been accepted if it had not transpired that Maugin had destroyed the triumphal arch erected in his village after the Emperor's coronation in Milan, and committed similar disrespectful acts. He went about sneering on public holidays, and insulted members of the General Council. In his letter the Magistrate of Security deplored that the laws as they stood could not help him in dealing with the impudent fellow and punish him properly, therefore he asked the Senator-Minister to take administrative measures against him. His request was granted.

The Prefect of the department of Aube, also the Sub-Prefect and the Magistrate of Security of Bar-sur-Seine, reported that the gendarmerie of Bar-sur-Seine had observed that a sabot-maker of the village of Fouchères on April 7 had put into the pillar box of Bar a parcel addressed to His Imperial Majesty. Questioned he explained that he was notifying the Emperor of a plot hatched against him. On the 8th the sabot-maker, whose name was Seuvre, gave the gendarmes a detailed account of the plot. On April 5 he found himself at nightfall on the Paris road near the castle of Vaux, owned by a M. Mony, son-in-law of Marshal de Montmaure, when two travellers on horseback stopped beside him. One of them said, "When I see this castle I truly feel unhappy, but all that will soon change". Another snatch of conversation Seuvre overheard was, "On his way to Italy the Emperor fell ill between Chalons and . . . he got out of the carriage to continue on horseback . . . what a pity that he did not die. . . ." The next was, "But how to get rid of him? One could achieve that only by the use of . . . the celebrations in May could help us . . . the Emperor and Murat must perish". Then again, "M. . . . (the sabot-maker did not catch the name) of Lyons had ridden through Langres. He knows Paris well, and will do all he can to succeed."

They rode on, Seuvre ran after them, but they soon outdistanced him. They did not stop in Fouchères, and took the road to Troyes. The description Seuvre gave of them was pretty vague, none the less the gendarmes went in search of the two horsemen. The sabot-maker was an entirely trustworthy faithful subject.

In the next report the sabot-maker began to look less trustworthy. The gendarmes had scoured the countryside, covered eight leagues in each direction without finding anyone who had seen the two horsemen. They stopped at no inn. No-one would travel such a distance without stopping for refreshment. On further enquiry the gendarmerie discovered that Seuvre was a poacher, a gossip and rumourmonger. His son had reached the calling-up age. Seuvre hoped to be sent to Paris to be presented to the Emperor. As a reward he would have asked for his son to be exempted and himself employed on the canal. Questioned again by the Sub-Prefect and the Magistrate of Security he persisted in his tale. In the next letter the Sub-Prefect and the Magistrate announced that the two travellers had been seen in different places along the road, collaborating in fact Seuvre's description of them. One of the four people who saw them was certain that he would recognise them. Therefore Seuvre could be believed. The two travellers were probably involved in no plot, but simply expressed a hope. None the less, the feast in May in Paris should be even more carefully controlled after the sabot-maker's evidence.

The High Police took immediate measures to find out who was the man from Lyons whose name the sabot-maker could not catch. A secret agent was dispatched to Troyes. The gendarmerie continued searching for the two men, but were to date unable to find out where the two horsemen had spent the night.

Then nothing more was heard of and about them.

On the 23rd the Prefect of Rennes reported that Admiral Villeneuve, thrashed by Nelson at Trafalgar, had been found dead the previous evening in his apartment. He lay half naked beside his bed with a knife stuck in his breast. He was alone in the bedroom; the door being locked from the inside the police had not succeeded in entering the bedroom until ten thirty. The servant, who had gone out after dinner with her master's permission, had several times knocked on the door, and receiving no answer thought that the Admiral had gone out. Police seals were put on the front door.

On the 28th it was reported from Morlaix that a seaman calling himself Opus and saying he was a Dane had arrived on a Prussian vessel, the *Brandenburg*. That was still in March. Opus asked permission to proceed to Emden via Antwerp as some money was due to him in that port. The Government Delegate granted his request, giving him as route Saint-Brieuc, Caen, et cetera. Opus did not keep to the itinerary, was caught in Brest, and sent back to Morlaix. The explanation he gave was that when he asked for the road to Saint-Brieuc he was directed to the road to Brest. Opus was under suspicion because he spoke English like a native. In any case he could not prove that he was a Dane. He was ordered to be kept in prison till further order.

On the 29th the Government Delegate had more important news

to report. On the 25th the English landed sixty men from a frigate between Concarneau and Orient. They overran a battery guarded by eight gunners of the coastal artillery, destroyed two cannons, took provisions, then re-embarked. The High Police could not help noticing that the reports of the Prefect of Quimper and the General commanding Brest made no mention of the English landing though both were written on the same date as the Government Delegate's.

On the 30th the Prefect confirmed the Delegate's report of the English landing. The National Guard was called out immediately after the English had made off. The National Guardsmen, the Prefect was happy to state, were full of zeal for and ardent love of His Imperial Majesty.

Lamor, a Paris baker, presented a petition to the Emperor, asking to be exempt from depositing fifteen sacks of flour with the authorities before opening his shop, as prescribed by the law. His previous shop had burnt down, and his good reputation and the poverty of his family forced him to make the request. The High Police refused him because other Paris bakers might then ask to be exempted even if they were not in as wretched a position as Lamor.

May

M. Fardel, police magistrate of the first district of the Sûreté, on May 5 announced that he was going to the country for a few days' rest. That was on Saturday. On Monday he sent in his resignation, and on Tuesday an investigation was ordered. As his whereabouts were not known it was presumed that he mismanaged funds.

The Secretary General of the War Ministry forwarded an anonymous letter to the Senator-Minister which came from Saint-Ciers-La Lande in the department of Gironde, dated April 20 and full of spelling mistakes; the handwriting poor. It spoke of a plot hatched against the Emperor and the War Minister, accusing M. Duparty, a nobleman, the priest Labadie near Bourg, the parish priest of Samonac, and the Magistrate of Security Blaye as the plotters. The captain of an English frigate had supplied them with money and a trunk full of arms. The conspirators had met on March 20 in Duparty's house. After the meeting two priests, one court usher and a nobleman, all of them heavily armed, were seen to leave the house. Though the letter seemed to deserve little credence the High Police decided to watch the men mentioned in it.

A secret agent reported from London that Windham was seriously thinking of setting alight Brittany and the Vendée by encouraging the royalists to start a new civil war. Once the trouble began a Bourbon, preferably the Duc de Berry, who was more resolute than his brother, would be sent to France. Then the Russians would land. But Windham's horrible plan had met two obstacles, the first: several members of the Cabinet were against it; second: Puisaye, the royalist leader, whom Windham wanted to employ, was not trusted by the émigrés. "But one can do so much with money," were the words with which the secret agent ended his letter.

On the 6th the colonel of the gendarmerie of the Nièvre reported that Massin, parish priest of Saint-Saulge, had refused to sing the Te Deum ordered by the Government. He refused to do so in the presence of the assembled local dignitaries. Fouché asked for more details. Massin, it transpired, did sing the Te Deum because his bishop had told him to, but sang it before the dignitaries arrived in spite of having been warned by the mayor to wait for them. The Prefect added that there were many similar complaints against him. Fouché ordered Massin to be sent to Dijon, and kept there under surveillance.

The ecclesiastical authorities came to Massin's rescue, averring that he was entirely innocent. The decree regulating the singing of the Te Deum before dignitaries surely did not include the mayor of a village. The Grand Vicar of France thought that though the whole village of Saint-Saulge acclaimed their parish priest, another parish should be found for him. However, the Prefect reported that only twenty-nine of the two thousand inhabitants of Saint-Saulge had signed the petition. The Senator-Minister decided to keep Massin under surveillance.

Derichaud, a market porter in Lyons, fared no better than the priest. He spread the rumour that the market building of the Market of Saint-Joseph was in such a bad state that it could easily collapse. Arrested he tried to deny this, but because he was a nasty and dangerous man he was sent back to his native village with the instruction that he should remain there for good.

On the 7th the Prefect of Police was notified that an Englishwoman, Mrs Garnett by name, domiciled in Valençay had arrived in Paris with a passport issued by the mayor of Valençay. She asked permission to live in Lille to be near the buyer of a machine (not specified) she had sold him, and which she alone knew how to work. Having verified the facts the Prefect granted the permission.

A small number of fishermen of Brest were taken prisoners by an English squadron while out fishing. The English sent them back, and one of them related that before their release they were taken to the English admiral who showed them fresh cabbages, saying that his sailors had picked them only the previous night at Pointe Saint-Mathieu, and they would do so every night. The coastal batteries were warned.

The Senator-Minister was informed that a Mlle Philippeaux, an orphan aged sixteen, who was to marry M. de Thermine of Miramont, had disappeared. The civic marriage was to take place in the house she lived in, and the witnesses were chosen by M. de Thermine. The religious ceremony was to precede the civil marriage; however Mlle Philippeaux ran off to a relation who then vanished with her. She left behind a letter accusing M. de Thermine of having coerced her. The groom obtained permission from the tribunal to look for her, and when found to have her brought back by the gendarmes. Their names do not crop up again.

A M. Thierry who had been dismissed from the army, was denounced in an anonymous letter which the Minister of War sent on to Fouché. Thierry boasted of his friendship with Pichegru, and said, according to the letter, that however proud the officers of the National Guard were of their epaulets he too would wear epaulets again; but by then they would have lost theirs. The police files showed that Thierry had been sent under surveillance to Besançon in March, therefore the letter must have come from Besançon. Counsellor of State Réal was charged with a further investigation.

On the 17th the Commissioner General of Police of Boulogne reported that Haquemet, a fisherman from Dieppe, was caught by an English man of war, spent several hours in the ship, then was allowed to return to port. He was sent to Brest to be questioned by naval security. Two other fishermen had spent an hour and a half conversing with the crew of an English brig. They were detained on their arrival in Fécamp.

A rebellion broke out in the department of Hérault. On the complaint of a M. Fabre the gendarmes entered a wood near Tarler in which were hiding about forty men who had illtreated M. Fabre. The gendarmes were greeted by a shower of stones, one gendarme and one horse being badly wounded. Two of the rebels received wounds, only twelve were caught, but they were immediately brought before a special tribunal in Montpellier. Those rebels, it was suspected, were led by General Villot who had left London the previous month.

An American vessel arrived on the 23rd in the port of l'Orient with a cargo of tobacco. The captain declared that before entering the port he had been stopped by an English ship. The English commander told him that the *Marengo* and the *Belle Poule*, two French men of war, had been taken to Plymouth by the Royal Navy. The American captain also reported to the Prefect that General Moreau was highly esteemed in England, and a house was built for him which cost the Government 100,000 piastres.

In the department of the Vendée Jausmet, a dangerous Chouan, had been arrested, but as there was insufficient proof against him he had to be acquitted. The Senator-Minister ordered his transfer to Bicêtre, where he would remain till further orders.

An Irishman was arrested in Bordeaux. He declared that his name was Richard O'Reilly, born in Dublin thirty-two years ago. He had been persecuted by the British Government, so sailed to America, where he went into business, but had no luck. The next year he came to France to join the Irish rebels under General O'Connor. He returned to Ireland after a three months' sojourn in Paris. Now he was back in Bordeaux still working for the Irish cause. As he could not find direct transport to Ireland he travelled through England, coming back the same way. That was why, he maintained, he had no identity papers. He mentioned the names of three Bordeaux merchants who were acquainted with him. The police interviewed the merchants who gave him a good reference. It transpired that this Irishman had been arrested in Bruxelles two years before, and released only when he gave proof of being an Irish refugee. The merchants knew him, the police in Bruxelles had checked on him, even so the High Police decided on having him shadowed because his frequent trips to England gave cause for suspicion.

The Irish were mentioned again in the police bulletin of the 27th. The Irish officers who formed the nucleus of the Irish Legion in Brest rebelled because they thought that they had been slighted when the English made a landing on the coast. The National Guard was called out, but not the Irish Legion. Adjutant-General Mayer had all of them put under arrest. In any case he suspected the Irish officers of going over to the English when the first opportunity presented itself, so this was a good excuse to put them out of harm's way. They would all be sent inland.

In the department of Aveyron the High Police found traces of fanaticism. Alpeuch, a brigand, shot dead by the gendarmes, was buried on the spot where he was killed. In spite of his life of crime Alpeuch had professed great devotion, and the priests of his native village had him exhumed, then buried with much pomp in the village cemetery. Such acts of fanaticism were truly to be deplored.

The Minister of Foreign Affairs communicated to the Senator-Minister the contents of a letter received from Alexandria. A certain Ahmed of the household of Efty-Bey appeared at the French Consulate, charged by his master to ask for a passport to France, also for letters of recommendation to the Emperor-King. Questioned by the Consul he gave rather vague answers about his mission, yet insisted that it was a matter of importance. The Consul gave him an "insignificant letter" to the Commissioner in Smyrna to whom he also wrote privately.

In April the Commissioner in Smyrna notified Fouché through the Ministry of Foreign Affairs that Ahmed, a Mameluk, had arrived there, bringing, so he affirmed, letters from three beys who begged the Emperor-King to take Egypt under his protection, and had authorised Ahmed to deal personally with His Imperial Majesty. He was carefully watched while he remained in Smyrna where he behaved decently, was affable and pleasant, never missing a chance to speak admiringly of the Emperor. On June 17 the Prefect of the Bouches-du-Rhône announced Ahmed's arrival in Marseilles. Ahmed declared that he was not on a mission, had invented the whole thing in order to get out of Egypt and find refuge in France. He handed a petition to the Prefect in which he begged the Emperor to grant him asylum and a pension as he had no means whatever. On July 18 the Senator-Minister instructed the Prefect to send Ahmed to Paris, and supply him with enough money to reach the capital. It was on Napoleon's order that Ahmed was given asylum in France.

Caseneuve, a native of Toulouse and a rebellious priest, who styled himself Bishop of Santo Domingo, was after a period of detention in Paris sent back to his village, but instead of going there he travelled to Germany, calling himself the Emperor's chaplain. Arrested in Munich he escaped from the escorting gendarmes. Shortly after he reappeared in Nancy, where the bishop complained of his presence. He was taken to his village, stayed but for a few days, then made his way to Paris. He was sent to the lunatic asylum of Charenton.

On the 28th Fouché received an anonymous letter, denouncing M. Henry Grandin of the Place Vendôme as an English agent. The last run on the funds on the Bourse had been prepared by the English for whom he worked. Grandin had been to Spain, his emissaries to England learnt his messages by heart; thus no letters would be found. While he was in Madrid he sent a messenger to Lisbon who embarked there for England. As he had not succeeded in murdering the Emperor he now planned to kill the Minister of Foreign Affairs. The police went into action, but no evidence could be found against Grandin. None the less, he was to be shadowed.

Several men who had finished their prison sentences were kept on in prison on Fouché's order because in their native towns or villages they would upset their neighbours if they returned. An English convict in Rochefort called Wilbraham, who had been sentenced for theft and forgery, continued to bombard the authorities with letters in which he asked to be taken before the Senator-Minister because he knew the names of everyone in France who plotted with the English, and could also tell him how to conquer England. The Senator-Minister ignored his letters.

Prefects were not as circumspect as the High Police, and often reached conclusions they should have thought of earlier or not at all. A case in point was the Sieur Asséré, an erstwhile monk, who had gone to live in Quimper in 1801. The Prefect of Finistère had no idea where he came from, how he managed to pay his way in the cafés he constantly frequented, and in the gaming rooms where he regularly lost, yet now in 1806, five years after the former monk's arrival, the Prefect began to suspect him of being an English agent. The High Police did not fail to point that out to the Prefect before beginning their own investigations.

June

Again a mail coach was attacked by brigands. The coach on its way from Lyons to Paris was held up on May 25 at eleven at night between Tarare and Pinbouchin by four armed brigands. The postilion did not stop when they told him to, so they shot his horse. The courier got off the box, and while he spoke to the brigands the postilion detached the dead horse, the courier jumped into the coach, and with the remaining two horses they made off, soon outdistancing the brigands. Nothing had been taken. The courier was later reprimanded for having neglected to ask for an escort in Tarare.

June seemed to be the right month for abortive plots. The Prefect of the Isère informed the High Police that a M. Segoud, landowner in the village of Mens, declared to the mayor that his cousin Lachaud, a physician by profession, had suggested seventeen months ago that they travel to Paris together to kill the Emperor. Segoud was horrified, and succeeded in persuading Lachaud to remain at home. Segoud told the mayor that he bitterly regretted waiting all that time to denounce his cousin. He offered to question him again.

As a result of their investigations the High Police discovered that Lachaud had in fact been to Paris seventeen months before, where he attended lectures connected with his profession. He kept his address from his friends and family, his letters were sent to a friend from whom he collected them without disclosing his own address. On May 2 Lachaud disappeared, leaving behind all his belongings. He told some that he was going home, others he asked to write to him poste restante to Melun. The police ascertained that his original intention was to take up medical practice in Egreville, between Melun and Nemours. But he remained there only four days, then left, saying he was returning to Paris. In Egreville he told the deputy mayor that he was sick of life, and wanted to kill himself. No trace of him could be found in Paris. However, on May 29 the High Police received a report that he was back with his father in Mens. Because the local Prefect had forgotten to notify the Senator-Minister he received a strong reprimand. The matter, wrote Fouché, was too important for any kind of negligence.

On May 5, the Prefect reported, Segoud signed the declaration in which he had accused his cousin. Arrested in his father's house, Lachaud denied the whole thing, swore that Segoud, with whom he was on bad terms, had wronged him. True he had been a strong Republican, but ever since the advent of the Emperor he was his faithful subject. Segoud was questioned again. He stuck to his declaration, yet added that he did not think his cousin capable of harming the Emperor or anyone else. Finally he admitted that he was on bad terms with his cousin because he had spoilt his chances

of marrying the girl of his choice. The Prefect found nothing
incriminating in Lachaud's papers, thought him harmless enough,
and believed the best solution was to put him under surveillance for
a time.

The next plot looked far more serious. His Serene Highness
Prince Berthier in a letter dated May 29 which reached the High
Police on June 6 revealed to the Senator-Minister the treacheries
of one Senger, a surgeon in the Grande Armée, concerning a man
called Princeps from Strasbourg who had been arrested during
Moreau's trial, and had escaped from Paris at the time. He suggested
that Senger take part in a plot originating in England, its aim to
poison Napoleon, the Kings of Bavaria and Württemberg, the
Elector of Baden, and all their armies. "Pestiferous poisons" would
be used. Princeps promised Senger the rank of surgeon-in-chief in
the English or the Russian army, and a similar position for his son.
Senger informed Berthier that he believed that several accomplices
were hiding in Strasbourg and assured him that he was certain that
Princeps would make the same sort of offer to other surgeons. His
Serene Highness sent Senger to the Prefect of Strasbourg to be
examined in order to find out whether his accusations had any
foundation.

The High Police were acquainted with Princeps. He was an
artisan from Strasbourg, spied under the name of Griffon in the
years 1796-7, was arrested in 1804 as Pichegru's agent but was
released for lack of proof the following year. The Senator-Minister
had heard rumours according to which Princeps was back in
Strasbourg, and had tried to gain admittance to the Empress-Queen.
The police in Strasbourg were ordered to check on that. The
Prefect reported that Princeps had never gone near the Palace.
Other sources said he had certainly been to the Palace. The Prefect
was instructed to have Princeps removed from the town. That was
in 1805.

In a letter dated June 4 the Magistrate of Security of Strasbourg
notified the High Police that he had sent a reliable agent to find
Princeps who was either in Mannheim or Heidelberg, and was

engaged in smuggling English goods into France. Senger, reported the Magistrate, was known as an ambitious man who tried hard to improve his lot. Therefore one should not rely on him too much. Senger continued to maintain that all he had said was true, and if helped by the authorities he could make Princeps confess. The Magistrate went on with the investigation, and eventually on the 27th Berthier sent to Fouché an intercepted letter, written by Senger to a friend in Munich in which he asked the King of Bavaria to send him a trustworthy man whom he could put in touch with one of the conspirators, and expressed his surprise at the King taking the matter so lightly. Could he not see that if Napoleon came a cropper he would follow too? "If I am helped by my Emperor and your King I can make you earn a hundred million, the other man fifty million, and I could force England to Paris to beg for peace, and Napoleon could go anywhere without having to fear for his life."

At the same time the Magistrate wrote to say that Princeps was in Heidelberg, occupied only with smuggling. The investigation was closed, and Senger remained on the police files as an intriguer who could not be trusted.

Bonard and Le Simple, who in 1804 had offered to assassinate the Emperor for the British Government (see page 154), were by June 6 in the Temple. Questioned, Le Simple explained that he and Bonard were taken to the secretary of Mr Addington on the day they reached London, and it was Bonard who offered to kill the Emperor, then First Consul. The secretary firmly told them that the British Government would never countenance any plan to assassinate Bonaparte. At that Le Simple spoke, saying they had been sent by friends of General Moreau who had made all the arrangements to free him. All Bonard and Le Simple really wanted was an English ship to take them to Emden and embark General Moreau and his friends. During their talk a man came into the room, and was treated with great respect by the secretary. That made Le Simple surmise that he was the minister. Their offer was accepted at ten at night, but later because of the duel they were detained for eighteen months, at the end of which time they were allowed to go. "You are free," Mr Reeves of the Alien Office told them. "We shall see about the rest when we hear from you." Le Simple admitted to the High Police that their only intention was to get money out of the English. The story about Moreau was pure invention. Bonard said the English accepted their offer, Le Simple maintained they did not. In any case at the end of 1805 Moreau was no longer in France. Bonard and Le Simple, the police concluded, were just a couple of despicable crooks.

One Sortel, a fisherman from Dieppe, had his vessel stopped by the English squadron, and he and his crew were interrogated by the English. On his return he was taken to police headquarters, where he declared that all the English asked him was whether he had fresh fish, and if there were corsairs in the port. His answers being in the negative the English let him go. He and his crew were thrown into gaol.

The treatment of the fishermen very much depended on the local commissioner of police. For instance, a pilot of Cherbourg (June 18), who thought (so he said) than an approaching ship was American, discovered only when going aboard that it was an English frigate. The captain let him go when he told him that he was but a poor fisherman, and not a single question was put to him. The police accepted his story, and he was not molested; whereas a Calais fisherman was put in prison because when stopped by an English brig he spoke in English. He was denounced by a member of his crew who did not understand English.

General Wirion, commandant of the English prisoner-of-war camp in Verdun, on the 11th, gave permission for Mr Dayne, an English bookseller, to go to Plombières for a cure. He would have to return on September 10. The General allowed Phillips, a Mr Forbes's man-servant, to join his master at Tours as Mr Forbes had guaranteed his good behaviour. Fouché ordered both of them to be kept under surveillance.

On the 13th the Prefect of the Dordogne reported a rebellion in Fontenille. When the gendarmes arrested a condemned conscript called Castagner a crowd of over two hundred people attacked them, and freed the prisoner. The rebels took him into the field, the gendarmes pursued them, and managed to catch one Vergnac who had the rope on him with which Castagner had been tied. It was the feast day of the village's patron saint, the reason why the crowd had been so large. Hidden in the fields the rebels shouted seditious words. A few of them had been wounded by the gendarmes' sabres.

Fouché asked for more details which he received on the 21st. Four gendarmes had gone to the village; on their approach several conscripts tried to get away; Castagner was caught, and tied with a rope to a gendarme's horse. The people shouted to him, "Defend yourself," the horse shied, the crowd surged forward, and freed Castagner. Later in the day the conscripts were caught, and the rebels returned to the village; one of them, having been trampled on by the horses, had died since. The Prefect did not wish to punish the entire village, but only the four ringleaders.

The Sub-Prefect of Chalon-sur-Saône reported on the 8th that the 3rd battalion of the Issembourg Regiment arrived in the town, and several officers took rooms in the *Cheval Blanc*, among them Captain Montaigu, known as a violent man. In the course of the day he had insulted and struck some of the servants. At ten at night a girl brought him a lamp: he kicked her, then chased her down the stairs. Mme Boisson, the innkeeper's wife, heard the girl's shrieks, and rushed to her help. The same treatment was meted out to her. Montaigu drew his sword and threatened Mme Boisson with it, and her daughter aged thirteen, who threw herself between her mother and the captain, received a sword wound on her right arm. M. Boisson eventually succeeded in disarming Montaigu. The colonel of the battalion was sent for, he came, and put Montaigu under arrest. The gendarmes had also been sent for by the innkeeper, but when they appeared the colonel refused to hand Montaigu over to the officer of the gendarmes because, he declared, the matter concerned him alone. Meanwhile a large crowd had gathered which included a number of officers belonging to the battalion who loudly proclaimed that they had only to give one single order, and the damned civilians would be properly dealt with. Yet order was maintained. The battalion left at dawn with Montaigu at the head of his company. Two officers of a more gentle nature went to the Sub-Prefect to express their regrets.

Police bulletins were full of similar clashes between civilians and Napoleon's army, for soldiers, especially officers, behaved provocatively and arrogantly. After all, they needed some form of compensation for fighting all over Europe.

There was trouble again with the postal service. The Prefect of the Bouches-du-Rhône complained of lack of horses; young, inexperienced postilions; and insolent postmasters. However, the postmasters also had their grievances. There were not enough passengers, extra horses had to be paid for out of their own pockets, and they received no remuneration for special work. The inspectors could not be counted on as their visits were known twenty-four hours before by the postmasters. Fouché sent a strongly worded circular to every Prefect, emphasising the importance the Emperor attached to mail and communications.

Le Clerc, a Chouan, was acquitted for lack of proof in 1801; since then he had been kept in prison on the instruction of the High Police. Originally he had served in the Republican army; when his company was disbanded he joined the Chouans; had been amnestied; but suspected of having dealings with Georges he was arrested. Captain Bourgeois of the Gendarmerie d'Élite asked for the young man to be freed, guaranteeing his repentance. Perhaps his long detention had brought him to his senses. Fouché ordered his release under surveillance after five years in prison.

On the 14th an English emissary disembarked in Calais, and went to see the naval commandant of the town to assure him that French fishermen would no more be interfered with while out fishing. The High Police were of the opinion that it was an English trap.

A stranger arrived in Niort at the beginning of the month, bringing letters of recommendation to the Public Prosecutor and the presidents of the law courts. He was cordially received. He gave his name as Dufriche-Fontaine, said he was a lawyer, would soon plead his first case and was on excellent terms with most of the high officials of the Empire. The Prefect was slightly suspicious, so instructed the captain of the gendarmes to check his passport. Dufriche-Fontaine had none, so he was thrown into prison. He had, it appeared, told a very different story to the local royalists, namely that he was one of them, and had been involved with Moreau at the time of his trial, which was the reason why he had to leave Paris. He was certainly a versatile man, for he also frequented workmen whom he taught songs ridiculing His Imperial Majesty and the Government. Since the High Police files showed that he had never been involved either with Georges or Moreau, and as his passport was found in his Paris lodgings, the songs were the only charge one could bring against him. He was ordered to be detained till further notice.

Huré, a landowner at Pont-sur-Yonne, had lent the postmaster two horses when in April the Emperor had travelled through the district. Shortly after Huré claimed payment for the horses, saying they had perished while drawing the Emperor's coach. The police discovered that both horses were sickly animals and died of natural causes. Huré's request was, therefore, refused. Huré would have done better to keep quiet, for having now earned the Senator-Minister's displeasure the High Police established that he had previously been known as M. de Saint-Flour, was an immoral intriguer, and had circulated a pamphlet in which he pretended that the Bourbons wanted him to join one of their schemes. That was completely untrue. Fouché ordered him to be taken fifty leagues from Paris and the Court, and put under special surveillance.

Jeanson, a native of Maubeuge, who had lived in Russia for fifteen years, returned to France on the pretext of having family matters to attend to. He was put under surveillance in Maubeuge. The High Police suspected him of espionage, so he was brought from Maubeuge and thrown into the Temple. His papers were examined, but nothing suspicious was found in them, though it did not go unnoticed that in spite of his low origins and lack of education he was in close touch with the Emperor of Russia's chamberlain. When his examination was concluded he was deported from the Empire.

On the 26th Fouché decided to send Bonard and Le Simple to Bicêtre.

July

The Empire was vast, and it was hard work to keep a constant watch on all of it. Moreover, it was an expanding Empire. On June 11 in the quarters of the 20th Dragoons a traveller called Quellet was arrested suspected of being a spy. Marshal Augereau had him transferred to Mainz. Quellet carried a passport delivered on March 24 in Buren in the Canton of Berne, giving Neuchatel as his place of birth, and to visit his parents as the object of his journey. His own signature was different from the one on the passport. He said he was twenty-seven years old, had served for several years in the Engineers in Holland without being able to give any coherent details. At the present time he was a schoolmaster, yet he had neither pupils nor a residence. A Polish gentleman, whom he had met in Lubeck, had offered to take him to Russia, then vanished leaving him without resources. He was on his way to Munich to offer his services to Marshal Prince Berthier. When he was arrested he was not on the Munich road, and in the dragoons' quarters he spent his time asking questions concerning military matters. He was ordered to be held in Mainz.

By order of Fouché the Prefect of Police seized in Leopold Collin's bookshop in Paris a book entitled, *History of Events in the months of July, August and September 1792*, written by M. de la Varenne, an attorney. The book was badly written, distorted facts, and gave wrong information on persons who were then in the public eye, including Fouché.

A M. Dupuy-Briacé, member of the General Council of the department of Maine-et-Loire, had some time before used insulting words when speaking of the Emperor. He was sent under surveillance to Saumur, the authorities not wishing to punish him further.

The Council called him back however, and to add insult to injury appointed him a member of a deputation going to Paris with a loyal address from the inhabitants of the department. The Sub-Prefect of Saumur refused to give him a passport before the Senator-Minister lifted the surveillance. Now the Senator-Minister heard with horror that Dupuy-Briacé was in Paris with the other members of the delegation. To be taken back to Saumur immediately.

Bordeaux was behaving rather disloyally. First pamphlets were distributed, all of them speaking disrespectfully of the Emperor, then the War Minister passed on a letter of the Captain of the Grenadiers of the 112th of the Line, accusing two civilians of having attempted to suborn his men. Auger, one of the civilians, had on July 11 drunk with several Grenadiers, and wanted to take one of them back to his house, but when the sergeant-major refused to let him go, explaining that he could not miss evening parade, Auger used insulting words about the Emperor and the army. He was taken to the guardroom. On the 12th Cadet Boucheu, former drum-major of the 7th Light Regiment, egged on by Auger, went to the Castle, where he used seditious expressions while chatting with soldiers, and spoke of his wounds which he now bitterly regretted, for it had not been worth it to sacrifice himself for men who had waxed rich at the expense of the nation. He told them that they too would discover that. He had fought for liberty, but under Napoleon there was no liberty left in France. His words were but echoes of the pamphlets. Fouché instructed the Prefect to find out why there was so much dissatisfaction in Bordeaux.

The Prefect of Deux-Sèvres reported on the 29th that Jagot, a former Benedictine monk, had returned to France. He had not got permission to come back as he had been secretary to the Supreme Council of the Vendéens during the civil war, and was also suspected of having had a hand in the attempt of Nivôse 3. The Prefect believed that at the moment he was in Civrac-en-Médoc, but would soon proceed to Thouars to see his mother. The Prefect ordered the Sub-Prefect of Bressuire to arrest him.

August

The Commissioner-General of Police of Genoa reported in a letter dated July 26 that the inhabitants of the Canton of Borzonasca had since time immemorial travelled to foreign parts with the intention of making money. They called that *andare in birba*. When they embarked on their journeys they dressed up according to their projects either as merchants or monks or bishops, now and then even as cardinals. Before setting out they studied their roles, if necessary even learning Latin. During their absence they preached, collected alms for themselves, in short used every possible means to obtain money. Invariably they carefully avoided committing crimes that would bring the death sentence on them. They visited France, Italy, Germany and Russia, did not hide their trade, and when some of them were called up the parents told the military authorities that their sons were *in birba*. The previous local government tolerated their trade as it brought in about 200,000 francs a year. The present mayor had made his fortune *in birba*. Two years ago the Roman Consul in Genoa complained of two of those vagabonds who, dressed as bishops and showing a paper which they pretended had been signed by the Pope, collected vast sums. On Fouché's instructions no more passports were to be given to the inhabitants of Borzonasca without the police investigating whether their errand was an honest one.

The Minister of France in Lower Saxony had arrested a Frenchman called Loiseau in Hamburg. It appeared that Loiseau had been deported from London at the request of the Baron de Roll. On reaching Hamburg he went to see M. de Gimel, agent of the Comte Delille, and offered to go to Paris to assassinate the Emperor. As he was being taken to prison he tore hidden papers out of his cravat, and swallowed them. The policeman escorting him managed to save a few fragments. One of them contained the words, ". . . murdered at Toulon, Malta, massacres in the mosque of Alexandria, cruelty in Cairo, Jaffa, shot and cut to pieces four thousand men three days after taking them prisoners. . . ." All that in Loiseau's handwriting. A letter of his to M. de Beauveau in London was intercepted. He was, he wrote, in such a miserable state that the only way out was to speak disrespectfully of the Emperor, and get himself locked up.

To be transferred to Paris.

The officer commanding the gendarmes of Savenay in the Loire-Inférieure reported that a pitched battle had taken place between two gendarmes of Muzillac and eight brigands. One of the gendarmes was badly wounded, two brigands were killed.

The Prefect of the Drôme notified the Senator-Minister that the parish priest of Chabenit had complained to him of his parishioners because when he sang the *Domine Salvum* for the Emperor not a single member of the congregation followed him. The priest asked for the reason: too high taxes, was the answer. But, added the Prefect, elsewhere in the department it was sung "with joy and serenity".

Cretin, a forty-seven-year-old former Lazarist born in the Jura, had been deported to Cayenne during the Consulate. He returned to France without permission, was sent before the tribunal of Montaigu in the Vendée, taken on the tribunal's order to Amiens, where he was locked up in a depot for beggars, then sent back to the Jura to stay in his native village. He eluded the watchful eyes of the gendarmes, took himself off to the Maine-et-Loire, was arrested for begging, pretended that he knew the Sieur Bunet, head of the missionaries in Paris, so the Prefect gave him a passport to Paris; but questioned there admitted that he did not know Bunet. As he could not give a good account of his actions the Prefect of Police sent him to the prison of Sainte-Pélagie. There were thousands like Cretin who roamed the Empire when not behind bars.

Is is not clear from the police reports whether the summer of 1806 was a good or a bad one.

September

On the 3rd two English deserters of the 5th of the Line arrived on the coast near Cherbourg in a stolen boat, declaring that their regiment was in Alderney, and that they had left in their major's own craft. They were put at the disposal of the military authorities.

A letter from Berlin, dated August 23, reached Fouché on the 4th. Preparations for war were gathering momentum. The agent who wrote the letter had recently left St Petersburg, where the English Ambassador, the agent reported, went to see the Emperor of Russia the same day he had received mail from England, and asked if the King his Master could still count on him. The Emperor's answer was that his separate peace with France did not prevent him from remaining a faithful ally and friend of the King of England.

On the 5th the gendarmerie announced that the brigade of gendarmes of Faucogney in Haute-Savoie had been manhandled by the mob at the local fair. The gendarmes had had to seek refuge in the mayor's house. The rebellion lasted the whole night; the rebels built barricades to stop the gendarmes from escaping; however they had managed to do so through the barn. The mayor was entirely unhelpful, allowing the gendarmes in only as a last resort. His own nephew was the leader of the rebellion in which the entire population had joined. The gendarmes had come without their muskets. On the 18th the Prefect gave a very different picture: there was a fight at the fair between two villages, and the gendarmes intervened in a complete state of drunkenness. The mayor and his deputy took no measures to stop the fight which in any case was not bloody, and nothing disloyal was said. Fouché seemed to believe neither version.

On the 11th Fouché received a letter from a trustworthy Piedmontese official, announcing the presence in Saint-Cloud of Sartoris, another Piedmontese, who pretended to be the son of the master of the horse of the King of Sardinia, whereas he was only a groom in the royal riding school. He had already solicited and obtained financial aid from H.I.M. the Empress. As a matter of fact, the letter stated, Sartoris was a dangerous spy. Fouché had him brought with wife, child and a servant from the inn where they stayed, to his mansion. The servant girl was called Catherine Ernoud.

Sartoris declared that he had left Turin a year before to marry his wife in Genoa. Three months before they had come to Paris to take advantage of the lull in the war with England and travel there in order to collect a legacy left by an uncle. Once in Paris he began to entertain hopes of being employed in the Emperor's stables. He made every effort to obtain a job, and while at Saint-Cloud in the kindness of her heart the Empress gave him a present of money. He maintained in front of the Senator-Minister that Her Majesty had promised to be the godmother of the child his wife had given birth to twenty-five days before.

On the previous day Sartoris, having sold all his belongings and being unable to pay the bill, sent Catherine Ernoud, the servant girl, to the Palace with the child and a letter. She got through because the guard knew her as she had often brought them food. The letter addressed to Joséphine was rather a menacing one, for Sartoris threatened to throw himself into the Seine if she did not come to his rescue. Fouché had the three of them detained, and after a short inquiry discovered that the child was a foundling. Sartoris and his wife were sent back to Turin to be kept under strict surveillance, the child was taken to the Hospital des Enfants trouvés, and Ernoud was detained in the prison of the Madelonnettes, where she swiftly repented, begged to be let out, explaining that Sartoris and his wife had taken advantage of her simplicity; moreover the nuns testified to her sincere repentance. She was discharged, and sent twenty leagues from Paris and the Court.

Detainees had the strange habit of disappearing, that is often no trace could be found of them. Napoleon handed to Fouché a petition he had received from a Mme Dargent, shopkeeper in Württemberg, requesting to be told the whereabouts of her husband arrested in 1798 as an émigré in Paris. Checking in the files the High Police found out that M. Dargent was detained for two years, then was taken to the Swiss frontier. Nothing had been heard from or of him since; thus Mme Dargent could get no satisfaction.

October

Censorship remained severe; even a book entitled *Essai sur la vie de Grand Condé*, a purely historical work, was confiscated because author and bookseller had not asked for permission to publish it, and had had the cheek to announce it in a gazette. Fouché ordered that no newspaper or gazette was entitled to mention a new book without his authority. On the other hand, he sent a circular to all Prefects that the bulletins of the Grande Armée should be displayed in every mairie and on every church door.

A M. Montaignac, aged seventy-three, kept under observation in Le Mans as a royalist, was allowed by the Prefect of Police to return to Paris because of his exemplary conduct and his deep respect for the Emperor. That was in July. However, since his arrival in the capital he had completely changed his tune. The police intercepted a letter he wrote to Denmark in which he asserted that in spite of his age he was still ready for the fight, and asked whether there was fresh news from Louis XVIII. Questioned he denied any serious intent: poverty alone had made him write to his former protector, the Chevalier de Montrichard, and he had written in those terms simply to please the Chevalier. His advanced age and infirmities notwithstanding he was considered a dangerous man, and was therefore ordered to be locked up in the Temple.

At the end of the previous month the Commissioner-General of Police in Strasbourg had informed Fouché that a large number of Frenchmen serving in the Prussian and Austrian armies had deserted, and now the Commissioner wanted to know what to do with them. Fouché sent the letter to the Minister of War who on October 27 replied that he had instructed the general commanding the 5th Division to send the men to Landau, there to be incorporated in the 1st Legion of the North. The same order was issued to the general commanding the 26th Division. Fouché exhorted the High Police to hand over to the military any deserters who turned up in France.

Fouché on the 29th received an anonymous letter about a gendarme called d'Abos who had married a noblewoman in Mainz, a Mlle d'Ormesson, whom he ill-treated. The Senator-Minister, whose entire time was taken up with royalists, Chouans, rebels, deserters, and the Emperor's comings and goings, none the less made time to make inquiries. The anonymous letter had not lied, yet nothing more was done about the gendarme in spite of the inquiry proving that he was a cruel husband. It had been sheer curiosity on Fouché's part.

The battle of Jena was fought and won by the Emperor on October 14. Of course, it had little to do with the police, yet a secret agent in Vienna did speak of it in a report. The Austrians were delighted with the rout of the Prussians. A young Austrian named Euler, who was making a sort of a grand tour, arrived from Vienna, and told Mr Walpole, an English prisoner, that the Archduke Charles had thrown himself at the feet of his brother the Emperor of Austria, begging him to take part in the war against France. The Emperor answered, "I gave my word to my brother the Emperor of France, and I wish to keep it".

November

A traveller arriving in Paris at the beginning of the month declared that on the 1st the stage coach from Rouen had been attacked near Ecouy, and that the brigands had taken his watch and the sum of 1,500 francs from his fellow passengers. The Prefect of Rouen confirmed this in a letter dated November 1. There were no funds belonging to the Government in the coach. The Prefect observed that the same stage-coach had been attacked in the department of the Eure on February 14. At the time he was Prefect of the Eure, and immediately arrested a few Chouans which put an end to further attacks. Unfortunately most of them had to be set free for lack of evidence. The Prefect went on to say that neither the postmaster nor the parish priest of Ecouy could be trusted as on several occasions both had expressed their sympathy for the Chouans. It would be advisable to remove them from the district.

The mail coach of Rouen had twice been attacked between Bounière and Roboise near the forest of Galisset. The number of the brigands was roughly the same. They were in uniform, and said to be deserters. The High Police wondered whether it was not the same band.

The London correspondent of the High Police sent a letter on the

8th to the effect that the émigré Puisaye had despatched an envoy to Windham who promised to help some of the Chouans in London; but the correspondent was unable to get hold of their names. Puisaye and Windham were encouraging the Chouans. They worked through hidden or infiltrated rebellious priests in Morbihan. From Hamburg Bourrienne sent on reports he had received from London. M. de la Chapelle was extremely busy there. A royalist agent called Marino or Merino had left with £1,800 for Paris, whence he would proceed to Brittany; another, whose name was unknown, had left for Holland. Bourrienne's agent had over-heard in London that a firm in Paris which was under contract to supply the army corps in Brittany with arms received a subsidy of about 50,000 louis from the British Government. In three or four weeks' time twenty more royalists would be sent to join Marino. They were hoping in England to start a revolt in Normandy, Brittany and part of Italy. They counted on Poitou and Gascony. Several plans were shown to Windham, but he had not yet chosen any. There was also talk of sending an expeditionary force to Le Havre. His Excellency the Senator-Minister instructed the High Police to run Marino to earth without delay, also to find the firm that was to receive 50,000 louis. The victory of Jena, His Excellency believed, might change Mr Windham's plans.

His Excellency was interested in everybody and everything. The wife of a cloth merchant of Lyons left her husband to follow a shop-assistant to Switzerland. Laligant, the merchant, and his family obtained her arrest thanks to the Imperial Ambassador. They begged the Senator-Minister to keep her in prison for six months in the hope that she would come to her senses. The request was granted.

In the town of Brest Bourdon, an artilleryman aged twenty-one declared to the police on the 19th that on the previous Sunday another gunner, Darras by name, confided in him that an unknown person offered him in a café the sum of two million francs if he went to Paris, stayed in his house in the rue Saint-Nicaise, waited for the Emperor's return, then killed him by firing a bullet through the window. Escape would be easy as there was a door at the back.

Darras, aged seventeen, was questioned. He said that on Friday the 14th, an artilleryman aged eighteen, whose name he did not know, invited him to the Café Valéry, where they sat in a corner, and were joined by a man aged about thirty who seemed to be a friend of the other gunner, and who asked him about his family. Darras told him that his father had perished on the scaffold during the Revolution. The stranger then offered him the two million if he went to Paris, where he would be waiting for him when the stage coach arrived. Thoroughly shocked and disgusted Darras turned down the proposition. On the following Monday he and Bourdon returned to the café in the hope of getting the stranger arrested. The third gunner was there, but explained that he had met the stranger only in the café, and all he knew of him was that he was generous with drinks. The police did not get any further.

The Prefect of the Loire-Inférieure reported on the 25th that the priests in his department refused to have the communiqués of the Grande Armée pinned to the church doors or inside the churches, because only religious announcements were allowed by the bishop to be put up there. The matter was referred to the Minister of Public Worship. Meanwhile the mayors of every commune had them read out in public.

December

The High Police were busy preparing new passports for the year 1807. They were printed on special paper which they believed could not be imitated. They entertained the pious hope that with the use of the new passports deserters would more easily be caught.

On the 6th the gendarmes arrested a tramp in Morlaix who possessed no identity papers. Taken before the Government Delegate he declared that his name was Salami, that he hailed from Turin, had been taken prisoner on a Spanish ship by the English who forced him to enter their service. He was put in a brig of fourteen cannons, and when the brig approached the French coast the captain called for volunteers to land and pillage the countryside. He stepped forward. As the party reached the shore Salami ran off into the nearest wood. He had no idea what became of the others. The Delegate was convinced that his declaration was a pack of lies and that the man was most probably a deserter from the Imperial Navy. No English landing had recently been signalled on the coast. Salami would be put in gaol pending further inquiries.

On the same day another suspect was caught, in this instance a surgeon called Leb, aged thirty-nine, a naturalised Frenchman established in Strasbourg for the past nine years. He had been employed by the secret police in Germany in the time of ex-General Moreau. In April he had asked for a passport, and because of his bad reputation he was restricted to keeping the route set out in his passport. He reappeared in Strasbourg towards the end of September, and asked to be allowed to go to the General Headquarters of the Grande Armée to offer his services to General Savary. When asked to produce his passport he did so hesitatingly, for he had rubbed out the names of the towns he should have passed through. Arrested and questioned he made the statement that in his youth he had deserted from the Austrian army, therefore thought it was more prudent to travel to Hungary by way of Lemberg, but the Russians sent him back. Utterly broke, he had joined a travelling fair with which he visited all the small towns in the department of the Roër and on the other bank of the Rhine. The alterations in his passport were made in Germany. He added he could neither read nor write French.

For a long time the police had had their eye on him because of his frequent trips across the Rhine during periods of military activity. As he could not give an account of his actions during his long absence, and as his presence in Berlin had been noticed shortly before the outbreak of hostilities, the Commissioner-General of Police suspected him of having intelligence with the enemy. To be detained till further order.

Once again superstition was the cause of trouble. In the parish of Lagers in the department of the Haute-Vienne which had been joined some time before to the parish of Chalus, the bells were ordered to be taken from the first village to the second. The peasants of Lagers objected, saying the bells had always protected them from hail, lightning and other scourges. The tocsin was rung, and the peasants assembled to stop the bells being taken away. Escorted by a detachment of the National Guard the gendarmes intervened, arrested two armed peasant leaders, and soon re-established order. The gendarmes explained their errors to the peasants, and guarded by the National Guard the bells were transferred to everybody's satisfaction.

Though Christmas and the end of the glorious year were approaching, rebellions, desertions, chouannerie, plots against the Emperor and subversion kept the High Police busy. And busy they were to remain for years to come.

XII

Some Latter-day Chouans

After the execution of Georges Cadoudal, in Normandy, the mantle of leadership fell on the shoulders of the Vicomte d'Aché, a man of irreproachable loyalty who went into hiding when Cadoudal was caught in Paris. He had emigrated in 1792, served in the royalist army of the Prince de Condé, and come back to France in secret when Cadoudal's first plot was hatched. He was denounced by one of his own men, yet managed to escape arrest and go underground. However, his wife and daughter were imprisoned in Gournay in the department of the Eure. Disguising himself as a peasant he visited them from time to time.

All his fellow noblemen in Normany offered to hide him. He chose the manor of the Marquise de Vaubadon, a pretty woman aged thirty-six divorced from her husband. (It is noteworthy that such an ardent supporter of the old regime did not hesitate to take advantage of the divorce laws established by the Revolution.) Arrested during Cadoudal's trial, Councillor of State Réal came to see her several times in her cell. Suavely he explained to her that if she were willing to serve the State, that is act as informer, she would immediately be released. If not . . . Réal sighed as he described the fate in store for her. Mme de Vaubadon thought that she was a master in the art of double-crossing, so she agreed and was released. D'Aché became her lover; when their idyll ended he left the manor and went to hide elsewhere. They remained friends and Mme de Vaubadon continued to support the cause of the Chouans. She quite forgot her promise to Réal.

D'Aché hid for a while in the town of Caen, but as staying on became dangerous he left and found refuge in a country house near the small village of Trévières not far from Bayeux, his host a M. de Montfiquet whose life was saved by d'Aché's wife when she hid him in her manor several years before. That was before the amnesty. M. de Montfiquet was a reliable man, though somewhat indolent, letting his wife boss him. His young daughter, Henriette, fell in love with the fifty-year-old vicomte, who took advantage of her infatuation to use her in the royalist cause.

The de Montfiquet family was frequently visited by a sixty-seven-year-old marquise, Mme Hély de Combray de Bonneuil, a widow. She spent part of her time in her manor at Donnai, the rest in her manor at Tournebut. Her daughter Rosalie lived near the manor of Donnai. She was the wife of the Baron Aquet de Férolles, but was separated from him. Rumour had it that Armand Le Chevallier, a former Chouan and a strikingly handsome young man, was her lover. His father had gone over to the Revolution; however the son, who at the time was sixteen years old, joined the Chouans and was wounded in a fight with Government forces. In 1801 a mail coach was held up on the road leading from Saint-Lô to Coutances. Le Chevallier was suspected of having organised the robbery and taken part in it. One of the attackers wore the uniform of a dragoon and a number of witnesses swore that Le Chevallier was the dragoon. Arrested, he was taken to Paris where Fouché would have given him short shrift had not a senator stepped forward, declaring that Le Chevallier was in Paris and not in Normandy on the day of the hold-up. The Senator-Minister could not accuse another senator of lying, so much to his regret he set him free.

Mme Aquet loved Chevallier dearly. She was his obedient mistress, her love so profound that she often said she would willingly die for him. D'Aché met him in Mme de Combray's manor. Le Chevallier made an excellent impression on him, and Le Chevallier promised to put his considerable influence among the Chouans at his disposal. D'Aché was in touch with the émigrés in London who urged him to organise a rising in Normandy. D'Aché moved into Mme de Combray's manor, which in plain language meant that she hid him on her estate. Theirs was a conspiracy of gentlefolk. However, that was not sufficient to start a rebellion. Lots of underlings were needed to achieve that. It was easy to find them since the countryside teemed with deserters, most of them conscripts.

D'Aché was an idealist, a man above suspicion, yet was ready to ally himself with the so-called brigands and even real brigands, for the sake of the royalist cause. He was, like many other royalists, expecting England to send ships to the Norman coast which would not only bring money and arms but also a Bourbon prince who would put himself at the head of the nobility, the peasants, and the deserters and march on Paris. In the course of d'Aché's last clandestine voyage to London he was promised an Anglo-Russian army of thirty thousand men who would disembark on the coast, bringing with them the Comte d'Artois, and once they landed d'Aché would raise the insurrection. As on previous occasions the Anglo-Russian army remained an empty promise, and d'Artois did not put in an appearance either. On twenty-two occasions he swore he would come, many Chouans and other royalists died for him. The heir to the throne came only after the Allies had defeated Napoleon. Nonetheless, the English Government put £1,200 at d'Aché's disposal. That was in 1805; by 1806 the £1,200 was used up.

Mme de Combray was no plotter. She was an honest, straightforward woman whose only wish was for King Louis XVIII to stay in her manor on his way to Paris. In her manor of Tournebut she had a room ready for him. Her son bought a printing press, waiting for the great day when the royal proclamation would be printed.

The provincial nobility of France had faith in the Divine institution of monarchy. Those of them who were not guillotined were set aside by the Revolution. They returned to their country seats if the country seats had not been pillaged or burnt down, and prayed for their king's return. For them the Republic, and later the Empire, was the only enemy. Prefects, police and gendarmerie were but the representatives of the foe; and living in their dream world they ignored that immense security organisation with its spies and *agents provocateurs* that Fouché led, one of the reasons why their plots miscarried.

From Tournebut d'Aché went to Donnai. In his new hide-out he saw a lot of Mme Aquet and Le Chevallier, her lover. The police was searching for d'Aché, but with an amiable prefect like Caffarelli there was little danger of him being run to earth. After a while d'Aché left Donnai and went either to Brittany or England. Anyway he was absent while Le Chevallier and Mme Aquet decided to rob a mail coach. One cannot start an insurrection without money; mail coaches carried vast sums collected in taxes; and robbing a mail coach would be no crime as the Usurper's treasury was not entitled to sums that belonged to the King. It was taking from Napoleon the money that was due only to the King. For the hold-up experts were needed.

The idea filled Mme Aquet with enthusiasm. Le Chevallier planned going to Paris, his excuse to recruit royalists among the civil servants, the truth to establish an alibi, for Fouché would at once suspect him. A friend of theirs, the Chevalier de Godet, had misgivings, but Mme Aquet and Le Chevallier brushed them aside. Mme de Combray remained in Tournebut ignorant of the plans evolved by her daughter and her daughter's lover. She knew nothing about the planned mail-coach robbery. She would have abhorred the idea.

Le Chevallier's first move was to recruit resolute men. The first recruit was Lanoë, the gamekeeper at Donnai, who, however, made it quite clear that he was unwilling to take risks that would lead him to the guillotine. The second was Fierlé, a Bavarian who remained in the district after the amnesty of the Chouans. D'Aché was still absent; therefore all that was to follow had nothing to do with him. Le Chevallier studied the time-tables of the different coaches that carried Government money in the district.

The summer of 1807 was approaching when the plotters decided to strike. No one was more impatient than Mme Aquet. Le Chevallier's final choice fell on the coach which regularly transported the money collected in Alençon and Argentan to Caen. Mme Aquet chose the site for the hold-up, the wood of Quesnai, which was nine miles from her house near the village of Langannerie. Suddenly Lanoë declared that he was not playing: Fierlé alone remained. Le Chevallier decided to appoint a well-known Chouan to collect the men he needed.

The Chouan was called Alain who ever since the Chouan War had been known as General Antonio. He too signed the concordat with the First Consul, none the less he continued fighting the government. His hide-out was near Caen, and his daughter acted as messenger between him and other disgruntled Chouans. When he received Le Chevallier's request he came out of his lair, collected six intrepid men, ex-Chouans and deserters, who were attached to Fierlé. One of them, Harel, had taken part with Antonio in a raid on the house of an old man over eighty who represented the Paris Government during the Terror. They beat him up in the name of their dead companions whom the old man had sent to the guillotine. Then they took 16,00 francs from him. Harel now hesitated because he feared the guillotine: Antonio reassured him. The Anglo-Russian army would soon land; therefore there was no reason for fear. The other five needed no reassurance: they were the scum of the earth, for not one of them was without a criminal record. They were promised money, and were hidden in different localities, one of them in the corn loft of Mme Aquet.

On the higher level the plotters were joined by Lefebvre, a notary in La Falaise and a friend of Le Chevallier, Dr Révérend, who practised in the same town, and Courmaceuil, a landowner, who provided the men with rifles, swords and even an axe to break open the treasury boxes. Joseph and Pierre Buquet, cobblers in Donnai, were willing to hide the loot. Léonie Pons, Mme Aquet's seamstress, brought the hidden men their daily food. The stable boy at the Hôtel du Point-de-France in Argentan promised to notify Antonio when the coach arrived from Alençon, also when it left for Caen.

Things began to move. Under Antonio's command the men chosen for the robbery assembled at the inn of Aubigny. They went there at night so as not to rouse suspicion. On the following day they killed time drinking heavily from morning till evening. Le Chevallier and Mme Aquet arrived at the inn on the second night. Mme Aquet was so pleased to be in the thick of things at last that she served the drunk men with more wine. Suddenly two men appeared in the inn. They came, they said, sent by a group of royalists to ask them not to proceed with their plan. The risk was too great. Antonio said it was too late. As the discussion continued some of the hired men began to show signs of fear. Le Chevallier intervened, saying they were subjects of the King, were fighting for him, and the King would recompense them. He made them swear to carry out the job. Then Le Chevallier and Mme Aquet left the inn. Since he was the first man the police would suspect Le Chevallier set out at dawn for Paris, his intention to establish an alibi. He reached the capital on the evening of June 7.

On the same evening Antonio and his men departed from the inn and went to hide in the wood of Quesnai. Lefebvre, the notary, accompanied them, but then left them as he wanted to wait for the results at Mme Aquet's. A mounted messenger, sent by the stable boy at Argentan, brought the news that the coach had arrived from Alençon, carrying 30,000 francs, remained in Argentan overnight and loaded as much again. It left early in the morning for Caen, thus it should reach the wood around eight in the evening. As the local brigade of the gendarmerie was elsewhere the coach was accompanied only by one gendarme who was going on leave.

Alain and his men were waiting. At last the heavy coach appeared, drawn by four horses. The gendarme walked at some distance behind it in the company of three travellers on foot whom the gendarme had met on the road. They were chatting and laughing. When the coach reached the wood Alain's men appeared, halted the coach, pulled the coachman down from his box and bandaged his eyes. The gendarme drew his sword, and rushed up, though not before telling his travel companions to race to the nearest village to have the tocsin rung.

By the time the gendarme reached the spot there was no coach left on the road. Alain's men had driven it into the thick wood, and were unloading the boxes containing the money. They used the boxes to fire from behind them at the gendarme. A bullet hit his arm. No longer able to defend himself the gendarme sought safety in running away. Alain's men found 60,000 francs in the boxes, which they put into sacks sewn by Mme Aquet and loaded them on three of the post horses. They had to abandon three thousand francs' worth of copper coins because of their weight.

Meanwhile the tocsin rang in Langannerie. Followed by a few villagers two mounted gendarmes rode into the wood. The night had come. As a ruse one gendarme shouted, "Forward, first section," then, "This way, second section". Unimpressed Alain's men opened fire on them, wounding one gendarme in the leg, and killing the other's mount. In the dark Alain and his men made good their escape, taking along the coachman. Before reaching Donnai Alain gave him twenty-five francs, and ordered him to remain under a tree he showed him, and wait there for the horses Alain would bring back. The horses were returned only in the morning. The coachman went to the village, complaining bitterly of the attack on the mail, but swore he had no idea who the attackers were. A few days later he received a second present of twenty-five francs.

The loot was taken to the brothers Buquet. The firearms were left in a field, each of the men received 150 francs on account, and they dispersed. The two cobblers hid the money, part of it in a hole they dug in a nearby field, some of it in their cowshed, and the rest in a disused kiln. Now the real trouble began.

First, Mme Aquet had a Mass said for the intentions of Alain and his men. Then she asked the cobblers for the sum of 3,400 francs. The cobblers gave her the sum, though ungraciously. They behaved as if the loot had become their property. She took the money to La

Falaise, where she handed it to Lefebvre, the notary, instructing him to pay with it the debts Le Chevallier had left behind. Lefebvre thought the sum far too small, and there was in La Falaise another old Chouan, Bureau de Placène, who believed he too was entitled to the loot. Mme Aquet promised them 12,000 francs each within a few days.

Mail-coach robberies were considered by the police an outrage and a personal insult to H.M. the Emperor-King. If the mail carried only passengers then the High Police looked at it as an ordinary crime, but if it also transported Government money and that money was stolen, then the shout went up, "Only the Chouans could have done it".

Prefect Caffarelli was pained when he heard the news, for he had convinced himself that no Chouans were left in the department of Calvados. Now the hold-up in the wood of Quesnai was proof of the Chouans being on the move again. Fouché was equally pained. Since Napoleon's departure to Poland in all his letters and reports Fouché assured him that perfect peace and quiet reigned in France.

When the last mail robbery in the Calvados had taken place four years before, each member of the band had been caught. Some were executed, others succeeded in producing watertight alibis, a number escaped from prison, nonetheless plenty remained under lock and key, serving their sentences. Fouché ordered Councillor of State Réal to take the matter in hand, Réal being the best choice. "Question them till their hearts and kidneys give way," he was supposed to have said after an interrogation that lasted for days. His first task, he thought, was to question the robbers of the other mail coach who were available since they were in prison.

The High Police reported that Le Chevallier was in Paris, staying in the rue des Martyrs with his sister-in-law, Mme Thibout, and showed himself most conspicuously in cafés, theatres, and even in the antechambers of cabinet ministers. Réal felt certain that he did all that to prove his alibi. As Le Chevallier was suspected of having been the dragoon in the previous mail robbery the simplest thing was to put him behind bars while the investigation went on. But Réal preferred to wait. The police made several arrests in the department of Calvados. The newly arrested were people who took part or were suspected of having taken part in previous Chouan ventures, or were friends of Le Chevallier, d'Aché, and General Antonio. Moreover, the Marquise de Vaubadon was in police pay. In the days of her affair with d'Aché she had met a number of Chouans through him. It is logical to suppose that she gave Fouché the names of many of d'Aché's associates.

Réal's policy was to fill the prisons with as many suspects as possible and only then start the investigation proper. The High Police being often frustrated by the judiciary, it was essential to make out a good case before sending them for trial. The gendarmes arrested two uncles of Le Chevallier and a number of vagabonds and ex-Chouans, and even some local merchants who had all to be set free as there was no evidence against them. But Réal was in no hurry. He did not forget that in the previous mail-coach robbery Le Chevallier, Antonio, Harel, and Lanoë, the gamekeeper, got off scot-free thanks to the judges. He did not want a repetition of that.

During this time old Mme de Combray remained in her manor of Tournebut. She did not care for Le Chevallier, disapproved of her daughter seeing so much of him, but was completely ignorant of their love affair. She knew nothing about the mail coach robbery, in fact heard of it only a few days later. However, when she heard that Habert, her farmer in Donnai, was arrested, she immediately set off to La Falaise, where she knew the magistrates, in the hope of getting her farmer released. She wrote to her daughter, who came to meet her in the village of Langannerie. Mme Aquet confessed everything to her mother. Horrified Mme de Combray put the blame on Le Chevallier, but her daughter said that it was d'Aché's idea. Mme de Combray refused to believe her, though Lefebvre, the notary, assured her that that was the truth. She then went straight to Bayeux, where she met a close "friend". It was later established that the close friend was d'Aché in person who, hidden by the de Montfiquets, was still waiting for an opportunity to embark for England.

The next move was to see the two cobblers, take the money from them and hide it in a safer place. (Mme de Combray wanted it to be taken as far as possible from her daughter's residence since its presence on the estate, if found, would totally incriminate her.) On the morning of July 18 Mme de Combray, her daughter and the notary arrived in a carriage before the cobblers' house. Lanoë, the gamekeeper, accompanied them. All they got out of the cobblers was 9,000 francs, which were put into a sack, then taken to Caen. On the notary's advice the money was given to a M. Gelin who promised to transport it in secret to a lawyer called Vanier de La Chauvinière. Then Mme de Combray drove back to the cobblers to take the rest. Categorically the cobblers refused to hand over more, with the excuse that the neighbourhood was watched by gendarmes. Mme de Combray returned to Caen empty handed. She asked Lefebvre to advise Vanier that for the moment no more money would be forthcoming. She lived in the belief that the money was intended for the King.

She went again to see her daughter from whom she heard that the gendarmes had made a search but found nothing. Next day she received a letter from her son, letting her know that the gendarmes searched her manor of Tournebut. The next news was that Pierre Buquet, the elder of the cobblers, was arrested, his brother Joseph, however, managed to escape. The net was slowly closing in.

Mme de Combray offered to take Lefebvre to Tournebut, where there were excellent hiding places. She asked her daughter to come too, but she refused, saying she was well in with the authorities at La Falaise. The sergeant of the local gendarmes was devoted to her, so she had no cause to worry. As a matter of fact Chauvel, the sergeant, had become her lover. He was a handsome fellow, and, in order to make him amenable, she had given herself to him. Chauvel just could not believe that a great lady, belonging to the high society of Normandy, could condescend to surrender to him. Mme Aquet did not lie to her mother when she said she could entirely rely on him. With the clever use of her charms she even turned him into an accomplice. Mme de Combray then went home.

On July 20 Fouché signed the order to arrest Le Chevallier. When the police burst into his sister-in-law's house they found that their bird had flown. He had gone to Caen, where, feeling safe, he did not bother to look for a hide-out. Thus when Fouché's warrant arrived he was at once arrested and taken back to Paris. Desmarets took him in hand and with his pleasant smile and friendly approach, interrogated him. Le Chevallier denied everything, Desmarets did not believe him, and sent him to the Prison of the Temple with the order that he should be kept in a dungeon, where he should communicate with no one, not even a lawyer.

Mme de Combray and Lefebvre arrived at the manor of Tournebut. They hid in a cellar, and not a soul except a gardener and her lady's maid was aware of their presence. Came the gendarmes again, arrested the gardener and the lady's maid, took them to Rouen, where they were kept incommunicado for several weeks. They were eventually released for lack of evidence. Suddenly Lefebvre decided to get hold of the money the cobblers had hidden. He took one of Mme de Combray's horses, never thinking that the police knew the number of the horses in her stable. A magistrate from Caen searched the premises both at Tournebut and Donnai to no avail, which was precisely what he wanted since he was a friend of the family and did not believe that they could have anything to do with the robbery.

But the police continued their investigations. It was reported to them that a washerwoman of La Falaise had talked to an acquaintance about the mail-coach robbery and mentioned a man known as Grand Charles as one of the robbers. Grand Charles was arrested. He gave the whole show away, that is as much as he knew. Fierlé was taken and brought to Rouen, where he refused to divulge the truth except in the Prefect's presence. Caffarelli was dismayed when Fierlé who had kept his council in the previous mail robbery, gave him all the facts. Mme de Combray and her daughter! He could not believe his ears. However, something had to be done: he sent

Fierlé under escort to Paris, where Desmarets took him in hand. Fierlé, who already had once escaped the guillotine, spilled the beans. He cried, fell on his knees, implored and, to please Desmarets which meant saving his skin, he even added details he invented on the spot. Desmarets gave him twenty francs and sent him back to Caen. A warrant was issued for the arrest of the Marquise, de Godet, General Antonio and d'Aché, but not Mme Aquet whom Fierlé had not accused. According to his signed statement she was the victim of filial obedience. Fouché decided that she would be spared "if she answered frankly".

Instead of summoning Mme Aquet to the Prefecture Caffarelli interviewed her in the town hall of La Falaise in the presence of the mayor's wife, Mme de Saint-Leonard, who was related to the de Combray family. Unfortunately for Mme Aquet she was not the person to stand up to questioning. She told the Prefect a lot of unconvincing lies. He gave her twenty-four hours to tell the truth. Her panic grew, she even tried, so Chauvel was to declare during the trial, to poison herself, and it was he who wrenched the poison from her hand. When the twenty-four hours were up she confessed everything. Caffarelli let her go home, but then he received formal orders from Réal to arrest her. The warrant was passed to the gendarmes in La Falaise, and since Chauvel was the sergeant there, he set out at once to see her, offering her refuge in a house outside La Falaise which he had rented for that purpose. She still was unaware of Le Chevallier's arrest. Mme Aquet's two small daughters were taken to Chauvel's sister who promised to look after them.

Mme de Combray was arrested on August 20 with her bailiff and her son. When the house was searched they found royalist pamphlets, also the printing press. The missing horse was traced to Donnai. It was really the absence of that horse that gave the show away. Lefebvre was arrested in September. Chauvel was present when the notary was arrested, and, naturally, he brought news of it to Mme Aquet. She was petrified as she had no confidence in the notary. She was right, for in his panic Lefebvre wrote a letter to Fouché, denouncing every one connected with the mail-coach robbery. The Chevalier de Godet, who took no part in the plot, was also put under lock and key.

By the end of the summer the prison of Rouen was full of suspects. Luckily for d'Aché he had managed to get to England, General Antonio was still in his hide-out outside Caen, and Dr Révérend made good his escape, taking with him a young girl who had left her parents for his sake.

After the notary's arrest Mme Aquet decided to leave the house Chauvel had put at her disposal, as she no longer felt safe there. Dressed as a peasant woman she roamed the countryside, spending the days in woods and inns, the nights in peasants' cottages. Peasants invariably opened their doors to her; for they were royalists at heart. Whenever Chauvel was reminded that there was a warrant out for her he took care to follow a false scent; and whenever he could get away he rejoined her. She kept him informed of every step she took. She went one day to Caen to see a young lawyer who at once fell in love with her, and promised to get hold of the remaining cobbler and force him to disgorge the rest of the loot. She spent a week in the house of the lawyer's mistress. Then suddenly she took fright again and wanted to move to Rouen, where, she thought, it was easier to hide. Vanier de La Chauvinière, who was involved in the robbery, persuaded her to stay on in Caen because he badly needed money and thought with her aid they could get the money out of the cobbler.

Eventually she went with Chauvel to see the cobbler who wrung his hands, burst into tears, but gave them not one sou. He averred that he had so well hidden the loot that he could not find it any more. Out of the kindness of his heart he gave them 160 francs. They left, but she was soon back with Antonio who was a much feared man. When the cobbler saw Antonio approaching he took to his heels and was not seen again. Vanier decided to send Mme Aquet packing. It was too dangerous to keep her in his house.

The police now concentrated on her mother who was in their hands. She put up a brave show, refusing to answer questions. The police decided to lay a trap for the daughter. Fouché and all his underlings were well aware that the peasants in Normandy sided with the Chouans. Their choice fell on one Liquet, secretary to the mayor of Rouen, a sharp fellow, utterly devoted to Napoleon and well in with the High Police.

His first move was to see Mme Combray in her cell, where he commiserated with her. A great lady like her should never have been arrested, it was monstrous, he would do all he could for her and bring along his own housemaid to look after her. Next morning he appeared with the maid who was in police pay. Mme de Combray was delighted with her, soon the woman became her confidante and Mme de Combray sent her letters through her, which, of course, were read by the police.

Liquet took himself to Donnai, where in the stable he found the missing horse. Then he saw Lefebvre, who spoke of the washer-woman in La Falaise who had put up Mme Aquet and Chauvel for one night. He hurried to La Falaise, took the washerwoman to the town hall and made her talk. Now he knew that Sergeant Chauvel was Mme Aquet's lover and worked hand in hand with her. "I do not work for glory but the police," Liquet said in one of his letters to the Prefect. Towards the end of September he wrote to Chauvel who had been a friend of his, advising him that he had a letter and a sum of money given him by Mme de Combray for her daughter. In the letter the old marquise informed her daughter that a skipper called Delaistre would take her in his boat to England. The three thousand francs were for her travelling expenses. Touched by Liquet's devotion to her and her cause, Mme de Combray gave him 12,000 francs which she had hidden on her person. First he modestly refused to accept the present: the old Marquise had practically to beg him to take it. When he had taken it he sent it to the police.

Mme Aquet did not want to leave the department of Calvados; for, so she argued, if she were caught in the department the magis-trates in Caen would acquit her as they were old friends of her and her mother. It was Vanier who finally persuaded her to leave for England. Their friends were in constant danger while she remained in Calvados. She rode off in the still of the night with the skipper, wearing a large cloak.

In the morning they stopped at an inn at Lunebaud. In the tap-room a gendarme asked for their passports. The skipper had no visa on his and she had none. They invited the gendarme to drink with them. They plied him with drink till he fell asleep. He was still sleeping when they rode off. When they reached Pont-Audemer Liquet stopped them, disguised as a sergeant of gendarmes. That put an end to Mme Aquet's wanderings.

She was kept for two days incommunicado in a prison cell in Rouen. On the third day Liquet came to question her. She had no fight left in her. She accused everybody she could think of, and denouncing d'Aché, Le Chevallier, Lefebvre and Antonio she gave herself away too. On the next occasion she denounced Vanier.

Liquet asked the authorities for his reward. "I have served the Government for twenty years . . . a paterfamilias and a much respec-ted man. . . ."

Le Chevallier from the dungeon in the Temple wrote to Fouché, swearing that he had nothing to do with the robbery. He admitted planning an insurrection, but as a man of honour he never had any dealings with brigands. Therefore, he was entitled to ask to be judged by a military tribunal, and if condemned to be shot and not guillotined. Liquet in the meantime succeeded in convincing Mme Aquet that it was Le Chevallier who betrayed her.

Le Chevallier escaped from the Temple, the whole police was mobilised, and he was recaptured two days later. Fouché decided to finish with him. Instead of having him taken to Rouen to be tried with his fellow-plotters he was sent before a military tribunal—after all it was his desire—was sentenced to death, and at once taken to the plain of Grenelle, where a firing squad was waiting for him.

The detainees in Rouen appeared before the tribunal on December 15. They were accused of every possible crime: Mme de Combray was supposed to have tried to poison her son-in-law. The trial lasted for a fortnight. Mme Aquet, Lefebvre, Fierlé, Pierre Buquet and seven others were sentenced to death; Vanier and three others to twenty-two years in irons; Mme de Combray to twenty years solitary confinement and to be exposed in public, also to repay the money taken in the mail-coach robbery (with which she had nothing to do); nine others were acquitted including Chauvel who was sent to a colonial battalion.

The old Marquise did not flinch when she heard the sentence. Her daughter's lawyer declared that Mme Aquet was pregnant. These sentenced to death were guillotined the same afternoon in the Place du Vieux-Marché, where Jeanne d'Arc was burnt. In spite of the hundreds of applications to the Emperor for mercy on February 17, 1809, Mme de Combray was taken from prison, led by the executioner through the streets of the town, and tied to a stake was left in the icy cold for several hours. Practically all the great ladies of Rouen came to keep her company, and dozens brought her flowers. Then she was taken back to prison.

When d'Aché returned from England, Mme de Vaubadon betrayed him to the police. He was ambushed and shot dead. The police pretended it was the work of brigands and Mme de Vaubadon received a handsome reward.

Mme Aquet remained in the Rouen prison as according to law a pregnant woman could not be executed. The President of the Rouen tribunal wrote to Réal on August 23, "The doctors are still uncertain. If she is pregnant she must be eight and a half months gone with child." The doctors, who were friends of the de Combray family, did all they could to gain time in the hope that Napoleon would reprieve her.

On the family physician's advice it was decided to send her two small daughters to the Emperor and beg him to spare their mother. Fouché agreed to give them, an aunt, and the physician passports to Schoenbrunn, where Napoleon was momentarily resting on the laurels of his victory at Wagram. This was completely in keeping with Fouché's policy. He, who never ceased contemplating the possibility of Napoleon one day losing the game and vanishing from the scene, was not averse to putting the blame on him in such matters. If Mme Aquet were guillotined the nobility of Normandy would hate him and become his bitter enemy. Let their wrath concentrate rather on the Emperor than his Police Minister. Let the daughters go to Schoenbrunn, and let Napoleon say no.

The daughters set out with the aunt and the family doctor. They reached Schoenbrunn near Vienna on July 20. The four of them were waiting on the steps of the palace when Napoleon appeared on his way back from a military review. He approached the four persons dressed in deep mourning. He imagined that they were the widow and children of an officer killed in battle. The little girls handed him their petition. Napoleon read it, frowned, then said it was beyond his power to reprieve their mother. The girls burst into tears. Napoleon spoke to the aunt and the doctor: as her accomplices were executed Mme Aquet should suffer the same fate. Then he turned his back on them and went into the palace. He was furious with Fouché for having allowed the little girls to come to him the whole way from France, knowing perfectly well that he could not reprieve the mother.

"If the mother were worthy of my pardon," Napoleon said, "why did he not write to me? As she was not why did he give them passports, forcing me to send them back heartbroken?"

The family had one hope left, namely to seek a reprieve from the Empress Marie-Louise. However, in the meantime the doctors of Rouen had to admit that Mme Aquet was not pregnant. By then Fouché was sick of the whole business, and through Réal he issued the order for the sentence to be carried out. Mme Aquet was guillotined in Rouen on October 7. Her mother was released from prison only when the Bourbons were restored.

XIII

The Ducs d'Otrante and de Rovigo and the Baron Pasquier

Benjamin Constant observed that Napoleon's police specialised in sending their secret agents among the discontented, hatched plots with them, encouraged them, then dragged them before the tribunals. That was the police's idea of preventing plots and risings. Joseph Fouché, Duc d'Otrante since 1809, called the police but an occult power whose strength existed only as long as it could impress with its force.

Fouché was an exceptional chief of police. He got away with such a lot that his courage or impudence had no limits. He had an answer to everything; moreover he was convinced that under no circumstances would his master dismiss him. For instance, when after the battle of Eylau in 1807 public funds dropped on the Bourse, Napoleon wrote him an angry letter, blaming him for allowing ugly rumours to be spread. Immediately Fouché got hold of a letter written by General Defrance, who was with the army, to his father-in-law describing the battle at the end of which his brigade of carabiniers took up the same position behind the Vistula it had held before the battle. Fouché in his answer quoted the General's letter, in fact enclosed it with his, saying that if the public funds fell that was because the father-in-law had circulated the contents.

Even before Napoleon began seriously to entertain the idea, Fouché took to himself the task of suggesting that Joséphine accept a divorce so that Napoleon should be able to marry a Russian princess, thus consolidating the dynasty. He told the Empress to sacrifice herself in her husband's interest.

She answered with admirable dignity that she was willing to do anything in the Emperor's interest as long as the request came personally from him. Displeased, Fouché withdrew. He had hoped for a long chat in the course of which he would have persuaded her to say to Napoleon that the idea was hers, yet all he had achieved was to annoy her. When she complained to Napoleon he only scolded Fouché; one further reason for the Minister of Police to believe that he was and would remain indispensable.

Fouché, who during the Revolution had united a terrified Convention against Robespierre, had no illusions about public opinion or elected majorities. In fact, he heartily despised them. However, he knew the importance of keeping public opinion in chains. He once remarked that when a journalist wrote but one word of attack ten pages were required for an effectual denial, and "a minister has something better to do". Journalists were his special bugbear.

Under the Emperor only four newspapers were published, *Le Moniteur; Le Journal de l'Empire; Le Journal de Paris;* and *La Gazette de France. Le Moniteur* was the least read though Napoleon wrote at times in it. *Le Journal de l'Empire* was the most popular because of the witty feuilletons of Geoffroy. It had 28,000 subscribers. The newspaper proprietors were in truth paid servants of the Emperor. They were allowed to print only what the Imperial Censor permitted. Every morning the Censor went to the Ministry of Police to receive his daily instructions. The newspapers contained little material, so it did not take long to print them. They had to be ready by seven at night, and taken to the Ministry before eight o'clock. Truly Fouché was the leader of public opinion.

His power was immense, yet he always wanted to increase it. In 1809 he was temporarily in charge of the Ministry of the Interior, and when the Allies landed in Walcheren he took it on himself, in the Emperor's absence, to call out the National Guard. He got away with that, too: in fact Napoleon praised him. Then Fouché decided to put out peace feelers, that is to negotiate with England behind the Emperor's back.

On June 2, 1810, the Emperor held a cabinet meeting in Saint-Cloud. His spies had already acquainted him with Fouché's machinations. He turned to the Duc d'Otrante, and asked him why M. Ouvrard had come to Paris from Holland. The answer was that M. Ouvrard believed that through M. Labouchère, son-in-law of Sir Francis Baring, he could sound the British Government about the possibilities of peace negotiations. Angrily Napoleon retorted that Ouvrard had gone further than that, had even suggested conditions. If he did so without Fouché's authority he was a dangerous and guilty man who should be arrested at once. Fouché protested that even if Ouvrard had shown too much zeal he deserved to be forgiven.

"Duc d'Otrante," said Napoleon, "you ought to carry your head to the scaffold." Then to the Minister of Justice, "What does the law say of a minister who treats with the enemy without the monarch's participation?"

"Your Majesty used the right words," the Minister of Justice said. "The law is precise on the subject."

In the meantime Ouvrard had been arrested by Savary whom Napoleon had specially called to Paris. Ouvrard was found in Mme Amelin's house where Talleyrand was also present. In Saint-Cloud the Emperor ordered Fouché to resign, leaving it to him to find any excuse for his resignation. Fouché went without much regret, for he was already convinced that Napoleon could not last, and now the English would appreciate what a true friend of theirs he had become. Anne Savary, Duc de Rovigo, the Duc d'Enghien's executioner, was appointed the new Police Minister.

Ouvrard's papers clearly showed that with Labouchère he had negotiated with the Marquis of Wellesley, the Foreign Secretary, suggesting that as a basis for negotiations Napoleon should give up

Malta, Naples, the Ionian Islands, Holland, and even Spain. England and France would come to an agreement on the United States by sending a French army there in English ships. Among his papers was found also a detailed account of Fagan's journey to England.

After the peace of Vienna in October 1809 which followed the victory of Wagram, Fouché thought the moment propitious for a little occult diplomacy of his own, well aware that in his enormous pride Napoleon would not approach England. So Fouché decided to act on his own. A Sieur Hannecart, an émigré who had returned to France, found the right man for him to send to England, François Fagan of Irish origin, a former officer in Dillon's Regiment. Hannecart took Fagan to see Fouché who chatted with him on all sorts of subjects, and only at their third meeting did he propose that Fagan travel to London. The Emperor, Fouché implied, frankly longed for peace, and Fagan could help by sounding out Lord Wellesley on England's attitude. Fagan had many friends in England. Fouché's plan was to enter into secret negotiations with the English, and if all went well reveal the results to Napoleon, who, in his earnest desire for peace, would not only forgive him but thank him. He told Fagan not to go into details, just speak of peace, and see how Wellesley reacted.

On November 30, 1809, Fouché gave Fagan a passport to travel from Dunkirk to Boulogne. Fagan saw Devilliers, Commissioner-General of Police of Boulogne, who, in spite of Fouché's strong recommendation, was unable to find a boat to take him to England. (The outlawed Chouans travelled far more easily to England.) In Dieppe Fagan fared no better, so he returned to Paris, where he fell ill, staying in bed six weeks. Though Fouché was notified of his presence not once did he visit him. When Fagan felt better he left for Holland, eventually embarking from Ostend for England. He saw Wellesley several times, Spain seemed the biggest stumbling block, still he and Wellesley parted on the best of terms, and Culling-Smith, Wellesley's brother-in-law, said to him as he left, "If you or anyone else comes sent by the French Government we will receive him with pleasure". Fagan reached Ostend on March

10, Paris on the 12th, saw Fouché who thanked him in the Emperor's name, then did not hear from Fouché again. Fagan was a rare honest man who paid for the voyage out of his own pocket, and never asked Fouché to reimburse him.

It fell to Desmarets to question Ouvrard who said he had been given to understand by Fouché that the Emperor had consented to his getting in touch with the British Government. Ouvrard was set free.

When Fouché was dismissed Napoleon sent Dubois, Prefect of Police, to put seals on the front door of Fouché's house. A few days later Réal went to the house: all Napoleon wanted from Fouché was the return of the letters he had from time to time written him. The house was not searched. Then Réal travelled to Fouché's country house at Ferrières, and because he wanted Fouché at once to see that nothing rigorous or underhand was contemplated, he came in an open carriage, accompanied only by his daughter, the Baronne Lacuée. As they approached a saddle horse disappeared from the yard: Fouché was no longer in his mansion. Réal waited till eleven at night. Fouché remained away the whole day, carrying a large sum taken from his farmer, uncertain whether to go to Paris or escape to England. Finally he decided to come home; Réal asked for the Emperor's letters. Fouché swore that he had burnt them without exception, and though neither Napoleon nor Réal believed him there was nothing more to be done.

Savary, the new Minister of Police, discovered that on leaving the Ministry Fouché had taken away almost all the papers and documents that could be useful to him. Savary asked the high officials to try to help him. "I was rather ashamed of being unable to issue orders," but he was encouraged by some of them. Luckily he had an extraordinarily good memory, he said, for names. Fouché had burnt practically everything that could help him, so he had to discover for himself how the High Police were organised and how the organisation worked. Fouché had done him in every sense, introducing to him agents who, it turned out, were of the lowest sort, and whom even Fouché had not employed. But Savary was cunning, so he prided himself, and in a short while succeeded in mastering it all.

Many of his contemporaries considered the Duc de Rovigo a fool. One day he was informed that an assassin from the New World would shortly arrive in France, sent to murder the Emperor. His name was Gabriel Timothée, a Kaffir sold by the English to the former King of Sweden, then to Louis XVIII, and finally to the Emperor of Russia. He would kill the Emperor with a poisoned needle, could disguise himself at will as a white man, so that one could not guess whether he were black or white.

Savary became truly alarmed, and ordered every prefect, sub-prefect and mayor to arrest him on sight. A large number of white and coloured people were molested as a result of Savary's order, but black and white Gabriel Timothée was never run to earth.

The system pioneered by Fouché almost reached perfection under Savary; namely the police acting as the Empire's marriage bureau. Prefects were asked to send lists of marriageable young ladies in their departments. Naturally, they had to have dowries, also had to belong to the old nobility, for Napoleon wanted not only to reward his generals with the right kind of wives but by uniting the old nobility with the new he wished to establish a new ruling class. In their lists the prefects gave the names, the amount of the dowries, a description of the girls' appearance, their deformities if any, and their religious feelings. In a confidential message dated July 1811 Savary asked the prefects to hurry with the lists. Receiving no reply he ordered them to send them without further delay.

The scheme did not work everywhere as well as Savary had hoped. For instance, the Prefect of the Vendée sent in a list containing more than a hundred names, none the less he heard nothing more about it. Still, quite a number of young girls were found husbands against their inclinations. Thanks to the scheme M. de Marbeuf married an heiress from Lyons coveted by M. de Polignac; the Marquise de Coigny, a staunch royalist, had to accept General Sébastiani as son-in-law; Mlle de la Rochefoucauld despite her and her father's protests married Count Aldobrandini, the youngest brother of Prince Borghese, Pauline Bonaparte's cuckolded husband. Mlle Dillon was forced to marry General Bertrand, and the two daughters of the Comte d'Arberg Generals Klein and Mouton. The Duc de Cröy managed to save his daughter because his friend the Prefect of Le Mans let him know in secret that on the following day he would receive the Emperor's order for his daughter to marry some General. The Duc married his daughter on the same night to her cousin Ferdinand de Cröy who purely by chance found himself in the neighbourhood.

After the Restoration copies of a list were discovered which the Prefect of Isère had in 1810 sent to Savary. "Mlle Blanche de Bellegarde, twenty-four years old, 300,000 francs dowry. Her parents are dead, her figure is attractive and she possesses wit. Mlle de la Cisterna, aged eighteen, most attractive, daughter of the Prince de la Cisterna of Turin, 80,000 livres of income." Followed smaller fry: a girl aged sixteen from a good Bourguignon family on the mother's side, the father from a distinguished one in the Berry, with 48,000 francs dowry, of middle height but the figure good, no flaw in her education. They had a house in Paris, where they spent the winter, owned woods in the department, and her mother possessed land near Dijon. They were thrifty people who avoided debts.

In the Dauphiné, the Marquis de Bérenger de Sassenage, an émigré who had returned in 1805, was officially made a member of the guard of honour of the Isère, formed to escort Napoleon to Germany, and was, therefore, given the rank of colonel in the French army by General Duroc, Prince de Frioul, Grand Marshal of the Palace. Bérenger went to Paris, pleaded with Duroc without success, and against his will remained a colonel. Also against his will he married Mlle de Boisgelin. After his marriage the new colonel was sent back to Germany, where he was killed in battle. His widow gave birth to a son seven months later.

Savary's zeal was boundless. He wanted to persecute poor, old Abbé Jacques Delille, translator of the *Georgics* and author of a poem, *l'Imagination*. Napoleon had to intervene in person. "Savary," the Emperor said, "genius is not within the police's province. For the sake of my glory and of your honour do not torment the muses. Let that worthy old man die in peace undisturbed in his convictions. If he has not my affection he still retains my esteem."

Spies, Savary believed, were thick on the ground, and he nearly drew his sword when he heard the word. The finesse of Fouché was beyond him. When he was informed by the High Police of the presence in Paris of a woman belonging to one of the great families of France, and who was supposed to have been sent by Louis XVIII to spy and make contact with other royalists, he had her arrested, then brought before him. She was pretty, and he thought her amenable. She agreed to spy for the High Police, in short promised to act as a double agent. Savary gave her a thousand francs a month. It never transpired how much she received from Louis XVIII, but she had a fortune of about 600,000 francs in the first year of the Restoration.

(After the Restoration and Savary's return from exile the King wanted to discover the methods used by the Imperial Government in finding out what went on in Hartwell while he lived there. Savary informed him that the secret agents who watched the King cost the High Police around 120,000 to 150,000 francs a year. On the King's formal order Savary divulged that the Duc d'Aumont, who belonged to the Court in exile, sent him two letters a month for which he received 24,000 francs a year. "You see, Monsieur le duc," said Louis XVIII to Savary, "how little one can trust people. He always told me that he received only 12,000 from you. He probably said that because he did not want to pay me my royalties, for the letters you received were really drafted by me.")

After Fouché's departure Dubois, the Prefect of Police, was also dismissed. He had been an industrious, diligent Prefect, and devoted to Fouché with whom he worked hand in glove. It was he who established the rules concerning the Morgue, organised the river police, and ordered women, who wanted to disguise themselves as men, to seek police permits before dressing up. He revived an order of de La Reynie forbidding hunting horns to be blown in taverns. His successor was Etienne, Baron Pasquier.

Born in Paris in 1767 Pasquier was no ordinary man. It was said of him that he was like a cat, for the cat is attached to the house, but little interested in the tenants. He was a Counsellor of Parliament during the old regime, Counsellor of State and Prefect of Police in the Empire, Director General of Public Works and then Garde de Sceaux (Lord Privy Seal) under the Restoration, then Foreign Minister, and having been Charles X's minister and made Pair de France by him, he presided over the tribunal that tried his ministers. By then, of course, he had rallied to Louis-Philippe who made him Chancellor in 1837, Duc in 1844. He lived till 1862, an urbane, civilised man whose company everyone enjoyed.

When Pasquier became Prefect of Police he found that the police still had the same habits as in the worst days of the Revolution. In vain, from the public's point of view, did the Consulate and Empire replace the Revolution and the Directorate; in vain had the quality of prefects improved: the police continued to treat the public rudely, harshly and brutally. In the splendour of the Empire, with all its pomp and decorations, the police behaved as if the *sans-culottes* still ruled. Pasquier forced better manners on them. Because of the immense number of servants in Paris he wanted each servant to have a certificate issued by the police, thus preventing dishonest persons from finding employment. But the urbane Baron had come a bit late on the scene: employers feared police spies too much to take into service men or women who showed their certificates of honesty.

While it lasted Pasquier got on exceedingly well with Napoleon. He quickly grasped that when the Emperor put a question one had to give a precise answer. All high officials had to be present at the levée. The Emperor spoke to almost everyone, putting questions to them connected only with their jobs. One could see in his eyes when the answer pleased him. He seldom praised, but his manner would show his satisfaction. He would ask Pasquier how many ships were on the river, or how many sacks of wheat had arrived in the Halle. One had to give the exact number.

The Prefect of Police sent a report every evening to the Emperor, giving a detailed list of everything important that had taken place in the course of the day. When Pasquier took over from Dubois the "fermier des jeux", the administrator of the gambling dens, brought him 5,000 francs monthly, explaining that that monthly sum was for the Prefect of Police's toleration of the gaming rooms. Pasquier handed the payments to the Ministry of Police, so Savary asked the Emperor what to do with them. "I always knew," Napoleon said, "that dear Dubois took from right and left, and that was why in spite of his requests I never raised his salary as high as that of the Prefect of the Seine." He told Pasquier to add the monthly sum to his salary.

One of Pasquier's biggest difficulties was dealing with the five or six different police forces which interfered with the proper working of the High Police. (Today they would be called *polices parallèles* in France.) They competed with each other, each spying on the rest. The Prefecture had its police, so did the Ministry, the Military Governor had his own, the same applied to Duroc the Grand Marshal of the Palace, and the Commandant of the Imperial Guard, Marshal Davout. Complaints and denunciations made the Prefect's life impossible; and Savary, the martinet, only added to the confusion. On top of it the Prefect had to deal with Marshal Moncey too, as the Gendarmerie d'Élite also employed a police. With all those forces, said Pasquier, it was surprising that Napoleon was not even more suspicious.

The man Pasquier got on best with was Grand Marshal Duroc who had organised the security service round Napoleon in a truly admirable manner. There was nothing ostentatious, yet everything was efficient in the Imperial Palaces. Each member of the service knew his job, confusion was eliminated when Duroc took over. Inside the imperial apartments only seven or eight sentries mounted guard, one detachment of guardsmen was in the inner court, another at the foot of the main staircase, and that was all. No man, thought Pasquier, had been better guarded than Napoleon. Duroc wisely insisted on only a very small number of people being allowed to live inside the palaces and castles of the Court. Only those who were on duty were permitted to stay the night.

Of course, the Post Office had to work with the police since letters were regularly opened, and if they contained anything that might arouse suspicion they were sent to the Ministry for the High Police to deal with them.

Next to the Minister and Prefect of Police were three directors-general in Paris who were responsible for the departments which were divided into districts. Every large town had its commissioner-general of police, and all others special commissioners. On top of that the gendarmerie also sent in daily reports from every district to the inspector-general in Paris. Even so Napoleon was not completely satisfied with the running of his police state. He had in his pay several persons who kept him informed of everything that went on in the world of merchants and savants. Their reports reached him whether he was in the Tuileries or Moscow. Mme de Genlis, Regnaud de Saint-Jean d'Angély, and Fiévée were among his informers.

Yet in spite of all those precautions and with all the spying, denunciations, vigilance and careful control of the citizens there came a brief moment when one man succeeded in becoming master of Paris, and arresting both the Police Minister and the Prefect of Police. The man was General Malet.

Claude-François de Malet, born in 1754 at Dole in the Jura, had fought with the Army of the Rhine, then with the Army of Italy, and was made a brigadier-general in 1799. He became hostile to the Consulate, then to the Empire. He conspired against Napoleon, and in 1808 was put into the prison of La Force, where he continued to plot the downfall of the Emperor. In time he was transferred to Dr Dubuisson's mental home at the Barrière du Trône, now the Place de la Nation. On the night of October 22, 1812, a sergeant of the Paris garrison arrived at the mental home. "Compiègne," he whispered to Malet. That was the code word of the conspirators. After the sergeant's departure the general sat down to dine with the other inmates; after dinner he played his usual game of whist, and retired towards ten. He waited till eleven, then tiptoed out into the garden. It was pouring with rain. In the company of the Abbé Lafon, a fervent royalist who was also a detainee, he let himself out of the grounds, using a stolen key. The Abbé carried a leather box crammed with the proclamations of the General's Provisional Government.

In a hovel in the rue Villehardouin the Abbé Caamano, a pock-marked Spaniard, was waiting for them. Malet donned the general's uniform Caamano had laid out for him, signed the proclamations and orders, then had a quick meal accompanied by a glass of claret. Rateau, a corporal of the Guard of Paris, joined him. At dawn as Malet was ready to leave the Abbé Lafon seemed to have second thoughts; "Too late, the guillotine is at the door," said Malet, and at half past four, followed by Rateau, he arrived at the barracks of Popincourt, where he announced to Colonels Rabbe and Soulier that Napoleon had been killed on the ramparts of Moscow, and the Provisional Government (himself) had made him military governor of Paris. On his orders Generals Guidal and Lahorie, both imprisoned as enemies of the Emperor, were released from the gaol of La Force, Guidal designated as Minister of Police and Lahorie as Prefect of Police. (Which in itself showed the importance of the two functions in Napoleon's empire.) The next move was to arrest Savary and Pasquier, who surrendered like lambs; Desmarets was caught in his bed.

Malet hurried on to General Hulin, who had presided over the tribunal that had sentenced the Duc d'Enghien to death, and was now the military governor of Paris, his residence in the Place Vendôme. "You are under arrest," Malet informed him. Hulin asked him to show his orders. "Here they are," said Malet, breaking his jaw with a pistol shot. Hulin's wife appeared, wakened by the bang; Malet told her to look after her wounded husband. Then, still accompanied by Rateau, he crossed the square to the head-quarters of the Paris garrison. Commandant Doucet, Chief of Staff, and his adjutant, Laborde, hesitated to accept orders from Malet who immediately drew his pistol. They had, however, noticed his movements in the looking-glass, and sensing that something was wrong, managed to overpower both him and Rateau. By then messengers had arrived from General Hulin. Tied with ropes, Malet was dragged to the balcony, and shown to the troops in the square. Guidal and Lahorie were arrested by Réal, and the Minister of Police and the Prefect of Police set free.

The conspirators were tried at once. No lawyer dared to defend them, and Malet conducted his own defence. When the President of the Military Tribunal asked him who his accomplices were, Malet replied, "The whole of France, including you had I succeeded."

All the conspirators—fourteen in number—were sentenced to death, and on October 29, in six fiacres, escorted by mounted gendarmes, they were taken to the plain of Grenelle, the usual place for military executions.

When Malet faced the firing squad he called to the soldiers, "It is my privilege here to give you orders. Aim! Fire!" He shouted "Long live liberty!" as he fell.

In his inscrutable fashion Napoleon never uttered a word of reproach either to Savary or Pasquier.

XIV

The Tragedy of Fauche-Borel

There was somebody who constantly and continuously betrayed the royalists. One does not think so much of the Chouans, whose conspiracies often were too cumbersome, and where too many people were in the know; but of the lone agents and emissaries sent from England or beyond the Rhine. They were almost inevitably caught in France, many of them disappearing without trace, unwept and unrecorded in the annals of the police. Notwithstanding the excellent organisation Fouché, Réal and Desmarets had built up it is difficult to believe that practically every agent that entered France could have been caught with such ease by the High Police if they had not been warned in advance. The man whom the restored Bourbons and posterity accused of having been the traitor and double-crosser was Louis Fauche-Borel. It is worth examining the evidence which, in spite of the missing links, throws a harsh light on police procedure and the intrigues in which the unfortunate Swiss got himself involved.

Louis Fauche-Borel, born in Neuchatel in 1762, a printer and bookseller in that town and a subject of the King of Prussia who used him as an agent, was a vain, childish man who loved his role of agent as a child wearing a mask or a false nose. He was convinced that the wind of history had brushed him, and that he had an important part to play. He espoused the cause of the Bourbons as part of his historic mission; and, because he wanted to mix with his betters. His opportunity came when he carried letters between the Prince de Condé and General Pichegru (see page 63). He also approached General Moreau and Barras, though he came into the public eye only in 1804 when he was imprisoned in the Temple as an accomplice of Moreau. The High Police took a poor view of him as he was known to have flitted from place to place for several years. They would have kept him for a long time if the King of Prussia had not claimed him as a subject. As Napoleon considered Neuchatel too near his frontiers Fauche-Borel went to Berlin, which was apparently not far enough, for the Queen of Prussia told him that three French agents had arrived in Berlin, and there was a serious risk of him being kidnapped. Fauche-Borel put down the new persecution to his having printed Louis XVIII's Declaration issued in Calmar in Sweden on December 2, 1804. However, as the King in exile wrote him flattering letters, Fauche-Borel gladly accepted the "new inquisition", as he called it.

After printing the Declaration in Berlin he had just time to escape from Prussia. He took the road to Luneburg, the general headquarters of Gustave IV, King of Sweden. He had several audiences with the King which boosted his morale. Truly he was in the thick of things, a friend of crowned heads. Persuaded by him, Gustave IV offered the Ducs de Berry and d'Orléans commissions in his army. Delighted, Fauche-Borel left Luneburg, hurried to the Comte d'Artois with the good news, but the evacuation of Hanover put an end to the plan. Still, he was now well in with the French royal family.

When he arrived in London in January 1806 Louis XVIII asked him under the direction of the Comte de La Châtre to follow the correspondence of one Perlet, writing from Paris in the interests of the Bourbons. That correspondence seemed to impress the British Government as they thought there existed in Paris a secret royalist committee composed of important people, totally devoted to

Louis XVIII, waiting for the right moment to strike. In his letters Perlet expressed his hope for quick concerted action, and asked for large sums which the secret striking force needed. Fauche-Borel knew of Perlet, had, in fact, had confidence in him since at the time of the Directorate he had been the editor of a periodical. The sentiments Perlet expressed in his letters were vehemently against the Emperor. Fauche-Borel found in them but one snag, namely that Perlet did not give the names of the members of the committee, though they were all supposed to be men of high standing. It was felt in London that there was some mystery which needed investigating; therefore it was decided to send someone over to find out who comprised the committee, and how much money was really needed. Fauche-Borel had several chats on the subject with Lord Howick, later Lord Grey. Perlet himself asked for someone to come over. He named Fauche-Borel as the ideal messenger. Now Fauche-Borel was perfectly aware that the French police were extremely interested in him, and had dogged his footsteps ever since he left the Temple. He declined to go.

Lord Howick chose a man, who was unable to leave so Fauche-Borel suggested his nephew, Samuel Vitel, an officer in H.B.M.'s service. Lord Howick received Vitel, gave him his instructions, adding that his mission was a perilous one. "My lord," answered Vitel, "one dies with pleasure for such a wonderful cause." Vitel first went to Neuchatel to see his mother. Shortly after Vitel arrived in Paris, Fauche-Borel received a letter from Perlet, advising him that Napoleon had had his nephew arrested, then assassinated "without reason or pretext". Fauche-Borel mourned the brave man. In his apologia, published as a pamphlet after the Restoration, Fauche-Borel stoutly maintained that he did not know, and could not imagine either, that Perlet was an employee of the Préfecture de Police in Paris.

Pasquier related that one day Counsellor of State Fiévée (one of the Emperor's secret informers on merchants and savants) recommended to him a fellow called Perlet, who was his brother-in-law, a wretched chap working in the Préfecture, not irreproachable, yet the poor devil deserved indulgence. Pasquier promised to look after him, and on the next day sent for him, but was unfavourably impressed by his effusive, humble manner. That impression was confirmed by a letter Perlet sent him two days later in which Perlet explained that because of the royalist friends he had made during his deportation he had become the Emperor's secret agent, carrying on a correspondence with Fauche-Borel, the best known agent of Louis XVIII, the aim of the correspondence being to discover when royalist emissaries were sent to France. He had persuaded Fauche-Borel and Louis XVIII that there existed in France an important royalist committee. Eventually Perlet was sent to England, where he was well received, and saw M. de Puisaye and d'Entraigues, returning to France as an even more trusted royalist. Pasquier spoke to the chief of the first division of the Préfecture to which Perlet belonged, and was told that he was held in awe by his colleagues. Perlet was a native of Geneva, and had entered the Préfecture while Dubois was Prefect.

To return to Samuel Vitel. On February 25, 1807, Perlet reported from the House of Detention of Sainte-Pélagie to Dubois that on the day before yesterday, which was a Monday, a young man came to his house at 6 rue de Tournon, asking to speak with him in private. He found only his wife at home, so told her that he had to meet her husband to discuss a work entitled *Les Oiseaux de Paradis* which Perlet knew to be a password of the royalists. Mme Perlet explained that her husband had given the book to M. Garnery. Then the young man wrote down his name and address, M. Vitel, Hôtel d'Hambourg, rue de Grenelle, repeating he wished to see Perlet urgently. After dinner Mme Perlet went to see her husband who at the moment was detained in Sainte-Pélagie for debt. Perlet wrote a word to Vitel, telling him to go in the morning to Gallay, his factotum, who would conduct him to Perlet. He did not want to divulge that he was in prison, so instructed Vitel to follow Gallay. The next day Vitel went to Gallay, but when Gallay told him that Perlet was detained he became frightened, refused to follow him, declaring that he had no business with Perlet, and left the factotum.

Gallay reported to Perlet who "much regretted being in prison" as he knew that Vitel could only be Fauche-Borel's nephew. So Gallay was sent to the Hôtel d'Hambourg, and succeeded in reassuring Vitel whom Perlet had met in London in 1800 on his way back from deportation. Gallay brought him to the prison at three in the afternoon. Perlet took him up to his room, and "confidence was restored". Vitel told him that he had been sent by the British Government, had left London on January 6, a ship had taken him to Usum, where he saw another English agent, then he had travelled to Gotenburg, then to Hamburg, arriving in Neuchatel a few weeks later. There he obtained a passport to which he was entitled since he was born in the town. His passport being valid Perlet did all he could to persuade him that he was in complete safety in Paris, and promised to hand him the papers he had come for without undue delay. Vitel declared that true harmony reigned between England and the Northern Powers, then, dropping his voice, he said he had matters of enormous importance to discuss, but did not think that a prison was the right place for it. Again Perlet reassured him, and when Vitel asked whether the Hôtel d'Hambourg was safe Perlet was truly delighted, for now he could send him anywhere the Prefect of Police wanted. Among other things Vitel confided in him that the King of Prussia was at the head of an army of 60,000 men, and the restoration of the Bourbons had been agreed to by all the Allies. After Vitel left him Perlet sent an urgent message to Veyrat, Inspector-General of the Préfecture de Police, to see him in his cell. Perlet ended his letter to Dubois bemoaning the fate which forced him to remain in prison, but assuring him that he was completely at his disposal. He signed the letter Charles, which was his code name.

Vitel was arrested, and Perlet wrote to Fauche-Borel, asking for a large sum of money to save his nephew. (Here Fauche-Borel contradicts himself: at the beginning of his apologia he spoke only of the one letter in which Perlet informed him of his nephew's "assassination".) Fauche-Borel sent the large sum which Perlet shamelessly kept. Not every one in London trusted Perlet as blindly as Fauche-Borel. MM. de Puisaye and d'Entraigues were convinced that the royal committee was a chimera; Fauche-Borel stood up for Perlet, and he and the two leading émigrés had a row.

After Vitel's execution when Perlet was sent by Desmarets and Veyrat to London he saw Louis XVIII whom he endeavoured to persuade to come to Paris in secret. The King did not play. Perlet tried to take money from him; however the King had practically no cash, and only managed to give him fifty louis for his return expenses. Perlet complained bitterly to Fauche-Borel who gave him an additional hundred and fifty louis. On Perlet's arrival in France the correspondence began to languish.

As soon as he became Prefect of Police Pasquier made inquiries about the Vitel affair. He discovered that the whole correspondence between Perlet and Fauche-Borel was in the hands of Veyrat. "I had no liking for him, and he had no more for me," wrote Pasquier of the Inspector-General of the Préfecture of Police. Veyrat was without a doubt the most cruel, venal and corrupt policeman of the Empire. His protector was Constant, Napoleon's valet, and Veyrat acted as his spy inside the Préfecture, where his son was employed too. "The worst pair I ever met," said Pasquier of them. When pornographic books were seized and locked up in a special room in the Préfecture, the Inspector-General helped himself to as many as he wanted; Dubois had done the same but Veyrat sold many of them back to the booksellers, whereas Dubois took them to present them to his friends.

Pasquier sent for Veyrat whom he told to show him Perlet's correspondence with Fauche-Borel. Pasquier found the whole business absolutely disgusting, and said it should cease. He heard nothing more about it till Savary had Perlet arrested for having kept back two letters he had received from London. Only then did Pasquier realise that egged on by Desmarets, Perlet had continued corresponding with London. Pasquier was delighted when Perlet was kicked out for good from the Préfecture.

Of course, Perlet had a different story to tell of his activities. He published it, also in a pamphlet, soon after the Restoration, refuting everything Fauche-Borel accused him of.

He was also a printer and a journalist to boot. He was, so he maintained, firmly attached to the Bourbons. Five days after the death of Louis XVII, he published an article in which he begged the nation and its rulers to set free the daughter of Louis XVI as it would be unworthy of France to keep her as a hostage. Madame Royale was eventually exchanged for the Conventionels Dumouriez had handed to the Austrians in December 1795. In his *Exposé* Perlet took the kudos for that. He had fought against the Convention, was sentenced to death, but escaped and was hidden by peasants in Brie. Caught he was deported to Cayenne in 1797. While out there the mob destroyed his printing works. He survived where others had died and was back in Paris in 1806, his loyalty to the King unshaken. (One cannot help asking the questions, how did he get back? Who allowed him to enter? What did he live on till he joined the police?)

In 1806 M. François Fauche-Borel, bookseller from Hamburg, came to Paris to solicit the release of his brother Louis, detained in the Temple. François called on Perlet as theirs was practically the same profession, and they soon discovered that they both had the same political convictions. Perlet invited François to stay with him, and François repaid his hospitality by giving him news of his adored King who was at the time in Mittau, and mentioned that his brother Louis was in the King's confidence. Perlet perceived that by becoming friends with him he could serve the King's cause. Perlet, who had served the King without asking for any reward, now followed the dictates of his heart: he would co-operate with Fauche-Borel to restore the King on his throne. That was the reason why he consented to correspond with the two brothers. "Alas! Why did I change my manner of serving the King! Why did I bind myself to intriguing with Fauche-Borel who on the pretext of serving the King thought only of increasing his private fortune!"

Perlet swore that it was Fauche-Borel who put him in touch with Veyrat, saying Veyrat could be useful to the King. Perlet had known Veyrat since 1797, yet found out only much later that he belonged to the secret police. Then he broke with him, in fact sent him packing with *éclat*. But Fauche-Borel and his brother forced him to enter Veyrat's service; and now Fauche-Borel dared to say he had betrayed the King.

Though there is no doubt that Fauche-Borel was set free on the King of Prussia's intervention, Perlet maintained that he regained his liberty thanks to his intervention with Veyrat. In the beginning Perlet corresponded only with brother François, an honest reliable man. However that did not suit treacherous Fauche-Borel who in his letters practically begged Perlet to spend a lot of money in the King's interest. Perlet spent his own money (where did he find it?) which Fauche-Borel did not reimburse, so poor Perlet was thrown into debtors' prison.

Perlet explained the arrest and execution of Vitel. Naturally, Fauche-Borel alone was to be blamed for his nephew's tragedy. In his letters Fauche-Borel counselled Perlet never to ask small sums from the British Government as that would make a bad impression. He should demand large ones, giving the English concrete plans at the same time. Anyway, Fauche-Borel would soon send someone to Perlet. In his reply Perlet advised caution, and insisted on being informed well before the departure of the messenger so that he should be able to prepare everything for his safety. But what did traitor Fauche-Borel do? When the British Government decided to send someone to Paris Fauche-Borel forced his nephew on them because he wanted to make extra money for his family. Without bothering to remember that Vitel had been announced to the High Police, and without taking any precautions or letting Perlet know in advance, the unfortunate young man was sent straight to Paris. Vitel had a letter on him from Fauche-Borel to Fouché in which he recommended his nephew to the Minister of Police. Fauche-Borel was really one of Fouché's agents, dedicated to the cause of the Usurper, whereas, of course, Perlet of the Préfecture was not.

Carrying the letter of recommendation Vitel arrived in Paris, two days later called on Perlet in prison, and Perlet's heart went out to him, for he feared that the dear young man might come to harm.

Vitel tried to reassure him, telling him that one of the most important men in the Empire was his protector. Perlet was far from reassured, though he did ask Vitel whether he had brought money for him. The answer was in the negative. Because of his fatal relationship with Veyrat, Perlet could not hide so important an event from him, especially as Fauche-Borel had assured Perlet that Veyrat was with them. He notified the Inspector-General of Vitel's arrival, asking him to do all he could for the young man. It was on that occasion that Veyrat made Perlet write the letters which now his enemies, and Fauche-Borel chief among them, held against him. He only wrote those letters to England to stop the police from arresting Vitel. It was in Perlet's definite interest, says Perlet, to send the young man back to England. What did for Vitel was Fauche-Borel's letter to Fouché which the police found hidden inside his cane. Perlet himself was persecuted by the police for quite a while as they were suspicious of his relations with Vitel. But the best bit in Perlet's apologia was his description of his visit to England after Vitel's execution. "Would I have gone if I felt guilty?"

In London he was brought into the King's presence, and Desmaret's and Veyrat's agent was overcome with emotion as he beheld his venerated sovereign master who "with the customary kindness of his family" bade him sit down. Perlet was enchanted with His Majesty. What a good, intelligent and extraordinary monarch he was, and how well acquainted with everything that went on in France was he who was rightly waiting for the day, when tired of tyranny the French nation would call him back. The King promised Perlet to send all future letters direct to him; however Fauche-Borel, who wanted to have a finger in every pie, insisted on the letters being sent through him. Fauche-Borel persuaded Perlet to return the fifty guineas the King gave him after he had handed him one hundred and fifty. That must have offended His Majesty, and was probably the reason, thought Perlet, why he was in disgrace ever since the King was in his own kingdom again. "If this ever reaches the King I humbly beg his forgiveness for my two enormous blunders which I made under Fauche-Borel's wicked influence, who feared that if he did not control the correspondence he would lose his own influence."

Perlet returned to Paris, where Veyrat took him back into the Préfecture on Fauche-Borel's recommendation. Perlet showed only insignificant letters to Veyrat whom he no more trusted, and if Fauche-Borel had not forced him he would have had no more dealings with him. Later Veyrat denounced him to Pasquier as conspiring against Buonaparte (sic), but Pasquier refused to arrest him because he considered him an excellent fellow. His Excellency the Baron Pasquier had often congratulated him on his probity.

On July 26, 1813, M. G . . ., a Paris merchant and intimate friend of Fauche-Borel, came to see Perlet, to invite him to his house as he had important intelligence to impart. Next day Perlet called on him. First M. G . . . showed him a letter written by Fauche-Borel in the agreed code, asking Perlet to travel to London. Perlet said he would at once prepare for the journey. Then M. G . . . told him that he knew all Fauche-Borel's affairs, and that his own journeys to London and their purpose were known to Desmarets. M. G . . . was protected by the Government, therefore did nothing against their interests. If Perlet took Fauche-Borel's letter he would notify the police; if he refused to leave for London they would burn the letter together, and no more would be said. When Perlet had agreed to the letter being burnt M. G . . . enlightened him on Fauche-Borel who corresponded with Desmarets, who wanted only to increase his fortune, and was trying to get 30,000 pounds out of the British Government though perfectly aware that the Bourbons' cause was hopeless.

Perlet went away, thought it all over, at last saw Fauche-Borel in his true colours, but how to warn the King? Meanwhile M. G . . . notified Desmarets of Perlet's loyalty to the King, so Perlet was thrown into Sainte-Pélagie again, where he was not even given the forty sous a day to which every prisoner was entitled. He stayed there till the arrival of the Allies on March 31, 1814. He wrote immediately to the King to acquaint him with all he had suffered at the hands of his enemies. Then Fauche-Borel descended on him and presented him to the Duc d'Havré who complimented him on his loyalty. Havré arranged for Perlet to see the Comte de Blacas, the King's Minister, but Fauche-Borel accompanied him because, so he said, Perlet would be better received if he went with him. However, it happened quite otherwise: when Blacas saw that Fauche-Borel was with him he refused to speak to them. Perlet did not get anything out of the King either. He saw d'Havré again whom he told that whatever Fauche-Borel did he did for money. "You tell me nothing new," cried d'Havré. In fine, Perlet was an innocent man whom Fauche-Borel had used for his wicked purposes, and Vitel's death was Fauche-Borel's fault too.

Here one has to go back to Fauche-Borel himself.

He arrived in Paris five days before the King who entered his capital on June 3, 1814. Fauche-Borel sought out Perlet who received him cordially, and practically forced his hospitality on him. Fauche-Borel decided to stay with him, plied him with questions, for he wanted to be enlightened on the circumstances leading to his nephew's execution; what became of the money he had sent Perlet; and who were the members of the royalist committee as he had to report to the King. Perlet was cagey about the committee, and in vain Fauche-Borel urged him that now with the Corsican Ogre gone there was no further cause for secrecy. Perlet remained adamant, though he was forthcoming where Vitel's fate and the money were concerned. Veyrat had taken the whole sum from him, and was the true culprit and double-crosser. Fauche-Borel tried to get in touch with Veyrat; however he had been sent back to Geneva, his native town. (The Swiss had contributed generously to Napoleon's police.) Instead of stringing up the lot Louis XVIII dismissed the men who had tortured and murdered his agents as one dismisses unwanted servants. Though they were under the same roof Perlet wrote Fauche-Borel a letter in which he complained of being calumnied, putting all blame on Veyrat. Fauche-Borel then went to the Préfecture, where he heard that when d'Artois had appeared in Paris as the King's lieutenant Veyrat became a member of his secret police, expecting to achieve a similar position to the one he had held under Napoleon thanks to Constant without reckoning with Pasquier who truly loathed him. Pasquier summoned Veyrat, bluntly told him that he was dismissed, annulled his French nationality, and gave him a passport to Geneva, ordering him to leave France within twenty-four hours. Veyrat left the Préfecture, and on the same evening Pasquier received a letter from M. de Vitrolles, commanding him in His Royal Highness's name to stop persecuting Veyrat and his son. Pasquier called at seven in the morning on M. de Vitrolles, asking to see Artois at once as he wanted to tender his resignation. Vitrolles was as frightened by his threat as Artois was when he received him, and both begged him to stay. Pasquier returned to the Préfecture, where he found a triumphant Veyrat installed in his old office. Pasquier told him to be gone from Paris before nightfall. Veyrat went. So Fauche-Borel could not get in touch with him.

Fauche-Borel could not keep himself out of the limelight. He accompanied the Allied Monarchs to London, then leaving with the King of Prussia he travelled to Neuchatel, where he received a letter from the Duc d'Aumont, advising him that the King of France would give him an audience on July 11 at 11.30. Fauche-Borel could not reach Paris before September. He had already been warned by the Comte de Moustier, Louis XVIII's envoy to Berlin, that Perlet was complaining to everybody, saying Fauche-Borel had done nothing for him in spite of their correspondence having been the cause of his losing his fortune. Fauche-Borel could not understand how their correspondence could have ruined him. As Fauche-Borel still wanted to find out who had been the members of the royalist committee he met Perlet in front of witnesses. "Speak up, M. Perlet," Fauche-Borel said, "and tell us who were the people who made up the committee. You must not bury them in your memory. They deserve to be rewarded by the King." After a lot of shilly-shally Perlet declared that he would not give the names in front of those present, though he would give them to the Duc d'Havré in private. Fauche-Borel insisted on going with him. The same thing happened before d'Havré: no names and a pack of lies.

Perlet, always according to Fauche-Borel, lied about him to the King, insinuating that Fauche-Borel was a double agent who had worked both for Napoleon and Fouché. As Fauche-Borel was a busybody flitting from place to place and from crowned heads to ministers, it was not difficult to convince the King; especially as Fauche-Borel had several enemies at Court, the Comte de Blacas included. While waiting impatiently to be summoned by the King Fauche-Borel went to the Préfecture to ask back the money he had sent Perlet to save his nephew, also a draft on the Bank of Gottingen which the police had taken ten days after Vitel's arrest. He saw the Comte Beugnot, the new Director-General of the police, to whom he showed the police receipt for that sum. Beugnot wanted to pay at once since no one was more deserving than Fauche-Borel, but because of formalities he asked him to return the day after tomorrow, which Fauche-Borel did. In the waiting room he found Comte Jules de Polignac who tenderly embraced him, saying, "My dear Fauche, how happy I am to see you again. I have not seen you since our stay in the Temple. We were very unlucky because of our dealings with that monster of a Perlet." Fauche-Borel stared at him stupefied. "It was he," continued Polignac, "who had your brave nephew killed . . ." Fauche-Borel rushed into Beugnot's office, and the Director-General confirmed what Polignac had said. He showed Fauche-Borel several letters Perlet had written to Dubois (one of which was quoted in this chapter). There could be no doubt that it was Perlet who had betrayed Vitel.

Beugnot promised to pursue the matter, though nothing could be done without the King's approval, and Perlet seemed to hang around the Tuileries. Beugnot kept his word, prepared a long report which he sent to the King, and there the matter rested for the time being. Then Beugnot moved to the Ministry of the Navy, Dandré took over, and allowed Veyrat to return to Paris.

Fauche-Borel rushed to see Veyrat in the Hôtel d'Hollande in the rue des Bons-Enfants on the day he arrived. Fauche-Borel explained that he had come not to recriminate but only to find out the truth. Veyrat put all the blame on Perlet, requested Fauche-Borel to return a little later as he had not yet unpacked. In a trunk were the letters Perlet had written him. (Those letters belonged to the police files, and when Pasquier kicked him out Veyrat had no business to take them away with him.) Fauche-Borel came back an hour later, and read them. His next move was to go to Desmarets who lived in peaceful retirement near Senlis. Desmarets received his erstwhile prisoner with open arms, asked him to forget the past, then pointing to his wife observed, "Thank her. She begged me twenty times on her knees to set you free." She also was from Neuchatel. Of Perlet Desmarets said, "It is unbelievable how much money he took from the two police groups, the Minister's and the Prefect's". Every letter Perlet received from England was immediately sent to Bonaparte. Before Vitel's execution the heads of the High Police had met in secret to decide whether it would be a good thing to postpone the execution in order to force Vitel to write to his uncle to entice him to Paris. It was on that occasion that Fouché remarked that one bereavement sufficed in a single family. So the trap was not set.

A royal commission was appointed to investigate Vitel's death. As it was in no hurry to reach a decision Fauche-Borel wrote a long report which he took to the Tuileries on the day the King held the child of the Marquis de la Rochejaquelein over the font. Fauche-Borel entered the chapel, the King smiled at him; when the King left he hurried to the Marshals' Room and the King smiled at him again, saying to Blacas, "Voilà Fauche". He repeated "here is Fauche" three times. The King came up to him, he thanked His Majesty for having appointed the royal commission, and begged him to speed up the investigation. He handed over his report which the King took, saying, "Yes, Louis, yes, my dear Louis, I will read it myself".

All Fauche-Borel got out of the royal commission was Perlet's opportunity to calumniate him. Perlet put the blame on Veyrat, Veyrat on Perlet, and things were still dragging when "came the fatal day of March 20," when the eagle rose from Elba to fly to the towers of Notre-Dame. Fauche-Borel ran to the Tuileries to offer his life for the King, then to Count von Goetz, the Prussian minister, who sent Fauche-Borel with some despatches to Vienna which he reached on the 23rd. He was in his element, hurrying to the Duke of Wellington by whom he was kindly received; then to Talleyrand who called him a godsend as he had not had news from Paris for twelve days. Fauche-Borel dropped straight into the world of intrigues, coming to the conclusion that the Congress was in favour of the King of Rome and no longer of Louis XVIII. Fauche-Borel became Louis XVIII's champion, and, so he boasts in his apologia, it was due to him that after a while the Congress veered to the true King of France.

He persuaded the King of Prussia that Louis XVIII deserved to stay on the throne, provided, of course, the throne could be recaptured. Then he set out for Ghent, taking a message of encouragement from the King of Prussia to the King of France who was once again in exile. Fauche-Borel saw the Duc d'Havré, whom he asked to arrange a private audience with the King. Havré told him to see Blacas. Now Blacas had been present when Louis XVIII had the previous year landed in Calais to take over his kingdom, and Fauche-Borel, who naturally was in the retinue, noticed that the scabbard of the King's sword was caught by the ribbon of the Garter, so rushed to help the King. "What are you doing, Fauche?" Blacas shouted. "Fauche is rendering me another service," the King said.

Fauche-Borel waited on Blacas with the despatches which the King of Prussia had given him. Blacas was ill, and received him in bed. "Your health will be restored with the news I bring," cried Fauche-Borel. Blacas coldly told him to leave the despatches with him, and he would give them to the King. In vain did Fauche-Borel insist, Blacas would not let him see the King. When he returned to his lodgings the Director of the police appeared, ordering him to leave Ghent. Fauche-Borel refused to budge, so gendarmes hustled him into a carriage, and escorted him to Brussels, where he was flung into gaol. Eventually the King of Prussia obtained his release. After the Second Restoration Fauche-Borel was back in Paris, and though he moved heaven and earth Louis XVIII refused to speak to him.

The King of Prussia notified Fauche-Borel that in a letter addressed to him Blacas called him a scoundrel who had been in Bonaparte's pay. The King of Prussia refused to believe him.

The Allied leaders were forced to listen to Fauche-Borel's tale of woe. Fouché, the King's Minister of Police, testified to his loyalty to Louis XVIII, so did Lord Grenville and Sir Charles William Flint. Fauche-Borel's enemies brought a new charge against him. In 1813 it had been planned in émigré circles in England to send the Duc de Berry from Jersey to Normandy, where, so agents and counter-agents reported, forty thousand armed Chouans were waiting to rise. Early in 1814 the Princes wanted to put the plan into execution, and Havré sent Fauche-Borel to Guernsey to find out what the exact situation was in Normandy. He came back with the depressing information that the forty thousand armed Chouans were but a dream. Now his enemies said that the expedition did not materialise because Fauche-Borel had wrongly advised the Duc d'Havré.

The fight against Perlet continued, but even there he got no real satisfaction and the suspicion that while he had spent his time flitting between England and Germany he sold royalist secrets to Napoleon's police was so strong that Lousi XVIII had definitely to discard him. For fifteen years Fauche-Borel tried to justify himself, but even the English statesmen whom he had served would have nothing more to do with him. Eventually at the King of Prussia's request, Louis XVIII gave him a small pension. That was not good enough for Fauche-Borel, whom the King of France in exile had promised to appoint the royal printer. He wanted to be vindicated, to be taken back with love by Louis XVIII. He published his Memoirs: nobody took any notice of them. In 1829 instead of consoling himself with the words Mme des Ursins had written of Philip V of Spain, "Kings are made to be loved though fundamentally they love nothing," he threw himself out of the window of his house in Neuchatel, and fractured his skull on the cobbles. It was the twenty-fifth anniversary of General Pichegru's death.

The truth, of course, will never be established, for too many papers and documents vanished on the eve of the Restoration. The present writer believes that though he was a fool and a braggart, and though he tried to play a part that was beyond him, Fauche-Borel was not a traitor. The real betrayer of the royalist cause in the royalist camp, the one who for the sake of money sent so many men to their death, remains the unknown fiend, far more evil than the wretched Perlet and his like.

XV

The Maubreuil Affair

On the night of December 30, 1813, Savary went to the Tuileries to see his Emperor whose future had looked dark ever since the battle of Leipzig, and whom many of the men whose fortune he had made were preparing to leave in the lurch. Savary, the faithful Achates, was not yet among them. He suggested to the Emperor that all members of the *Corps Législatif* be arrested. The moment had come to put an end to what he considered as subversion. "Sire," he said, "this must be the second volume of the Duc d'Enghien."

"You fool," said Napoleon. "The success the first volume had should discourage us from writing a second. Besides, in those days I had made a pact with Victory; now we have been beaten."

When Napoleon set out for the campaign of France which was to be one of his most brilliant, he gave his Duc de Rovigo virtually absolute power. Except for the Empress, the King of Rome, Mesdames Montesquiou and de Montbello the Minister of Police was empowered to arrest anybody in the Empire, the Emperor's brothers included. Even then Napoleon remained unable to take decisive action against Talleyrand. He warned Savary to do nothing against him without his handwritten approval.

Savary entered into the spirit of the Emperor's last but one game with his usual enthusiasm and sabre-rattling. The result was that public opinion turned against him, and he was, as a contemporary put it, as much hated by the French as by the Allies. Then all of a sudden the *fidus Achates* became a frightened man, and sensing the cause lost he tried to sever his connections with his Imperial Master. Though the road between Paris and Fontainebleau remained open Napoleon asked his Duc de Rovigo to join him in vain. The Minister of Police was busy negotiating with the Allies, pointing out to them that it was thanks to him that Marie-Louise could "escape with the King of Rome". He also approached Artois, and when Joseph and Jérôme Bonaparte let him know that they wanted to continue the war in Napoleon's name Savary turned against them. But as with many others his loyalty to Napoleon was reborn during the Hundred Days, and he was appointed Inspector-General of the gendarmerie. His reconversion, as it were, was pretty sincere (or did he appreciate that the Bourbons would have nothing to do with him because of the part he played in the execution of the Duc d'Enghien?), and he followed Napoleon into exile. However, he was arrested in the *Bellerophon*, then interned in Malta. In 1816 he escaped to Smyrna, where he lost most of his fortune in unlucky business ventures. Condemned to death in his absence he returned to France in 1819, was tried, acquitted, and retired as a General on half pay. Still, there was a kick left in the old Achates: in 1831 he was at the head of the French troops in Algeria. He fell ill, went back to France, where he died peacefully in his bed two years later.

In 1814 his Prefect of Police, the Baron Pasquier, approached the problems of the Restoration and the downfall of Napoleon in a distinctly more subtle manner. As Prefect of Police he was informed on March 30 that Napoleon, who had arrived in Fontainebleau, had sent the Duc de Vicence (Caulaincourt) to Paris to do all he could to approach the Czar. Pasquier had no illusions about Vicence's mission since he was in touch with the Russian Emperor. Naturally, he was also kept informed by his police spies on what went on in Fontainebleau; thus he heard that some of Napoleon's marshals were as convinced as Napoleon himself that the war was not lost, and the Allies ought to be attacked instead of continuing the retreat. On April 1 Prince Schwarzenberg left Paris to establish Allied headquarters in Chevilly between Essones and Paris.

The next morning Pasquier visited Talleyrand. The Duc Dalberg was present and while they discussed Napoleon's chances, Pasquier observed that the Allies were still afraid of him, their numerical superiority notwithstanding, therefore they might lose the war.

"You are right," answered the Duc Dalberg. "One will have to find other means."

"Where do you expect to find them?" Pasquier enquired.

"Certain measures have already been taken to forestall the possibilities we fear."

Dalberg, with Talleyrand always present, explained the measures they were taking. A number of determined fellows led by a vigorous chap (*bougre* was the word he used) would be dressed in the uniforms of the Chasseurs of the Guard which had been found in the stores of the École Militaire, and would approach Napoleon before or during the next battle and kill him. Pasquier was indignant, and did not hide his indignation. He asked where those men would be found. "That is not difficult," came the reply. "There are men of every colour, Chouans, Jacobins and so on."

Pasquier went home, and a few minutes later received a note from M. de La Valette, Director of the Postal Service, saying, "I know how completely incapable you are of taking part in the infamous project planned against Napoleon . . . do all you can to frustrate it".

Practically at the same time Pasquier received a similar warning from police inspector Foudras, a man he trusted. However the snag was that neither M. de La Valette nor Foudras could give details or the names of the men who would don the uniform of the Chasseurs of the Guard. Towards the evening another note was handed to Pasquier, brought by a countryman. Pasquier recognised the handwriting of Hugues Maret, Duc de Bassano, one of the ministers still faithful to Napoleon. He enquired in the Emperor's name what was going on in Paris, adding that the little news that reached him seemed almost unbelievable. Pasquier took a quick decision, in fact two, the first to notify Napoleon that his life was in danger, the second: that he should not address himself any more to his Prefect of Police as the Prefect of Police considered himself no longer in his service. Then Pasquier took Bassano's note to Talleyrand, who was once again closeted with Dalberg.

Dalberg approved Pasquier's decision, though insisted on Napoleon being told that the Jacobins were the people who planned to murder him. Pasquier's reply to Bassano went as follows:

"Here are the facts: eighty-two members of the Senate have organised a provisional government; the Senate has declared the end of the reign. The government has addressed the French army. Several generals have declared themselves in the government's favour (here follow the names of the generals). . . . One is assured that there are several plans afoot on how to approach the Emperor, and among the persons who are intent on it several Jacobins are to be found. The bankers have offered twelve millions. The Legislative Body will meet this morning, they will be even more decided than the Senate . . . one should not contact me in any way as one should understand which side I have chosen."

The countryman came to fetch the cat's goodbye letter to the leaving tenant. Bassano gave it to Napoleon who observed, "This one seems in a great hurry; one could say he put on his hunting coat to go quicker". Such remarks made no more impression on Pasquier, who did not forget his chat with Talleyrand and Dalberg of which he was forcibly reminded when Marie Armand Guerri de Maubreuil, Marquis d'Orsvault, usually referred to as the Marquis de Maubreuil, entered the picture.

Born in Brittany in 1782 he joined the army of the Vendée in 1797, and since he was a congenital liar and intriguer he later managed to insinuate himself into Napoleon's good graces, and was for a while equerry to Jérôme Bonaparte, King of Westphalia. After he fell into disgrace he took part in shady business speculations which did not improve his reputation as a plain adventurer. When

Napoleon's cause began to look lost Maubreuil discovered that he was an ardent Royalist, and on April 4, 1814, led a mob into the Place Vendôme to the shout of "Down with the Usurper, long live the King!", and under his guidance horses were attached to ropes tied round Napoleon's Column, skilled workers were hired, and on the fourth day the Emperor's statue crashed to the ground. He also strung his Cross of the Legion of Honour on a string to his horse's tail, dragging it in the gutter to the applause of the onlookers.

The moment was ripe for adventurers, for chaos seemed round the corner. The Provisional Government needed money, and money was scarce as Napoleon was in possession of most of the funds. They sent envoys in all directions to collect the revenue and whatever else they could lay their hands on. A M. Dudon went to find the diamonds and treasure of the Empress Marie-Louise which had been taken to Blois. Dudon encountered no difficulties, and M. de La Bouillerie, Treasurer of the Civil List, undertook to have them sent to Paris, but at the city-gate of Paris the convoy was stopped by a troop led by a M. de Lagrange who, he declared, was sent to seize the Empress's treasure, which instead of being taken to the Treasury should be delivered to the Tuileries. That caused an angry altercation between Louis, the Minister of Finance, and the counsellors of Artois. Louis maintained that they belonged to the Treasury, whereas Artois insisted on keeping them since the diamonds, the gold and the rest were of the Civil List, therefore the King's property. The cases remained for a time in the Tuileries without being opened, and guarded by the Garde Nationale and the gendarmerie whom Louis despatched.

The agents Louis had sent around France to collect moneys the Provisional Government considered as theirs though they were still in the hands of Napoleon and his family, needed volunteers to help them in their task. Naturally, only true royalists were allowed to offer their services. As Maubreuil had shown before the Column in the Place Vendôme the stuff he was made of, he was one of the many who filled Talleyrand's ante-chamber, hoping for lucrative employment. Laborie, the assistant secretary of the Provisional

Government, presented him to Talleyrand and some other members of the Government. What he and Talleyrand discussed has never been precisely known, yet for the rest of his life Maubreuil maintained that they talked in M. de Lagrange's presence not only of the treasures and funds of the Civil List. There were supposed to exist two cases containing a vast fortune, probably including the Crown jewels which Napoleon had retained. Maubreuil volunteered to find them. He asked for a written authorisation which was granted by General Dupont, the Minister of War, ordering all French troops he might meet or appeal to during his mission to give him all the assistance he needed. The other members of the Government were not consulted, and when the Maubreuil affair, as it were, exploded, General Dupont could not remember what exactly passed between them, but seemed to think that Maubreuil had asked for the order because he intended to collect some material belonging to the Ministry of War.

Be that as it may, Maubreuil proceeded to Comte Anglès, the new Minister of Police, and on the strength of Dupont's order received almost full powers from Anglès, "M. de Maubreuil being on a secret mission of the highest importance". Then he repaired to de Bourrienne, who was in charge of the Postal Service, and from whom he obtained a permit to use post-horses whenever he needed them. He also obtained from the Prussian General Sacken an order to the Allied troops similar to the one General Dupont had given him. With these papers he set out to find the treasure in the company of a man called Dasies whom he had encountered in the Place Vendôme while busy with the Emperor's statue.

On the day they left, that is on April 18, the Queen of Westphalia, Catherine of Württemberg, wife of Jérôme Bonaparte, began her journey to Germany, taking the road to Nemours. As Maubreuil had been her husband's equerry, and retained connections with her suite, it was easy for him to find out the direction she was taking. He must also have known that she was taking her jewels and other valuables with her. Showing General Dupont's order to the commandant of the garrison of Montereau he was given a piquet of

Chasseurs of the Guard and Mameluks. On his command they stopped the royal coach, Maubreuil stepped forward, forced the Queen to alight, then go into a barn, and would not let her continue on her journey before she handed over eleven cases containing her jewels and 84,000 francs in gold. She had to give him the keys too. There were twelve keys, the twelfth case being in her husband's possession. The reason Maubreuil gave for his highway robbery was that the Provisional Government, whose agent he was, suspected her of taking with her the Crown jewels. This took place on the 21st.

Maubreuil reached Paris on the night of the 23rd-24th just after midnight, and waited in the Tuileries for M. de Vitrolles, bringing with him four sacks filled with gold; (or so Maubreuil said). In the course of the day the cases were also delivered. However, the Emperor Alexander had heard of the outrageous affront to a royal princess, and he was furious. The Queen of Westphalia was travelling with a passport issued by all the Allied sovereigns, one further reason to consider the matter as a grievous insult. Therefore, M. de Vitrolles and the Provisional Government heaved a sigh of relief when the sacks and the cases reached the Pavilion Marsan. M. de Vitrolles made an error which was to have repercussions, namely that he had not checked the contents of the sacks, and was satisfied with Maubreuil's declaration that the Queen of Westphalia had kept the keys of the cases. When a locksmith came to open them, the same one who had made the locks, they were found to be almost empty, and the money inside them was only silver coins of twenty sous instead of gold pieces of twenty francs. Maubreuil protested that he had delivered the cases untouched, consequently only they who had taken the sacks from him could be held responsible for the disappearance of the gold. The cases and the sacks had been in the custody of MM. Vantaux, Geslin, Sémallé, de Vitrolles and Anglès, the Minister of Police; therefore the culprit was one of them. To accuse the Minister of Police of theft was no laughing matter in the eyes of the Allied monarchs.

Maubreuil strutted about the streets of Paris with the aplomb of the innocent; and the foreign sovereigns asked the police to act. On the night of the 25th Anglès went with a police commissioner to the Tuileries, where he questioned both Maubreuil and Dasies, then a bit belatedly police seals were put on the cases, and Maubreuil and Dasies were taken to the Préfecture. It was after midnight, and Pasquier, the Prefect, was already in bed, but Anglès had him wakened. He instructed Pasquier to deal with the matter urgently. Pasquier appreciated the serious aspects of the robbery since the Allies had been in touch with him on the previous day, moreover it was feared that some of the more imprudent members of Artois's suite might be connected with the affair. So the investigation began before dawn, Pasquier mobilising most of his inspectors.

The first discovery was a diamond in a flat Maubreuil rented: he had three other flats in Paris. The diamond was found in the bed, and the police had no doubt that it belonged to the Queen of Westphalia. Ten police agents went along the road Maubreuil and Dasies had taken after leaving the Queen. That took, of course, some time, in fact several days. Meanwhile the Emperor Alexander daily sent an officer to the Préfecture to ask for the latest developments; the other monarchs did the same. They worried and irritated Talleyrand to the extent of his offering Maubreuil, through Pasquier, a sum of money if he returned all he had taken. If he did so he would at once be released and no more molested. Pasquier had Maubreuil brought before him. That was their first meeting as only his inspectors had questioned him before. Maubreuil declared that he had not opened the cases, and though Pasquier tried hard to make him admit the truth he stuck to his guns. He wanted to serve the King's cause and that was all. He scorned Talleyrand's offer.

The agent sent along the road to Fossard returned to Paris. Maubreuil, they had discovered, had left the Paris road near the Croix-de-Bernis of Versailles. He went to an inn in the company of Dasies, took a room, called a locksmith who opened the only case whose key did not fit. That case contained the most valuable objects. Three hours later the same locksmith was sent for to close the case.

Maubreuil was again questioned, and he repeated exactly what he had said before, then loudly proclaimed to Pasquier and his aides that he was well aware that they wanted to ruin him because of the awful secret they had imparted to him; in fact had chosen him to commit a terrible crime. Before he left Paris Talleyrand had entrusted him with the mission of assassinating the Emperor Napoleon, and in spite of the horror he felt he accepted lest somebody else were chosen, somebody wicked enough to commit the crime. Frustrating their evil scheme he did not go to Fontainebleau, but, in order to appease them, he brought them back the treasure of the Queen of Westphalia to satisfy their thirst for money. He had left the lot with M. de Vitrolles, and it was no fault of his that others had helped themselves to it.

In vain Pasquier put before him his agents' reports. Maubreuil refused to budge. Pasquier was convinced that the whole story of Talleyrand having sent him to murder Napoleon was a sheer lie invented by Maubreuil as his best form of defence. Pasquier notified the Government of Maubreuil's allegation, pointing out the disastrous consequences his accusation would have on the general public and on the soldiers who still worshipped their Emperor. The Government decided to take no drastic action, but keep Maubreuil and Dasies in prison. After all, the Provisional Government found themselves in an embarrassing situation since like Artois they would immensely have profited by Napoleon's assassination. Maubreuil did not cease emphasising this during his interrogation. And what would the Czar and the King of Prussia think if they heard of it, though Maubreuil maintained that General von Sacken's order to the Allied troops was proof that both those monarchs were in favour of it?

Pasquier could not pretend to have forgotten the Duc Dalberg's words, especially as Maubreuil told him that he was offered men dressed in the uniform of the Chasseurs of the Guard. Looking back on the Maubreuil affair many years later he reached the conclusion that Maubreuil could have been the *bougre* Dalberg had chosen when contemplating the plan of having Napoleon killed.

However, the idea must have been abandoned, that is became unnecessary, when Marmont defected. Maubreuil did not lie when he said he had been approached, but his robbing the Queen of Westphalia had no connection with it. The question remained: who approached him? Pasquier remained convinced that it could not have been Talleyrand who was too subtle, too clever and possessed too much experience to discuss a matter that could have such far-reaching consequences as the assassination of Napoleon with a virtual stranger.

This dirty business put Anglès in an awkward position, for Maubreuil and Dasies calumniated him as their chief persecutor and the one who had taken the Queen of Westphalia's treasure. They appeared before a tribunal; their lawyer brought up the intended assassination of Napoleon; the tribunal declared itself incompetent to judge them; a court martial decided the same; Maubreuil and Dasies were taken to the prison of the Abbaye: then Louis XVIII set them free. Came the Hundred Days, Napoleon put them back into the Abbaye, but Maubreuil managed to escape. The Bourbons returned, they were set free again, and when it was thought that the affair had finally been forgotten Maubreuil was hauled before a tribunal which came to the same decision as the previous ones. From the Paris courts the case was taken to Rouen, then to Douai; however in the meantime Maubreuil disappeared, then was caught again. In thirteen years he was thrown into twelve different prisons, was arrested ten times, six times set free, escaped three times and spent six hundred and eighty-five days incommunicado. Eventually in 1818 the tribunal of Douai sentenced him to five years for having stolen the Queen of Westphalia's treasure. When he came out he attacked Talleyrand in two pamphlets, publicly maintaining that he had been sent by him to kill Napoleon, and in 1827 he boxed Talleyrand's ears as the old man left the church of Saint-Denis after Mass. Maubreuil lived till 1855.

Anglès was superseded by Fouché during the Hundred Days: Napoleon seemed truly to have gone out of his way to surround himself with his enemies. Fouché, who had been in communication with the Allies ever since 1809, now got in touch with the Chouans who had remained faithful to the cause. Though Napoleon needed every man he could get hold of, he still had to keep an army corps on the Loire in fear of Cadoudal and La Haye-Saint-Hilaire rising from their graves. The Chouans and Vendée leaders did not trust Fouché, none the less the Comte de Malaric came to see him in secret, and Fouché insinuated that he had always been on their side. Malaric was unconvinced, and went to consult the other Vendée leaders, Antichamps, Suzannet and Sapineau who got in touch with General Lamarque of the Army of the Loire, but their conditions were so stiff that Lamarque could not accept them. Still, Fouché could boast after the second Restoration that not only had he tried to help the Chouans and the Vendée leaders but was instrumental in an army remaining on the Loire which was of help to the Allies.

Fouché accepted the same portfolio from Louis XVIII after Waterloo, but in September was sent as envoy to Dresden, rather a come-down. When in 1816 the law against the regicides was passed his career came to an end. At last he paid for the only blunder he had ever committed. He moved to Prague, became an Austrian citizen, and died in Trieste in 1820. Réal, his right-hand, lived till 1834. He had come back to Paris after he was pardoned in 1818.

The Ministry of Police was abolished in 1818, and only the Préfecture of Police remained. When the police were thus downgraded many who had suffered from them began to hope that the police power might diminish: but what the police had learnt under the Revolution, the Directorate, the Consulate and the Empire the police did not forget.

Selected Bibliography

Beauchamp, Alphonse de. *Histoire de la guerre de Vendée et des Chouans.* Giguet et Michaud, 3 vols, Paris, 1806.

Bourrienne, Louis-Antoine Fauvelet de. *Mémoires.* Ladvocat, 10 vols, Paris, 1829.

Broc, Vicomte de. *La Vie en France sous le Ier. Empire.* E. Plon, Nourrit et C., Paris, 1895.

Bulletins de Police—Ministère de la Police Générale de l'Empire, Paris, 1806.

Cadoudal, Georges. *Georges Cadoudal et la Chouannerie.* E. Plon, Nourrit et C., Paris, 1887.

Castanié, François. *Comte Réal. Les indiscrétions d'un préfet de police de Napoléon,* Tallandier, Paris, 1912.

Coquelle, P. *Napoléon et l'Angleterre 1803-1813, d'après des documents inédits des archives des Affaires étrangères: des Archives nationales et du Foreign Office.* E. Plon, Nourrit et C., Paris, 1904.

Daudet, Ernest. *Histoire de l'émigration 1789-1793.* E. Kolb, Paris, 1889.

Daudet, Ernest. *La Police et les chouans sous le Consulat et l'Empire: 1800-1815.* E. Plon, Nourrit et C., Paris, 1895.

Desmarets, Charles. *Témoignage historique ou Quinze Ans de haute police sous Napoléon.* A. Levasseur, Paris, 1833.

Dulaure, J. A. *Singularités historiques, contenant ce que l'histoire de Paris et ses environs offre de plus piquant et de plus extraordinaire.* Baudouin frères, Paris, 1825.

Fauche-Borel, Louis de. *Mémoire contre Charles Perlet, ancien journaliste.* Mr Lombard Delangres, Michaud, Paris, 1816.

Fauche-Borel, Louis de. *Mémoires,* redigés par A. de Beauchamp. Moutardier, 3 vols, Paris, 1829.

Fauche-Borel, Louis de. *Précis historique des différentes missions dans lesquelles j'avais été employé pour la cause de la monarchie.* Paris, 1815.

Forgues, Eugène Daurand. *Le Dossier secret de Fouché.* Daupeley-Gouverneur. Nogent-le-Rotrou, 1906.

Forssell, Nils. *Fouché, the man Napoleon feared.* Allen & Unwin, London, 1928.

Fouché, Joseph, duc d'Otrante. *d'après une correspondance privée inédite.* Dominique Caille, Vannes, 1893.

Fouché, Joseph, duc d'Otrante. *Mémoires.* France, Editions, Paris, 1944.

Glachant, Victor. *La Police impériale: documents des Archives Nationales.* E. Plon, Nourrit et C., Paris, 1906.

Gohier, Louis-Jérôme. *Mémoires.* Bossange frères, Paris, 1824.

Guillon, E. *Les Complots militaires sous le Consulat et l'Empire: d'après les documents inédits des Archives.* E. Plon, Nourrit et C., Paris, 1894.

Hauterive, Ernest d'. *La Police pendant la Révolution.* Picard, Paris, n.d.

Maubreuil, Cte. Marie-Armand de Guerry de. *Extraits des plaidoyers et mémoires des avocats.* Germain et Pinet, Paris, 1855.

Maubreuil, Cte. Marie-Armand de Guerry de. *Précis de ce qui a été dit par M. de Maubreuil à l'audience de 31 juillet 1827 et supprimé par la censure. Réflexions sur l'affaire dite de Maubreuil.* Guiraudet, Paris, 1827.

Madelin, Louis. *Fouché 1759-1820.* Plon, 2 vols, Paris, 1955.

Nodier, Charles. *Nouveaux souvenirs et portraits.* Magen et Comon, Paris, 1841.

Nodier, Charles. *Souvenirs de la Révolution et de l'Empire.* Charpentier, Paris, 1850.

Pasquier, Etienne-Denis, baron. *Histoire de mon temps. Mémoires du chancelier Pasquier, publiés par M. le duc d'Audiffret-Pasquier.* E. Plon, Nourrit et C., 6 vols, Paris, 1893, 1894, 1895.

Pelet de la Lozère, Cte. Privat-Joseph-Claramont. *Opinions de Napoléon sur divers sujets, recueillies par un membre de son Conseil d'Etat.* Firmin-Didot frères, Paris, 1833.

Perlet, Charles-Frédéric. *Exposé de la conduite de Perlet relativement à l'auguste famille des Bourbons depuis 1789.* Foucault, Paris, 1816.

Peuchet, Jacques. *Mémoires des archives de la police.* A. Levavasseur, 3 vols, Paris, 1838.

Raisson, Horace. *Histoire de la police de Paris 1667-1844.* Levavasseur, Paris, 1844.

Saint-Edme, Edme-Théodore Bourg. *Biographie des lieutenants-généraux, ministres, etc.* The author, Paris, 1829.

Savant, Jean. *Tel fut Fouché.* Fasquelle, Paris, 1955.

Savary, Anne-Jean-Marie-René, duc de Rovigo. *Mémoires pour servir à l'histoire de l'empereur Napoléon.* A. Bossangre, 8 vols, Paris, 1828.

Index

INDEX

Martin, 125, 126, 127, 133
Martyrs, rue des, 194
Marville, Claude-Henri Feydeau de, 19, 20
Maubreuil, Marie Armand Guerri de, Marquis d'Orsvault, 234-244
Mauduisson, Comte de, 113, 114, 115
Mayenne, 8, 42, 57
Mayer, 165
Mazarin, Jules, Cardinal de, 16
Melun, 139, 147, 168
Mercier, 131, 150
Mercier La Vendée, 62
Mercier La Vendée, Lucrèce, 62
Merille, Jean, 93
Merlin de Douai, Philippe-Antoine, Comte de, 29-30, 31, 32, 33, 34, 35
Milan, 44, 149, 158
Mirabeau, Honoré-Gabriel, 29
Misedon, 53, 54, 55, 56
Mittau, 65, 223
Moncey, Bon-Adrien Jeannot de, Marshal of France, Duc de Conegliano, 95, 96, 122, 145, 146, 148, 150, 156, 213
Monge, Gaspar, 78
Monk, George, 48
Monsieur, Louis XIV's brother, 16
Monsieur-le-Prince, rue, 87
Montagne Sainte-Geneviève, rue de la, 86
Montaigu, 178
Montaigu, Captain, 172
Montbello, Mme de, 234
Monterblanc, 120, 121, 123, 125, 129
Montereau, 239
Montespan, Françoise Athénaïs de Mortemart, Marquise de, 17
Montesquiou-Fezensac, Abbé François de, 34, 35
Montesquiou, Mme, 234
Montfiquet, M. de, 188, 196
Montfiquet, Henriette de, 188
Montpellier, 76, 164
Montrésor, 110, 111
Monville, M. de, 30
Morbihan, 59, 60, 64, 65, 66, 73, 77, 81, 119, 120, 122, 125, 126, 127, 128, 129, 130, 131, 132, 133, 135, 136, 150, 151, 183
Moreau, Jean-Victor, 63, 64, 78, 79, 80, 81, 82, 83, 85, 86, 88, 89, 90, 91, 93, 100, 146, 155, 164, 169, 170-171, 174, 185, 218
Morlaix, 124, 125, 160, 184
Moscow, 214, 215
Moulin, 36
Mounet, 113

Moustier, Comte de, 228
Mouton, General, 210
Munich, 166, 170, 175
Murat, Joachim, King of Naples, 83, 99, 100, 104, 105, 107, 140, 159

Nantes, 41, 119, 120
Nantes, prison, 150
Naples, 116, 207
Napoleon I, 7, 8, 32, 35, 38, 39, 40, 45, 46, 47, 48, 49, 50, 51, 52, 57, 58, 63, 64-65, 66, 68, 69, 70, 71, 72, 73, 74, 75, 76, 77, 78, 79, 80, 81, 82, 83, 84, 85, 86, 88, 89-90, 91, 92, 93, 94, 95, 96, 97, 98, 99, 101, 102, 103, 105, 106, 107, 110, 111, 113, 115, 116, 117, 118, 122, 124, 130, 133, 134, 135, 136, 137, 138, 139, 142, 143, 144, 145, 146, 147, 148, 151, 154, 155, 157, 158, 159, 161, 165, 166, 167, 168, 169, 170, 173, 174, 175, 176, 177, 178, 180, 181, 182, 183, 186, 189, 190, 191, 194, 200, 202-203, 204, 205, 206, 207, 208, 209, 210, 212, 213, 214, 215, 216, 218, 219, 226, 227-228, 229, 230, 231, 234, 235-239, 242-244
Napoleonville, 132
Nation, Place de la, 214
Nelson, Admiral Horatio, 160
Nemours, 168, 239
Neuchatel, 175, 217, 218, 219, 221, 228, 230, 232
Niort, 156, 173
Nogent-sur-Seine, 153
Noisy, Comtesse de, 19
Normandy, 8, 52, 57, 83, 109, 126, 183, 187, 188, 189, 196, 200, 202, 232
Noyers, rue des, 90

Observance, rue de l', 87
O'Connor, General, 165
Opera House, 19, 68, 69, 70
Ordoner, Michel, 96
O'Reilly, Richard, 164
Orient, 130, 161, 164
Orleans, 65, 114
Orléans, Louis-Philippe-Joseph, Duc d', 29, 30, 218
Ouvrard, 206, 208

Paillard, General, 136
Palais-Egalité, 70
Palais-Royal, 30

351. 74

France: police work